NOT MY CHILD

PATRICIA CROWLEY

AVON BOOKS ◆ NEW YORK

AVON BOOKS
A division of
The Hearst Corporation
105 Madison Avenue
New York, New York 10016

The Doubleday edition contains the following Library of Congress
Cataloging in Publication Data:

Crowley, Patricia.
    Not my child : a mother confronts her child's sexual abuse / by Patricia
Crowley.—1st ed.
        p.   cm.
1. Child molesting—New Jersey—Essex County—Case studies.   2. Day care centers—New Jersey—Essex County—Case studies.
I. Title.
HQ72.U53C76   1990
362.7'6—dc20   89-17242
                                                                             CIP

First

AVO   TRIES, MARCA
REG

Pri

RA

For the Wee Care children

ACKNOWLEDGMENTS

Contrary to what I'd always thought, writing a book isn't a solitary effort. It involves a lot of give-and-take and back-and-forth with the people whose lives you're chronicling, not just in formal interviews but in late-night telephone conversations or whenever the mood strikes.

Writing a book this personal also means exploring one's own feelings and coming to terms with one's life, both of which can be painful and difficult. You can sometimes feel inadequate, insecure, and frazzled, and you've got to be able to bounce your thoughts and fears and hopes off those closest to you. Working on this book, I never lacked for love, support, or encouragement.

So many people were there for me that it's hard to list them all. But I express my gratitude to each and every one of you. I could never have done this by myself. Thank you to:

My husband, who baby-sat countless hours, taught me to use his computer so I could write this book at home, and put up with me on a daily basis, which I know wasn't easy.

My five children, who mean more to me than anything in the world and whose love, honesty, and generosity gave me the strength I needed to keep going during a difficult period of my life.

My mother, whose life is a shining example of what motherhood should be and whose editing of my manuscript reminded me of what a good English teacher she was before she became a lawyer.

My father, who has always been there for me and whose finely tuned sense of humor and optimistic outlook have enriched the lives of all of his children.

My sisters and brothers, who always made me feel as if

being the oldest was a privilege, not a chore, and whose genuine interest in this book made me realize anew how much they all mean to me.

A very special aunt, who died of cancer while I was writing this book and whose grace and dignity both before and during her illness taught me a lot about how to live.

The Wee Care parents, for their candor, their willingness to discuss a chronically painful subject, and most of all, their trust in me.

Casey Fuetsch, my editor, for her endless patience and for all her help on the manuscript, and Jill Roberts for her keen eye.

Sara McArdle and Glenn Goldberg, who gave generously of their time and expertise.

Susan Esquilin, who encouraged me to write this book by myself and who provided valuable insights into why children act the way they do.

A long-time journalist friend, who talked me into writing this book and believed in me when I didn't believe in myself, and to all my other friends who read parts of the manuscript and offered their comments.

My housekeeper, for her trustworthiness and devotion, and for laughing at my jokes, no matter how awful.

To protect their privacy, the names of the Wee Care children and their families, as well as their parents' occupations, have been changed. And in the interest of protecting the privacy of certain other persons whose real identities are not essential to this true account, some other names have been altered.

C H A P T E R

1

For the first four years of her life, I thought I knew my daughter Hannah nearly as well as I knew myself. We were so close that I could read her mood by looking at her face, and accurately predict what would make her laugh or cry or even which lunchbox or charm necklace she would choose out of a display at the dime store.

Although Hannah never showed it openly, I sensed her disappointment when the librarian didn't choose her to bang the drum that signaled the start of the preschoolers' story hour. And I felt her quiet pleasure when an out-of-town aunt unexpectedly turned up at her ballet recital.

Hannah was so candid she once inquired of my father why he had hairs growing out of his nose, and asked her great-grandmother why she had such fat legs. She was blithe and easygoing, with an infectious giggle, a droll sense of humor, and the conversational ease to prattle on for hours with me about anything—clothes, friends, or her future career plans.

I had unshakable faith in this child, with whom I felt deeply bonded and who had regarded me as her confidante since she was old enough to talk. If anything was happening at school to upset Hannah, I felt certain she would tell me.

Until the day before her fifth birthday party.

The year Hannah turned five, she wanted to invite her entire nursery school class to her party as well as her assortment of cousins. I mailed out nearly two dozen invitations, hoping the appointed Sunday would be pleasant enough to hunt for chocolate kisses outside. And if it was unbearably hot the way early June sometimes is in northern New Jersey, the two wading pools could be unearthed from the basement and set up in the backyard.

I'm a feature reporter for a large suburban newspaper, and I usually write at home on Fridays. But on this particular Friday—June 7, 1985—I was up earlier than usual. I helped my oldest daughter, Caroline, pack her suitcase for her first sleep-away birthday party that night. After dropping her off at her first-grade classroom, I went home to finish cutting two dozen round noses out of red construction paper. My husband Jim had drawn a poster-sized picture of Ernie from "Sesame Street." I intended to break out of the Pin-the-Tail-on-the-Donkey routine by letting Hannah's guests play Pin-the-Nose-on-Ernie instead. While our live-in housekeeper, Maria, fed five-month-old Robert, I let Hannah and two-year-old Ellen help me fill the goody bags for Sunday.

Midway through the morning, I remembered that a friend with two children Caroline's and Hannah's ages had bought tickets for all of us to see a local production of *The Three Little Pigs* and *Little Red Riding Hood* that weekend. I called Judy to plan where we should meet. But when I got her on the phone, she told me that I had confused the dates. The play was Sunday, not Saturday, and the time coincided almost exactly with Hannah's party.

At first I wasn't sure what to do. I could give the tickets away, but any children I could think to give them to were already planning to attend the party. The only other alternative was to reschedule the party for Saturday, which

2

meant calling two dozen parents as quickly as possible. I dug Hannah's class list out of my file cabinet and sat down at the phone.

Working my way slowly down the list, I reached a few mothers who said their children would be able to attend the party. I was relieved that Hannah would still have enough classmates to help celebrate her birthday and that all the hot dogs and hamburgers I had bought wouldn't go to waste. But as the afternoon wore on, I was puzzled when I couldn't reach my sister Kathleen.

On weekdays, Kathleen could always be found in her office. Her little girl Emily, who was three, attended the same day-care center as Hannah, though Hannah only went two days a week. With a housekeeper I loved and trusted, I didn't need day care for Hannah, but I wanted her to have the exposure to other children her age.

The Wee Care Day Nursery was housed in a rambling, ivy-covered brick church in Maplewood, the next town over from South Orange. Kathleen and I frequently car-pooled on the days when Hannah and Emily were both at school. Despite a fourteen-month difference in their ages, the two girls were very close.

On that Friday, Kathleen wasn't at work or at home. Sharon Bethel wasn't home either. Sharon, a social worker, was one of the few mothers I knew from Wee Care. Hannah was friends with her daughter Melissa, and I knew Sharon in the casual way you become acquainted with another mother when your children visit back and forth. She usually arrived home by three-thirty in the afternoon.

I looked at the clock. It was well past three-thirty now and yet Sharon's phone kept ringing and ringing. How strange, I thought.

While I was rifling through a closet for ribbon and tissue paper to wrap Caroline's gift, a stuffed animal, the phone rang. It was Kathleen, and she was nearly hysterical. She was crying so hard I could barely make out what she was saying. That morning, she had gotten a call from a friend whose daughter also attended Wee Care. She told Kathleen to come down to the school immediately, because a social worker with the state Division of Youth and Family Services (DYFS) was there and he was interviewing children. He had information that they might have been sexually abused. And Emily was one of those he was interviewing.

As Kathleen poured out her story, sobbing uncontrollably, I remembered the letter I'd received from the school's board of trustees a month earlier. The tersely worded note went out to all the parents and said that the county prosecutor's office was looking into allegations made by one of the children that a former Wee Care teacher had sexually abused him. No charges had been filed, the letter said, as if to anticipate and deter our fears. It worked.

A few days later, a letter from the center's director was placed in our children's cubbyholes at school. A meeting was called to discuss the investigation. A representative from DYFS would be there to answer questions.

Looking back, it seems incredible that I didn't attend that meeting. But the name of the teacher in question—Margaret Kelly Michaels, known to the children simply as Kelly—had never been mentioned in our house. Hannah wasn't even in Kelly's class and, moreover, the allegations were that Kelly had fondled little boys. And the knowledge that Kelly had resigned her position more than a month earlier, as far as I knew, was a further comfort. Besides, if Kelly had done anything to hurt my daughter, I knew Hannah would have told me.

My daughter was open and forthright, even as a toddler. At dinner, if she sneaked a piece of unwanted meat in a napkin and hid it under her chair so that she wouldn't have to eat it, she inevitably told me about it later. If a friend called with an invitation for Hannah to play with her child, I would have to ask my daughter before making the play date. Even at age three, she might refuse to go along somewhere if she didn't like the child.

4

"She's too bossy," Hannah might tell me about a child in her class, or, "She never wants to play anything."

Hannah was mature for her age, right from infancy. She sat unsupported at six months, gave up baby food at seven months, was completely toilet-trained by the age of two, and tied her shoes by age four. She talked early, too.

By the time she was a year old, Hannah not only babbled all the expected words—nose, mama, daddy, cookie—but mimicked what she overheard. When the phone rang, she crowed hello before I picked it up. Watching her father get into his car to go to work, she would invariably shout, "Bye, 'hon!"—my daily farewell to Jim.

Soon after she turned one, as she sat with Caroline in front of the television, Hannah gleefully uttered her first complete sentence—"I see Big Bird!"

A cheerful, dimpled baby with a round face framed by straight bangs, Hannah liked to sit in her high chair and empty onto her head bowls of anything—soup, cereal, ice cream. Once she sat happily on our kitchen counter while I demonstrated some quick-fix dishes for a photographer shooting pictures for a story I had written on how working mothers could streamline the dinner hour. A few months later, a national woman's magazine ran a picture of Hannah wearing one of my saucepans like a hat and looking quite pleased with herself.

She was probably a bit precocious because she had an older sister to emulate. Hannah and Caroline were very close, and Hannah was determined to do whatever Caroline did. Her desire to be like her older sister extended to her clothing. By the time Hannah turned two, she was insisting on wearing whatever Caroline wore. If her older sister had on a jumper, Hannah put one on too. If Caroline wore a sleeveless top, Hannah tore apart her dresser drawers until she found one.

She always loved music. A nursery rhyme could soothe her no matter how agitated, and I spent many a long car ride singing her my off-key renditions of "The Farmer in

5

the Dell" and "Twinkle, Twinkle, Little Star" just to keep her quiet. Her favorite toys were always musical ones, and her battered "Hickory Dickory Dock" wind-up clock was an essential item that went everywhere she did.

I took Caroline and Hannah to see *The Nutcracker* ballet when Caroline was six and Hannah was four. Caroline was restless in her seat and kept asking to go to the bathroom or for a snack, but Hannah sat raptly through the entire performance and said she never wanted it to end.

"It made me feel like dancing," she whispered later.

Hannah whispered only when she wanted to tell me something others weren't supposed to hear, so we often had conversations in hushed tones. Since she was a toddler, Hannah had confided in me about everything, so I knew that Kelly Michaels couldn't possibly have done anything to her. Or so I thought.

Except for selling Kelly Michaels Girl Scout cookies the preceding spring and occasionally chatting with her in the gym when I picked up Hannah and Emily, I had no contact with her. Nor did Hannah, as far as I knew.

Now my sister was sobbing out to me a horrifying litany of activities in which Emily said she had been forced to participate at school. On that sunny Friday afternoon, Emily told Lou Fonolleras, the DYFS (pronounced "DIE-fus") social worker, that she had watched Kelly sit at the piano nude and play "Jingle Bells." Emily said that during naptime Kelly had stuck a knife and a wooden spoon into her "bootie"—Emily's word for vagina.

I listened mutely, feeling nauseated as I tried to absorb the fact that my darling dark-haired niece had been sexually assaulted by a teacher she had trusted. Feeling inadequate and helpless, I tried to console my sister. After she hung up, saying she'd see me at Hannah's party the next day, I was engulfed by feelings of shock and sadness.

Emily is an only child whose parents were divorced. My sister had custody, and Emily saw her father a couple of times a week. She loved playing with my girls, who were almost like sisters to her. Whenever she came over, she would fling her arms around me for a cuddle. Then she would head straight for my bedroom closet and unearth all my old high-heeled shoes and purses. Emily loved playing dress-up, and she and Hannah would clomp around the house for hours, toting pocketbooks stuffed with small toys.

At times, Emily seemed lonely and almost waiflike. She was endearing and lovable, but she could also be moody and high-strung. I thanked God for Hannah—sweet-dispositioned, well-adjusted, and always candid. Had she been one of Kelly's victims, she would have confided in me immediately. I was sure of that, although I never came right out and asked my daughter if she had been a victim.

We parents had known a few weeks earlier that four little boys—not one—were involved in the scandal, and that Kelly Michaels was going to be indicted. These scant bits and pieces of information trickled down to us from the school's administrators. But we didn't really know very much. Wee Care director Arlene Spector treated the whole affair like an inconvenient nuisance that would eventually go away if she downplayed it.

Although none of the parents I knew were certain who the four victims were, we had our suspicions. I was friends with the parents of one of the boys—Benjamin Baird—but not close enough to come right out and ask if he was involved. At our house for a Memorial Day barbecue just one week earlier, neither Donald nor Cathy Baird had broached the subject. Not wanting to seem as if I was prying, I didn't ask them.

Kathleen hadn't mentioned any names when she said the DYFS investigator was interviewing other children. Now I wondered which other youngsters might be victims. Surely they must all be in Kelly's class. But how, then, to explain Emily's involvement. She was in Joan Higgins's class. Perhaps Kelly had been Emily's teacher when Joan was sick? I was so preoccupied with thoughts of my niece that nothing seemed to make sense.

When my husband got home from work, I pulled him aside and told him about Emily. He listened silently, but I could see he was shaken. He went out to cut the grass while I got dinner on the table and Maria bathed the girls and helped Caroline into a party dress. At seven o'clock, I decided to try Sharon Bethel's number once more.

This time, she answered immediately. Her voice sounded subdued, hushed, as if she were in the same room with a sleeping child she didn't want to awaken. I told her about the change in party plans and she promised to have Melissa at our house at the appointed time.

"I was trying to reach you all day today," I said finally. "Where were you?"

She hesitated. I felt suddenly tense, filled with inexplicable feelings of foreboding.

"I was going to call you a little later on this evening," she said slowly, as if each word were an effort. "I got a call from Arlene yesterday, asking permission for Melissa to be interviewed. I was at the school all afternoon, and it turns out that Melissa is one of the children who was abused by Kelly."

I stood there in the kitchen, cradling the phone to my ear so that the sounds of the running water and clattering dishes wouldn't drown out her voice. Sharon said Arlene had telephoned her the day before to say that the investigation at the school was widening. Lou Fonolleras had a list of names of children believed to be Kelly's victims. Some of the youngsters interviewed by Lou at the school had named Melissa when he asked them who else Kelly had "hurt."

Arlene asked Sharon if Lou could interview Melissa, and Sharon gave her permission. She drove to the school after her Friday classes and waited out the afternoon in an unused office she shared with other somber-faced parents whose children's names were on this list. She had to wait a long time because Lou was talking to other children.

"When Lou finally got to Melissa, she had things to say," Sharon told me. "Lou said it took her a long time to talk.

They finally went on a little tour of the school and it was in the choir room where she began to talk. She told him that Kelly made all the children take their clothes off and pile up on each other. Sometimes there would be silverware. Melissa said that Kelly would take a knife and a fork and a spoon and put them on the floor. She would take off her clothes and then all the kids would take off their clothes. Kelly would lie down on the silverware and have the children lay on top of her and they would make a stack."

Sharon paused several times; I knew she was crying. I stood immobilized to my spot on the kitchen floor, listening, fascinated with horror. It was seven-fifteen. Almost time to drive Caroline to the party.

I had about two minutes left before my world would be shattered.

"Lou told me that Melissa said that Kelly had touched her, so perhaps I might want to take her to the pediatrician for an examination," Sharon said. "I was absolutely in shock. I was just sitting there, answering him, saying, oh, yes, I will certainly do that, and yes, that's very unusual behavior. But inside I was screaming."

When I had called her, Sharon had been sitting at her kitchen table talking with her husband Pete and another Wee Care parent whose daughter had disclosed that day that Kelly Michaels had sexually abused her.

Now Sharon told me that while she was talking with Lou Fonolleras, he left the room to take a phone call. On the table before her was a yellow legal pad filled with notes he had taken while interviewing Melissa. His notes were scribbled all over the pad. Sharon leaned over to see if she could decipher his small handwriting. All she could read were six or seven names of other Wee Care pupils. Since Lou had told Sharon just minutes earlier that some of the children he'd interviewed named other youngsters as having been hurt by Kelly, Sharon inferred that this was a list of suspected victims.

"I don't like to be the bearer of bad news," Sharon told me, "but Hannah's name was on that list."

And at that moment, I had a terrible feeling that my daughter was a victim. My mind was flooded with images of Hannah in recent months, engaged in behavior that was so unlike her. Acting violent with her siblings and angry with me, wanting us to move away from home. They were images which until that moment I'd managed to repress, and suddenly it all made sense.

Oh, I would still try to pretend it wasn't so for two more days, until Hannah talked to Lou. Over the course of that endless weekend while we waited for her to be interviewed, I would look at my fragile, fair-haired middle daughter over and over and try to convince myself that it was all a mistake, that things like this don't happen when you're a good parent and when your child is as forthright as Hannah. But on the Friday I talked to Sharon, the comfortable complacence I'd been living with since we had gotten that first letter from the school suddenly evaporated, exposing raw anguish and utter shock.

I felt dizzy and short of breath, as if someone had just knocked the wind out of me. I heard myself murmuring the appropriate responses to Sharon. I thanked her politely, as if she had just reminded me about an upcoming PTA meeting that had slipped my mind. Somehow I said good-bye and hung up. Aware of Maria with me in the kitchen, humming and silently rinsing suds from the dishes, I mechanically put away the leftovers and excused myself. If I didn't tell Maria or anyone else, then maybe life would go on as before.

But I had to tell Jim. I walked out the front door and down the driveway, where he was busily washing the car. When I'm upset, I always pick up the phone and call my mother or one of my sisters. When Jim is troubled, he finds an excuse to do something by himself outside. Now he vigorously scrubbed the fender of our already gleaming white Renault with a soapy sponge. I hated what I had to tell him. Trying to focus on speaking calmly, I filled him in on what I'd just learned.

"I don't know what to do," I finished. "Should I call Arlene Spector? Do you think we should try to get Hannah interviewed as soon as we can? Maybe it's not true. Maybe Hannah just saw some of these things happening but she wasn't really in on them."

I was scanning my memory, trying to recall some of the odd behavior that Hannah had displayed in the past few months. I sat numbly on the front steps, watching her and Ellen as they rode their tricycles up and down the sidewalk in front of the house. Their laughter sounded foreign and faraway.

I knew how I could find out. I would take Hannah with me when I drove Caroline to the birthday party. And when we were alone, I would ask her if anything had ever happened at school that she didn't like. I knew my daughter, and I knew she would truthfully answer a direct question.

C H A P T E R

■ ■ ■ ■ ■ ■ ■ ■ ■ ■

2

With Caroline and Hannah buckled into seat belts in the back seat, I backed out of our driveway, wondering how to initiate a conversation about Wee Care without seeming too obvious. Trying to keep my tone casual, I asked Hannah where Kelly had been lately.

"Oh, she's on vacation," Hannah answered without missing a beat. Obviously, she wouldn't be taken in by such subtle questions. So I came right out and asked her if Kelly had ever done anything to hurt her. When Hannah assured me that Kelly hadn't hurt her, I asked if Kelly had ever touched her.

"Well," Hannah replied. "Sometimes she rubs my back at naptime. But that's all."

And that was the end of that. Caroline, sitting next to her sister, was so excited about the party she appeared not even to have heard our little exchange.

I went up to the door when I dropped off Caroline, who was clutching a sleeping bag and a small suitcase. The birthday girl had been at Wee Care with Caroline two years earlier, and although I knew her mother only slightly, I had to fight a sudden, irrational urge to tell her that my daughter had been sexually assaulted. Feeling like a robot, I hugged Caroline good-bye and chatted for a few minutes about the evening's plans—pizza and watching *Ghostbusters* on the VCR.

Back in the car, I buckled Hannah into her seat belt next to me in the front seat. "Hey, Mommy," Hannah asked suddenly, turning to fix me with her huge, guileless brown eyes. "When am I not going to have to take my nap at school anymore?"

My daughter had been asking me this question—in the same, almost offhand manner—for months, and I had never gotten to the bottom of why she didn't want to take a nap anymore. At first, I assumed that perhaps she was simply outgrowing her need to sleep in the afternoon. And the previous winter, when I had been on a three-month maternity leave, I had considered changing her weekly schedule from two full days to four half-days. I would be at home and could pick her up right after lunch instead of at five-thirty in the afternoon.

But I was exhausted after Robert's birth. Some post-delivery complications meant I had to stay in bed for a couple of weeks. The winter was unusually severe. It seemed pointless to drag Hannah out four mornings a week instead of two, and would be easier all around if she just kept to the same two-day schedule.

When I told Hannah about the change in plans, she didn't seem to mind. But she continued to inquire often, usually at breakfast, when she would no longer have to take her naps at school. And I kept gently reminding her that we'd decided to stick to her old routine.

Now, it was as if a light bulb suddenly went on in my head. I saw with horrible clarity why Hannah had been so eager to avoid naptime at Wee Care. I slammed on the brakes and shouted, "Hannah, why don't you want to take your naps at school anymore?"

Startled at first, she shrugged noncommittally. Her reply

was one I would hear her repeat often in the coming months.

"I don't know, I'm Forgetful Jones," she said, referring to a character on "Sesame Street."

After stopping at an ice cream parlor, we walked slowly up South Orange Avenue, the main street in town, licking our cones and looking in shop windows. I was feeling more and more uneasy. Even though Kelly wasn't Hannah's regular teacher, I wondered if my daughter was in Kelly's nap class. This, then, would be a regular period during the day when Kelly would have had easy, unsupervised access to Hannah. Now I tried to get Hannah to talk about Wee Care without having her raise her guard.

"Hannah, did anything ever happen at school that you didn't like?"

"No," she giggled, looking at me as if I had just told her the sky was purple.

"Did Kelly ever try to hurt you? No? You're sure? Did she ever do anything in naptime that you didn't like?"

"No," Hannah said firmly.

A tense, unfamiliar silence filled the car on the drive home.

Back at the house, I pulled Jim aside and summarized my unsatisfactory effort to pry anything from Hannah. "Either she's a great liar," I finished grimly, "or she wasn't involved in any of this."

Later that night, as soon as the younger three were asleep, I called Arlene Spector at home. She had a special fondness for my husband, who had donated his time to help erect several outdoor play structures at the school. Arlene and I shared a love of cooking, and we often traded tips on good restaurants. But tonight my tone of voice made it apparent that I was in no mood to socialize. I told her about my earlier conversation with Sharon Bethel and insisted that Hannah be interviewed first thing on Monday by Lou Fonolleras.

At first Arlene demurred, saying the list of suspected

victims was long and that she just couldn't promise anything. When I told her flatly that I intended to come on Monday and wait in her office until the investigator would see my daughter, she realized that she was no longer dealing with a rational feature writer. She said she would do her best to squeeze Hannah in at some point on Monday. After I hung up, the sheer insanity of our conversation—having to jockey with the authorities so my daughter could describe how she had been sexually assaulted—made me start shaking all over.

I called my mother. I'm the oldest in a large family, and we're all very close to one another and to my parents. My father and mother have always been there for us. I knew this weekend they had gone to their lakefront cottage in western New Jersey, about an hour from their Maplewood home. My Aunt Ginny and Uncle Jim were visiting them, and the four of them probably were playing bridge.

Though it was past eleven o'clock, my mother's voice on the other end of the line sounded as alert as if it were noon. She was used to getting calls at odd hours from her grown children, and she didn't sound the least bit surprised to hear from me. I got to the point right away.

"Did I tell you about that letter we got from Hannah's school in May about those four little boys being sexually abused?"

I could hear her inhale sharply, and I winced. The letter was so inconsequential to me that I hadn't even mentioned it to my mother. If such a letter had gone home with one of us when we were small, I bet my mother would have gotten to the bottom of it right away. What a terrible parent I was.

Unaware of the feelings of guilt that were making breathing a tremendous effort for me, my mother pressed me for information. An attorney in a prominent Newark law firm, she has an insatiable appetite for—and an enviable retention of—even the smallest details. I filled her in, beginning with the first letter and ending with my conversation with Sharon Bethel.

Together we started looking back over the months, jogging one another's memory to recall anything unusual in Hannah's behavior.

Hannah had always fit in well with other children. Not that she hadn't gone through her possessive periods—I could remember stretches when she was a toddler when she not only refused to let any other child including Caroline handle her toys, but wouldn't even let them touch her diaper bag or her bottle.

But once Hannah had outgrown this phase, she was very adaptive, playing well in groups of youngsters at school and at home with her sisters and cousins.

By nature she was a happy soul, not given over to Caroline's moods or Ellen's tantrums. Caroline could fly into a snit over the most innocuous remark. If Jim mentioned that he didn't much like the cookies she had picked out in the supermarket, she would burst into tears and fly off to her room, slamming the door.

And Ellen, well, Ellen could initiate a tantrum over anything at all. Some mornings, I would be practically limp with exhaustion before it was time to leave for work just from trying to maintain equanimity in my youngest daughter. She might have a tantrum after requesting ice cream for breakfast and getting no for an answer. Or she might lose emotional control if her hair wasn't combed the way she wanted it, or if she didn't get the particular juice glass that she desired, or if the bandage covering a scrape on her knee wasn't in the proper position, or if her sweatsuit was too tight or loose, warm or cold.

Life with Caroline and Ellen meant some tightrope-walking, lots of delicate balancing. But Hannah was affable, easy, and generally content with her life and herself. Now I found myself mentally reviewing what she'd been like of late. The way she seemed angry so often. The way she had been inconsolable while I was in the hospital to have Robert. At the time, we'd all thought it was because she'd just gotten over a flu and was still feeling clingy the way kids sometimes do when they're convalescing. But Hannah cried almost constantly the whole three days I was away, saying she was afraid that I might not come home.

And then there was the way she had hit the baby hard, on his head, the first day we came home from the hospital. Hannah had been two at Ellen's birth, which hadn't seemed to ruffle her placid temperament at all. In fact, as my mother had tucked Caroline and Hannah into bed the first night I was in the hospital with Ellen, two-year-old Hannah had grinned her sunshiny smile and said proudly, "Grandma, I'm not the baby anymore!"

But when Robert was an infant, she looked for opportunities to hurt him and was sullen when I insisted on sitting right next to her when she held him. I really was afraid if I didn't she might just toss him out of her lap onto the floor. Still, she'd seemed to get over the jealous feelings after a few weeks. We all just figured it was "a stage."

It wasn't until my mother and I began recalling the several occasions last winter when Hannah tried to stick objects like pencils and toothbrushes into her vagina that the first fingers of cold fear crept over me. She'd even attempted to insert things into her sisters' vaginas—something I'd never known Caroline to do. There was something so unsettling about watching a four-year-old run giggling from the bathroom, toothbrush in her hand, chasing one of her sisters. I'd scolded her sharply at the time, told her not to do that because she could hurt someone. And I'd sought the advice of my mother, who told me it was probably nothing to worry about.

"I didn't want to upset you, and Robert had just been born," she said now. "But I'll tell you something, honey. Not one of you ever did anything like that."

I couldn't sleep that night, so when Caroline called after midnight to say she was homesick and wanted us to come and get her, I didn't mind going. My eyes refused to close, preferring instead to stare blankly at the ceiling. I didn't cry. There would be plenty of time for tears tomorrow.

But at Hannah's birthday party the next day, it was the other mothers who had tears in their eyes while I ran around like an army drill sergeant, trying to keep two dozen five-year-olds busy for two hours in the balloon-festooned house while a steady drizzle outside made the steamy day that much muggier. The hunt for chocolate kisses—had I been crazy when that seemed like a good idea?—was staged in the living room and playroom. And because of the heat, the candies melted and were smeared everywhere as the guests pulled off the silver foil and gobbled their fill.

The mothers stood around in little knots and tried to compare notes on who had been called by Arlene and whose children were to be interviewed by DYFS. At some point, while the kids sat at the long dining-room table and stuffed themselves with ice cream cake, conversation among the young guests deteriorated into bathroom language. Various children shouted "doo doo and poo poo," "pissy" and "diarrhea house" to the great amusement of their peers.

Listening to this bawdy talk made some of the mothers look tearful again, and the contrast between their grieving expressions and the boisterous laughter and shrieks from their kids lent an aura of craziness to the party.

What's wrong with this picture? Why are all these women crying? Why is my daughter spouting the same kind of toilet talk she's been using for months, and why is it only now that I'm really listening to it for the first time and recognizing that it's not typical? Why have I glossed over her overtly sexual behavior of the past months, not wanting to overreact to what seemed like a preschooler's natural curiosity about the private parts of her body? How could I have failed to protect this child, whom I would die for, from harm?

I felt almost physically ill as I thought about all of this, and suffused with guilt as I watched my child tear the wrapping paper off her presents, then hand out the goody bags and say good-bye to all her friends. Having to hide my

18

feelings from Hannah was immensely difficult, for I was used to being as honest and open with her as she was with me.

◾

Somehow, I got through that endless weekend without letting Hannah see how upset I was. Arlene Spector had stressed the importance of not asking Hannah any leading questions because it could taint the interview, so I resisted the almost overpowering desire to say to her, Did Kelly stick a knife into your vagina? Did you really all take your clothes off and pile on top of each other? Did she sit at the piano nude and play "Jingle Bells"?

I waited until the kids were in bed at night and then I went out and sat on the front steps by myself to do my crying. Right from the start, Jim and I weren't good at comforting each other through any of this. We both were consumed by it, of course, but he didn't want to discuss it, while it was all I wanted to talk about. I snapped at him for not caring, he became disgusted with me for the uncontrollable fits of weeping that I allowed myself each night when the kids fell asleep. It set the tone for the coldness that would pervade our marriage in the next couple of years, and—as I found out later—it was a common behavioral pattern among other Wee Care parents.

On Monday, June 10, the day before Hannah's actual birthday, I dropped her off at school at 9 A.M. as usual, drove to my office, and worked until lunchtime. Hannah didn't know I got to her school hours earlier than usual that day because I slipped up the stairs past her classroom and went right to Arlene Spector's office. The interviewing procedure that had evolved informally in the previous two weeks consisted of Lou talking to the child alone in an empty office he'd been using, and then meeting with the parents to discuss his findings.

After telling me that Hannah would be taken in to see Lou about three-thirty, Arlene kept up a one-sided, cheerful conversation with me about restaurants she had recently visited. I watched the clock, tried to read the newspaper, and tried to compose myself for what I knew was going to come.

But still I wasn't prepared for the shock I felt when Lou escorted me into his makeshift office, closed the door, and told me sorrowfully that he was fairly certain Kelly Michaels had molested my daughter with tableware and forced her to participate in some bizarre sexual games.

In her interview with Lou, Hannah was reluctant to admit her involvement, and she began by denying that anything "bad" had ever happened to her at school. But Lou Fonolleras—a big, gentle man with a shape like Tweedledee—was soft-spoken and nonthreatening. Children soon learned that when they told him about what had gone on at Wee Care, Lou didn't get angry or start crying or say they should be punished for the bad things they had done.

Like the dozen or so Wee Care victims before her, Hannah eventually relaxed enough in Lou's presence to describe for him how Kelly had penetrated some of her classmates during naptime with knives and forks. And she reacted violently to the anatomically correct girl dolls set out on the desk in front of her, jamming knives and wooden spoons into their vaginas.

"That must have really hurt you," Lou commented to her at one point, and Hannah grimaced at the obviously painful memory and nodded. Then she caught herself.

"But it didn't happen to me," she told Lou quickly. "Only to the other kids."

At Lou's suggestion, the two of them took a walk up to the choir room, which was on the third floor of the church in an area that was supposed to be off limits to the day-care center. However, other children had told Lou that Kelly had taken them to that room, disrobed, and sat at the piano to play "Jingle Bells." Some youngsters said Kelly had directed them to beat her naked body with a wooden spoon and to fondle her pubic area. Some children said Kelly had sucked the boys' penises in the choir room (some children called it the music room or the piano room) and that she had inserted the handle of a knife into the children's rectums. Other children told of being forced to urinate on each other and on Kelly, and being made to drink urine.

Hannah wasn't ready yet to give information like this. But she showed Lou where she had sat during Kelly's rendition of "Jingle Bells" in the choir room, and she told him that Kelly had touched her vagina.

Lou said I should take Hannah to the pediatrician as soon as possible for an examination to see whether there was physical evidence of sexual abuse. He told me to watch her behavior closely over the next few days. She might feel like opening up to Jim or to me and telling us more about what had happened. Or she might start feeling tremendously guilty and begin misbehaving or acting babyish.

Feeling dazed, I picked up Hannah from her classroom and automatically checked the school refrigerator to see if there was a brown lunch bag of leftovers with her name on it. No bag. I recalled the frequent occasions the previous winter when at the end of the day I would find Hannah's entire lunch in the refrigerator. Exasperated, I would ask her why she hadn't eaten it. She would say that she hadn't had time or wasn't hungry, and then proceed to wolf down the fruit and sandwich in the car on the way home. I had mentioned this once or twice to Diane Costa, her teacher, who assured me that children weren't always hungry at mealtime but that they got nutritious snacks in the morning and afternoon.

No wonder Hannah hadn't had time to eat! She was kept too busy with Kelly's bizarre games. It was so hard not to show my grief. I got Hannah's jacket from her cubby and picked up the day's artwork from her spot on the bulletin board.

"Can we bake cupcakes tonight for me to bring to school tomorrow, Mom?" Hannah asked. "And can I bring my new Cabbage Patch doll?"

Cupcakes. Birthdays. Happy occasions for safe children whose parents care enough about them to see that they're not abused. How could Hannah face coming to school tomorrow? I never wanted to enter this building again.

Yet when I asked her if she wanted to go to school tomorrow, Hannah nodded emphatically. "But can I not take my nap at school?" she asked hopefully, wrinkling her nose.

I hugged her, wishing I'd recognized months earlier this innocent request for what it was—a cry for help, a plea to stop Kelly from hurting Hannah and her classmates.

"No, Hannah," I told her. "You don't ever have to take your nap at school again."

That night, Jim took out Hannah's class picture and showed it to her. Fourteen well-scrubbed preschoolers were arranged in three rows, those in the bottom row on little wooden chairs and those in the top row apparently standing on a bench. The children were flanked on one side by Diane Costa and on the other side by Kelly, who—since it had been taken in October 1985—was then an aide. In the picture, most of the children were grinning, and everyone was looking right at the camera.

"Who did Kelly hurt?" Jim asked Hannah. She carefully pointed to each child in the photograph, naming them one by one.

"All of them," she said simply. "Kelly hurt everybody."

CHAPTER

■ ■ ■ ■ ■ ■ ■ ■ ■ ■ ■

3

I remember reading, with a kind of detached fascination, the first few newspaper accounts that trickled east of the now-notorious day-care center sex-abuse scandal in Manhattan Beach, California. The case first made national headlines in 1984, when the founder and some staff members of the prestigious McMartin Preschool were charged with molesting more than a hundred children in their care.

Newsweek's cover story on May 14, 1984 was entitled "Sexual Abuse: The Growing Outcry over Child Molesting." The piece noted that "experts estimate that between 100,000 and 500,000 kids will be molested this year alone."

But even though the media was reporting that unspeakable atrocities—rape, sodomy, fellatio—were being committed on children the same ages as mine, I was every bit as naïve and sanguine as the other parents I knew. The "it-can't-happen-here" mentality was all-pervasive in the circle of mothers with whom I shared coffee, car pools, and an interest in Little League and the PTA.

That the besieged day-care center was in California made

perfect sense to me. In a state I perceived as having a higher-than-average concentration of serial killers and illicit drug users, it was no surprise to me that some kinky pedophiles had infiltrated a day-care center.

Neatly, I rationalized that sexual abuse doesn't happen in solid, middle-class communities populated by stable, comfortably well-off families like mine. And South Orange and Maplewood, the adjacent towns where most of the Wee Care parents lived and socialized, snugly fit the profile of the ideal suburb to raise kids. Young, growing families settle and stay here because the public schools are excellent and the community-run recreation programs for children are varied, abundant, and affordable.

Situated less than fifteen miles west of New York City, the towns are highly desirable for professionals who want to raise their families in a tranquil, tree-lined suburb.

We had two-year-old Caroline and three-month-old Hannah when we sold our Soho loft and moved out of Manhattan. My husband and I loved living in the city when we had no children and could take advantage of shows, restaurants, and museums. Even after Caroline was born in 1978, we still went out frequently, taking her with us to Chinatown, street fairs in Little Italy, and concerts in the parks.

By the time Hannah came along twenty-one months later, we'd left our one-bedroom Upper West Side brownstone apartment and bought an unfinished loft in Soho. Jim became an overnight expert on plumbing, carpentry, and electrical wiring, installing all the kitchen and bathroom fixtures, erecting walls where there had been none, and spending his nights after work nailing down a hardwood floor.

I was commuting to my job as a feature writer for a New Jersey newspaper, dropping Caroline off each morning with a loving, warm Haitian family in the West Eighties, and picking her up on my way home at night.

But it became increasingly clear that, unless you're very wealthy, the city is no place to live with children. Wheeling

24

the two girls to Washington Square Park in Greenwich Village during the hot summer of Hannah's birth, I tried to graciously sidestep the winos and panhandlers along Houston Street and the Bowery who gaped in astonishment at the sight of a young mother with two babies invading their territory.

We lived on the fourth floor of an industrial building with a temperamental freight elevator that would stall between floors without warning or ascend at heart-stopping speed to the roof. I preferred to walk, which often meant staggering up the stairs clutching both girls, a diaper bag, and a sack of groceries.

Our neighbors were mostly young, childless singles who had bought their lofts for investment purposes. And surrounding buildings that hadn't yet been converted to residences hummed with Spanish-speaking factory workers by day and stood eerily dark and silent by night.

Though health-food cafés, gourmet shops, and nouvelle cuisine restaurants were within walking distance, the closest place to buy a loaf of bread or a gallon of milk was Greenwich Village. And looking toward the future, we knew we could not afford to send our children to private school.

So we put our loft on the market and began looking for the traditional all-American dream—a house of our own. After we checked out Westchester County, parts of Brooklyn, and Long Island, it was Jim who suggested, "What about South Orange?"

I was reluctant at first. My family had moved there when I was eight, and we'd grown up in an oversized white elephant of a house on a street with dozens of children. Some of my younger brothers and sisters still lived at home with my parents, and most of the others were within a ten-minute drive of one another. I hadn't lived in South Orange since going away to college fifteen years earlier, and much as I loved everyone in my family, the prospect of being right on top of them was stifling.

But within a couple of weeks, Jim and I had found a cozy Colonial house with six bedrooms and a good-sized backyard. It was half a block from a small, pleasant park and an easy walk from a public elementary school. Best of all, it didn't cost much more than a young medical student was willing to pay for our refurbished loft.

On a sultry September afternoon in 1980, my brothers helped haul our furniture down the recalcitrant freight elevator and load it onto a rented U-Haul truck. Then we headed west through the Holland Tunnel. After seven years of life in the Big Apple, we were about to become suburbanites.

The village of South Orange has distinctive, turn-of-the-century houses set in generously sized yards and surrounded by towering oak and maple trees. When we have houseguests, they love being driven on a tour of the village, with its steep, winding roads, gently shaded parks, and quaint gas streetlights. Many of the stately, single-family homes are architecturally unique—pastel-colored, gingerbread-festooned Victorians sit next to majestic Tudors with leaded glass windows and doors. English country cottages, surrounded by painstakingly tended gardens, flank regal brick Colonials and Southern-style mansions fronted with columns and balconies. Mixed in with these one-of-a-kind homes are huge, rambling houses of no particular style but with a homespun charm of their own. Built in the days when families were larger and servants were easy to find, they boast eight or nine bedrooms; four or more tiled bathrooms; and libraries, butlers' pantries, and mud rooms. Now that families are smaller, these houses are likely to be lovingly restored by professional couples with just two or three children.

A measure of how much South Orange residents love reveling in their town's eclectic architecture is the enthusiastic turnout for the annual house tour, which is sponsored by a local civic group. Visitors pay six dollars apiece to view a half dozen or so houses. The event is traditionally held in the spring, when the village seems like one lush garden. Forsythia, crocuses, and daffodils, and later, azaleas and rhododendrons, provide dramatic splashes of color in spacious yards graced with delicate magnolias, flowering dogwoods, and weeping cherry trees.

The town's main thoroughfare, South Orange Avenue, is a perpetually busy street that zooms down the hill from the wealthy Newstead section of town, where homes have a spectacular view of Manhattan. From there it bisects the business district and snakes through the largely black Vailsburg section of Newark on its way to that city's downtown. Traffic is always heavy in "the village," as South Orange residents call their central business district, and the shortage of on-street parking sends many motorists scurrying to the shopping malls.

Still, I'm forever driving down to the village to pick up the newspapers and go to the bagel bakery. And it's traditional to celebrate our daughters' good report cards with hot fudge sundaes at the local ice cream emporium. But when I need basic items—socks or pajamas for the kids, or supplies for our aquarium—I drive five minutes to Maplewood.

Here the business district is cozy, family-oriented, and cohesive. Stores are arranged in Tudor-style buildings on one street that meanders out of a quiet residential area. In Maplewood village, you can get a good haircut, buy oatmeal and bran in bulk at reasonable prices, and choose good-quality meat and produce in a first-rate supermarket.

Maplewood is larger than South Orange and its racial mix and median income is nearly the same. Residents here get involved in government and civic affairs, and neighbors know and look out for one another. The annual Fourth of July celebration draws hundreds of revelers, as does a mid-December Christmas festival that features caroling and a visit from Santa Claus.

The towns share a single school system. But when we first came to South Orange, we were more interested in day

27

care than in the public schools. I had to return to work from a three-month maternity leave after Hannah's birth. We'd decided to look for a live-in person now that we had extra bedrooms. Our first sitter was Alva, a nineteen-year-old girl from Barbados whom we'd hired through a child-care agency. She weighed eighty pounds, was painfully shy, and moved noiselessly and unsmilingly through the house. By Thanksgiving, she had fallen ill with so many colds and assorted viruses I finally took her to the Maplewood doctor we used to see as children. Right before Thanksgiving, Alva told us she was so homesick she wanted to return to her family in Barbados.

But disaster—being left without day care when you have to go to work—was temporarily averted. My oldest brother's wife agreed to come to our house every day with her one-year-old daughter. It was a nearly ideal arrangement. Bernadette is a former nurse, the two of us felt comfortable with each other, and Caroline and Annie played well. But Bernadette was expecting a baby in June of 1981, so we had to find other day-care arrangements. After our experience with the stone-faced Alva, I wasn't eager to hire a live-in baby-sitter again. The idea of leaving my kids with another mother in her home didn't appeal to me either. I wouldn't know whether she parked them in front of the television all day. And though I had no sound basis for this theory, I felt sure the woman's own children would receive more of her attention.

A day-care center seemed like the best solution. And after looking at several in the area and talking at length to friends and friends of friends, we chose the Wee Care Day Nursery in Maplewood/South Orange. Children at the reputable, well-established school were divided according to age: three-year-olds through five-year-olds attended the Wee Care preschool, situated in St. George's Episcopal Church on Ridgewood Road in Maplewood. Those from nine months to three years were cared for at the toddler center, which was housed in St. Andrew's Church in South Orange.

Jim and I visited the toddler center and were shown around the spacious classrooms by the director, a capable, motherly woman with two children of her own. She answered all of our questions thoroughly, and the children seemed comfortable around her.

I was apprehensive about putting our two little girls, not quite one and not quite three, into a day-care center at all. But the toddler center was a bright and well-maintained place, and the two- and three-year-olds looked happy and closely supervised. We liked that the teachers appeared warm and caring, and the director was a highly visible presence. In the spring of 1981, we decided to enroll both girls there.

Hannah was the youngest child at the toddler center that spring. Just eleven months old and not quite walking, she joyously cruised around the smooth, toy-littered floor in her walker.

We kept our two daughters at the toddler center full-time until the fall of 1982, when Ellen was born. By then I'd decided I couldn't work full-time with three preschoolers in a day-care center. Ear infections, strep throats, and assorted colds and viruses had a way of attacking so that no two were ever ill at the same time. One would just be recovering from something when another would succumb. I knew I would be forever arguing with Jim about whose turn it was to take off from work and stay home with the sick child. We had to find a baby-sitter to come to the house, but I was afraid of getting someone as joyless as Alva.

While I was relating my fears to my twenty-year-old brother, Johnny, one day, he proposed (to my great surprise) that he become my baby-sitter. He was the lead guitarist in a band at the time, and working nights as a supermarket cashier. But his days were free and he needed the extra money.

To get a feel for what he would be letting himself in for,

Johnny took care of the girls one day while I disappeared to the mall. My mother and I felt certain that several hours with a four-year-old, a two-year-old, and a newborn would convince him that he wasn't cut out for baby-sitting. Much to everyone's surprise, he did well and took the job.

Johnny is gentle, kind, and unfailingly patient. My daughters loved him. He didn't mind folding diapers, enjoyed constructing huge ice cream floats for himself and the girls, and in his spare time he played his guitar and sang. He read my books on child care and development, and often quoted passages from them when advising me the proper time to introduce solid food or initiate toilet training. He taught Ellen all her colors before she was two. To help Caroline and Hannah learn about currency, he once made them a "money chart," gluing different combinations of real coins to a large piece of cardboard and printing how much each combination was worth.

When Caroline started kindergarten and began inviting little girls over to play, the children often begged Johnny to make them his Tuna-Mac, a combination of Kraft macaroni-and-cheese and canned tunafish. By the end of the year, their mothers were asking Johnny for his recipe. Several of them told me how lucky I was to have him, and I knew it.

And despite the way everyone in our family teasingly called Johnny Mr. Mom, he ended up baby-sitting for us for nearly two years. It wasn't until I was pregnant with Robert that Johnny decided to return to school full-time, and we hired Maria to be our housekeeper.

During the years Johnny baby-sat, Caroline had continued to attend Wee Care part-time. Jim and I wanted her to be able to play with other children her own age and to have the nursery school experience. When Caroline was four, she "graduated" from the toddler center to the preschool in Maplewood. Things were run quite differently over there. For one thing, the ratio of staff to children was about one to eight instead of one to four, as it was at the toddler center. Supervision seemed looser. The school was larger and more spread out, and it didn't seem as light and cozy as the toddler center. Arlene Spector, who co-directed both the preschool and toddler center, wasn't around much.

But Caroline adjusted well, and when Hannah turned three, she began to attend the preschool two days a week. (She'd been staying home with Johnny, but we felt she needed to be in a program.) Even though it was a financial struggle to pay for a baby-sitter in our home and for nursery school, we—like most parents—wanted the best for our children.

And Wee Care had a reputation for being one of the finest schools in our area. It first opened in 1975 with five pupils. The toddler center was opened in St. Andrew's Church in South Orange in 1980.

One co-founder of Wee Care, who had primary responsibility for the toddler center, had her degree in day-care administration and supervision from the Bank Street College of Education, one of the foremost schools in the East for early childhood education. She had impressed me immediately as a competent professional. And there seemed to be a lot more about the school to like.

Parents of prospective pupils were given a brochure about staffing and programs. Wee Care's goal was to provide "a safe, child-oriented environment which offers diverse activities such as art, music, movement, creative play, science experiences, and an individualized math and language arts program."

It sounded like paradise in a day-care center. And many parents were eager to sign up. Between 1975 and 1981, the budget increased from $15,000 to $165,000. The number of families serviced per year went from 25 to 125, and the staff increased from 4 to 14. There was a tremendous need in our community for a center like Wee Care because most other schools were traditional nursery schools geared to nonworking mothers. They offered programs for a few hours each day, but no all-day programs.

The programs were varied. At the preschool once, to

31

stimulate the children's awareness of the problems facing the handicapped, pupils simulated what it would be like to be disabled—they painted while blindfolded, tied their shoelaces while wearing gloves, and tried out wheelchairs and braces. Another time, youngsters took a trip to a local gas station, where a woman mechanic explained the uses of natural resources like water and oil.

There were gymnastics classes, trips to the library, family picnics, baseball games, and a series of music lessons entitled Piano Preludes. Visits to the local firehouse, the library, and the Papermill Playhouse were planned throughout the year.

Wee Care also offered occasional programs during the evening for parents. Not parents' discussion groups, but instruction in craft-making, for instance, or how-to parenting workshops.

The year before Robert was born, when Caroline was in kindergarten and Hannah was in her first year at the preschool, I was asked to be a panelist at a Wee Care parenting workshop on how working mothers can effectively manage their time. I was surprised and a little amused. I'd written first-person articles for *Family Circle* and other women's magazines on how working mothers can cope. Arlene had always hung them on the bulletin board with an arrow pointing to my byline. Still, privately I considered myself one of the least organized mothers I knew. But I spoke at Wee Care anyway, and the workshop was a huge success. Several listeners even laughed at my jokes—a first!

Each spring, an auction at the school featured goods and services donated by the parents. Jim and I always attended this fundraiser, because it was fun to socialize and hear some of the offbeat things you could bid on: a parent/child dental examination and teeth cleaning, bridge lessons, a ride in a private plane, help with one's income taxes, an interior design consultation, and having one's will drafted.

My contributions to the event were always much more mundane—baked goods and hors d'oeuvres for the refreshments table, or new baby clothes I'd received as gifts after my kids were too big to wear them.

The auction reflected the diverse nature of the Wee Care parents' occupations. They were mostly professionals—they had to earn fairly decent salaries because Wee Care was expensive. Among them were dentists, home economists, teachers, bankers, accountants, lawyers, and artists. There were an advertising executive, social workers, a pop-music composer, and a clothing designer.

Theoretically, both the toddler center and the preschool permitted parents to drop in during the day. But in reality few of us did. When you're forty-five minutes or an hour away from your child's day-care center, you can't exactly drop everything and rush back to the school at lunch hour or on a coffee break.

Coming to the preschool at naptime was definitely frowned upon. I can remember arriving early once to take Hannah to the doctor for a checkup. The door to the nap room was closed and an annoyed-looking Diane Costa made it clear that she did not want me in there disrupting the children. Instead, she brought Hannah out to me in the hall.

Wee Care parents were kept up to date on school events and schedules with newsletters and monthly calendars. These were cheery bulletins, illustrated with drawings of flowers and puppies, dinosaurs and goldfish bowls, that highlighted each month's upcoming activities for children and their parents. The calendars listed each month's "curriculum units": March was the month to discuss weather, animals, and ecology; April featured dinosaurs and music; and that May, the teachers planned instruction in plant growth and the use of building blocks to learn math, science, and language.

Two notes on those calendars seem particularly ironic to me now. In January 1985, a performing group called Tales à la Puppetry presented an educational puppet show to the children called "Don't Talk to Strangers." Entertaining as the show may have been, its lesson—that children's bodies are their own and that it's okay to say no to anyone who tries to touch you—was lost on the youthful viewers at Wee Care. And if it taught the youngsters not to trust strangers, it unfortunately didn't warn them not to trust their teacher.

The other note, about a workshop Arlene planned to attend, appeared on the calendar for June 7, 1985. I doubt Arlene ever got to her workshop—the seventh was that grim Friday when life seemed to fall apart.

While the monthly calendars portrayed the preschool as a safe, stimulating environment for young children, there was a lot going on during the 1984–85 school year that wasn't conveyed to parents via these monthly bulletins— such as the lack of supervision of teachers, the difficulty in hiring qualified staff members, and the absence of a concerned, involved director.

The toddler center and the preschool were two very different places, and those differences began with the physical layout. The toddler center was housed completely in the church basement, a huge, bright playroom that doubled as a nap room, and two smaller rooms used for lunch and structured activities. The outdoor play area wasn't ideal, but it was adequate: a long, narrow, fenced-in yard with toys and a sandbox.

The teachers at the toddler center were extremely conscientious about keeping track of how much their charges ate, slept, and played. When parents came to pick up their children at the end of the day, they could refer to a notebook in which the teachers had entered notes on each child's behavior and food intake for the day.

The preschool, for older children, occupied parts of three floors of St. George's Church. Stairs led down to a basement corridor that opened onto three classrooms. To the right was the block room and to the left was the "work jobs" room, where pupils worked on various projects. This room also had a refrigerator, and it doubled as a lunch room.

A third room, called the art room because it contained blocks and other toys for building, was darker than the others because it had fewer windows. The art room and the block room really comprised one large, L-shaped room that could be divided into two by shutting an accordion-pleated divider. Both these rooms were darkened after lunch and used as a nap room.

Artwork and papers to be taken home were stored in open cubicles, labeled with the children's names, that lined the walls of the three classrooms. The small corridor onto which these rooms opened was lined with the children's cubbies, where coats, boots, and extra clothes were kept.

On the second floor, Wee Care only used the gym and a bathroom, while the kindergarten and director Arlene Spector's office were on the third floor. The rest of the space on these floors were church offices and meeting rooms. Also on the third floor, beyond the kindergarten, was a room with a piano and choir robes. This, along with the other rooms used by the church, was definitely supposed to be off limits to Wee Care.

Teachers didn't monitor children at the preschool as closely as they did at the toddler center, but that seemed logical. A written record of a one-year-old's day was practically essential, but you didn't need to look in a notebook to find out if your four-year-old had slept at naptime or eaten all his lunch. Perhaps if records had been made of how the children spent their days, administrators might have noticed that something was disrupting the youngsters' eating and napping patterns.

Hannah seemed happy at the preschool during the 1983–84 school year, and we signed her up for the 1984 summer session. It wasn't until that fall that twenty-two-year-old Margaret Kelly Michaels got a job there as an assistant teacher. I was pregnant with Robert at the time, and after he was born in January I was going to take a three-month maternity leave. Although we planned to keep Maria while I was on leave, we enrolled Hannah for the 1984–85 school year at Wee Care. Among her friends that year were Benjamin Baird, who had been with her at the toddler center, Melissa Bethel, and Casey MacKenna.

Hannah scarcely knew Joshua Peterson, a blond three-year-old who was just starting at the preschool that fall and was not in her class. But before the 1984–85 school year ended, Joshua's words would have a profound effect not just on Hannah and our entire family, but on the other Wee Care children and their families as well.

Joshua's mother Anna thought highly of the center and frequently recommended it to friends looking for child care. She felt very positive about Wee Care, and was glad that Joshua would be attending a Maplewood preschool so that he would be able to make friends in his hometown before entering kindergarten the following fall. In good weather, she used to bicycle over to the preschool to pick him up. On the way home, they often talked about Joshua's day.

"He, of all my children, is the one who talks the most about stuff day to day," Anna would recall later. "And you'd say what did you do in school today and he'd tell you 'We painted, we drew, we did sounds.' He'd just talk about it."

Despite Anna's high regard for the center, though, she soon realized that Joshua didn't seem happy. In January 1985, after just four months of attending Wee Care, the child began complaining about having to take his naps at school. He would tell Anna, "I don't want to go to school 'cause I'm going to have to take a nap."

She figured he was just outgrowing his need to sleep in the afternoon. But he made such a fuss about not wanting to take a nap at school that Anna sometimes asked her girl friend to pick him up early so he could avoid taking a nap.

Anna also talked to Joshua's teacher, Joan Higgins, about his aversion to naptime, which lasted from 1 until 2:30 P.M. Joan suggested that Anna send something special from home, such as a stuffed toy or a book, for Joshua to play with in the nap room if he didn't feel like sleeping. Joan went home at one o'clock, and then Kelly was in charge of one nap room (the block room) for the first half of the nap period, from one to one forty-five. Another teacher, Brenda, had the second half of the nap period—one forty-five to two-thirty—and Anna always assumed that Brenda was Joshua's teacher during the entire nap. Anna didn't even know who Kelly was.

As the school year wore on, Joshua became frightened of being left alone on any floor of his house by himself, and he would go around turning on lights. He started to sleep with his parents in their room.

By March of that year, the little boy began stating flatly that he did not want to go to school. He shoplifted small items out of stores, and in February, he drank a sample bottle of dishwashing liquid that had arrived in the mail.

Joshua had always been "real sweet," according to his mother. "He was very friendly and I would say he was outgoing and huggy," she would recall later. "He loved to hug and be hugged. He liked visiting. He was a very social creature. On the weekends he loved to go to my girl friends' houses and visit with their children, and he was always up for a party. And he was just a fun-loving little kid."

But the outgoing, friendly child began to change around January of 1985. Joshua began verbally abusing visitors who came to the house. On more than one occasion, he bit or kicked people who knocked at the front door or walked past on the sidewalk. His mother had to remove her son from several friends' parties because of his disruptive behavior. "And everybody kept saying to me, 'What happened to Joshua? What is the matter?' " Anna said later. "He changed very drastically. I couldn't take him places."

But Anna and her husband were having problems of their own. Dan was in the process of switching jobs, and he had to work nights in his new job as a computer operator. At the height of their marital troubles, Dan left the house twice and stayed away for several days each time. Joshua was anxious when his father wasn't living at home, and Anna attributed his jarring behavioral changes to the difficulties she and her husband were having.

That winter, Joshua frequently complained about "his bum" being sore, and when his mother examined the area she saw that it was inflamed. Assuming that his sore bottom was due to sloppy toilet habits, she put Vaseline on the area, and bought packaged "wipes" so that he could clean himself better than he could with toilet paper.

Around February of 1985, Joshua began asking whether he needed to have his temperature taken. He would ask his parents and his older brother, "Do I need my temperature taken? Am I hot?" No, they would tell the little boy, you're not sick.

On April 30, 1985, he woke up with his upper body covered with a chicken-pox-like rash. Anna made an early-afternoon appointment with her pediatrician.

Joshua didn't seem at all upset to be missing school. He and his mother walked the two-and-a-half blocks to the doctor's office, and because they had the first appointment, they didn't have to wait long. Joshua played with puzzles until it was their turn to go into the examining room, where nurse Laura Hadley instructed him to lie down on the table. When she inserted a thermometer into his rectum, he looked up at her and said, calmly and matter of factly, "This is what my teacher does to me at school."

The nurse looked at Anna and asked, "What teacher?" And Joshua said, "Kelly. . . . Her takes my temperature every day at school."

The nurse was standing behind Joshua because she was taking his temperature, and she mouthed the words to Anna, "Who is Kelly?" Anna just shook her head. She had no idea.

Anna managed to maintain her composure. "I was shocked," she says. "But I was very calm. It just seemed like time stopped for a moment. It just seemed so amazing. It was totally out of my experience as a mother. I didn't want to upset him. Since I didn't know what to do, I thought the best thing was to do nothing."

When the doctor entered the room a few minutes later, Anna didn't even mention it to him. She didn't want to alarm Joshua. Back home, though, she asked her son what else Kelly had done to him at school.

"He leaned back against the refrigerator, put one leg up in the air and the other leg kind of out like this, so he was sort of balanced on the back of his spine," she recalled. "He put his hand over his genitals, and started rubbing it, and he said, her uses the white jean stuff."

"The white jean stuff?" Anna asked.

"The white jean stuff," Joshua said. "You have to be real careful not to get it on your pants because if it does it will turn your jeans white and everyone will know."

"Know what?" Anna asked.

"Know her takes your temperature," Joshua replied.

He told his mother that Kelly had taken the temperatures of several other small boys at the school. Specifically, he named Timmy Frankel and Brian DeLuca.

Anna is a self-possessed, dark-haired woman in her mid-thirties who grew up in north Jersey. She tends to state what's on her mind without caring about what others might think. She is a graphic artist who runs her own business, and is not known to be reticent or indecisive.

Although she never doubted for an instant that the incidents described by her youngest son had actually happened, she didn't have the slightest idea what she ought to do about it. So she telephoned her pediatrician to ask his advice. He suggested that she call the New Jersey Division of Youth and Family Services (DYFS). And he told her not to worry about contacting the parents of the other children Joshua had mentioned, because that was the school's responsibility.

Anna didn't call any parents. But she did call the preschool and speak to Arlene Spector. It was Arlene who explained that Kelly had the first part of naptime, before Brenda. Arlene also described Kelly to Anna: "She said she had brown hair, a big face, and was overweight, and she [Arlene] told me Kelly lived in Pittsburgh," Anna recalled later.

At DYFS, Anna's phone call was referred to Lou Fonolleras. DYFS authorities contacted the county prosecutor's office, and an investigation began.

Anna outlined for the prosecutor's office what her three-year-old son had told her Kelly did to him and to other Wee Care children. She said Joshua told her that almost every day, Kelly would pretend to be a nurse and take the children's temperatures rectally. First Kelly would put "gasoline" on the thermometer, Joshua said, and Anna finally figured out he meant Vaseline.

Then thirty-five-year-old assistant Essex County prosecutor, Sara Sencer talked to Joshua.

"Do you like school?" she asked him, and he answered yes. But when asked whether he liked naptime, he said no, because Kelly took his temperature.

"Does she take it in your mouth?" Sara asked.

"No," he said. "You don't put gasoline in your mouth!" And he gestured to his rectum and said that was where Kelly inserted the thermometer.

Sara then showed Joshua her anatomically correct dolls. They resembled any other floppy-soft rag dolls with an important difference: the girl dolls had breasts, pubic hair, rectums, and vaginas, and the boy dolls had rectums and penises. Investigators of sexual abuse cases use the dolls to help very young children verbalize what happened.

Joshua pulled down the doll's pants and pointed to the rectum as the place Kelly had put the thermometer. He also reiterated for Sara the names of the other two children.

Joshua also was taken to the Maplewood police station, where he identified Kelly's photograph out of a group of pictures of Wee Care teachers.

Now the prosecutors faced the difficult task of calling the

parents of the children Joshua said Kelly had hurt, and asking permission to interview the youngsters. Blond, shy little Timmy Frankel, just turned five, readily admitted his involvement and said that Kelly had touched his penis and backside, and that she hit him on the leg. But dark-haired, big-eyed Brian De Luca, who had turned five a month earlier, seemed terrified, and he denied having been victimized.

Meanwhile, Sara Sencer asked Wee Care's Board of Directors not to notify all the parents until the investigation was completed. The board, which was made up of about a dozen parents, had never been faced with anything like this before. They began holding emergency meetings at night in one another's homes, trying to decide how to proceed. They wanted to cooperate with the prosecutor's office. But at the same time, they felt a responsibility to let all the parents know—as soon as possible—what was going on. At this point, Sara thought the acts committed were fondling and touching.

Meanwhile, the rest of us parents were blissfully unaware that anything was amiss at the school. I had returned to work two weeks earlier from maternity leave, and I was learning what it's like to be a working mother of four children under the age of seven.

C H A P T E R

■ ■ ■ ■ ■ ■ ■ ■ ■ ■

4

After being home for three months, I missed my kids terribly when I returned to work, especially baby Robert. Sometimes my eyes would fill up with tears while I was driving to the office in the morning, and I couldn't wait to get home to them.

In the evening, there never seemed to be enough time to cuddle Robert, help Caroline with her first-grade homework, and still read as many stories to Hannah and Ellen as they felt they were entitled to. My job as a reporter seemed more complex and high pressure than ever, the forty-five-minute commute each way ate up so much precious time, and I often felt as if I was living on a roller coaster that never stopped.

So when I first heard allegations of sexual abuse, it was almost like hearing about a war on the other side of the world. I felt saddened and sympathetic, but it had nothing to do with my family, my life.

The Wee Care Board of Directors sent a letter in early May from the board's co-presidents. It was maddeningly unspecific:

There is currently an investigation being conducted by the Essex County Prosecutor's Office regarding serious allegations made by a child against a former employee of the Maplewood Center. We are cooperating with the prosecutor's office in this matter.

The Board has met to discuss these allegations and their implications for the children, their families, and the school. While we are very concerned, it is important to emphasize that no formal charges have been made. The Board has discussed a variety of measures, and has appointed a committee to determine what actions need to be taken in this matter. As we receive more information we will be communicating with you further.

My sister Kathleen and I discussed the letter at the time and tried to figure out who the "former employee" in question was. For all we knew, it might be someone who had taught at the school years earlier. Neither of us was aware that Kelly had suddenly left her job at Wee Care a few weeks before. We learned later that Kelly had told Arlene Spector she was leaving for personal reasons.

Kathleen and I hadn't noticed her absence, and we didn't know who her alleged victim was. We certainly never thought our own daughters were involved. And a week later, when we got a handwritten note from Wee Care director Arlene Spector about a parents' meeting to be held at the school, neither of us went.

As it turned out, the parents who attended the meeting on Wednesday, May 15, learned very little about the specifics of the abuse at Wee Care. The name of the accused teacher was not divulged, although it was conceded that more than one boy was involved.

It was frustrating for the parents, who were anxious about any possible effects on their own children, and a couple of mothers later telephoned Arlene at the school to probe further what kinds of things the boys had accused the teacher of doing.

"It was very benign stuff," Arlene told them dismissively. "On a scale of one to ten, I'd say it was about a three."

One of the speakers at that first meeting was Peggy Foster, a social worker from DYFS. Ms. Foster discussed a host of symptoms that sexually abused children exhibit, such as bed-wetting, nightmares, clinginess, tantrums, and a change in eating habits.

Julie Minetti, whose four-year-old, Jodie, attended Wee Care that year, couldn't believe how closely the symptoms described her daughter's behavior in the past six months.

"That's Jodie!" she kept thinking in amazement each time another symptom was described. And she even raised her hand at one point and asked Ms. Foster what it meant if your child displayed just about every symptom. She asked the question facetiously. And as Julie recalls, Ms. Foster didn't take it real seriously.

No parent suspected, back on that warm May evening in 1985, that dozens of Wee Care children had been molested by Kelly Michaels. And none knew that she had threatened to harm the youngsters and their parents if they told anyone.

But interviewing Joshua Peterson had been like scratching the surface of a skin boil. Once probed, pus begins to ooze and, before long, to pour from the wound. And so it was with the giant infection that was Wee Care. Slowly at first, a few children began to put into words the monstrous acts that had been committed on them by a trusted teacher. Then, more youngsters verbalized the degradation they had endured, until by the end of June, it became clear that many of the children at the school were involved.

In early May, something happened that gave the investigators a preview of the multiple horrors yet to unfold. The father of a Wee Care pupil questioned his son and learned that Kelly had sexually assaulted him. The child disclosed

44

to his father that the teacher had used a spoon to molest him.

The boy was five-year-old Benjamin Baird, whose father, Donald, is a tall, husky guy who looks as if he could just as easily be a football quarterback as the highly successful stockbroker that he is. Donald is a devout Catholic, warm and loving to his family, and adored by his two children. He is eminently calm, low key, and as solid as a rock. The kind of man whom others automatically look to as a natural leader, Donald is popular with his colleagues, neighbors, and the parishioners in his church.

Donald's wife Cathy is blond, sweet-faced, and sensible. A schoolteacher, she decided to return to work after Benjamin's birth. After having Benjamin cared for by a baby-sitter for a while, the Bairds decided to put him in a day-care center when he was a year old. Donald and Cathy were diligent about researching every available facility. Donald took some time off from work to look at different schools. They talked to the schools' directors, observed classes, and watched the children interact with each other. Finally, the Bairds chose Wee Care's toddler center. They felt it was the finest they could do for their son.

Benjamin was enrolled at the toddler center for more than a year before his brother George was born. After the birth, Benjamin moved over to the preschool and was a favorite with all the teachers there. He has the same rugged good looks and easy self-assurance as his father, and he was popular with the other children.

Cathy had the option of not returning to work after George was born, and she decided to stay at home with the kids. But Cathy kept Benjamin at Wee Care part-time so that he would be able to play with children his own age in a nursery-school setting.

Cathy and I grew friendly when Hannah and Benjamin were at the toddler center together, and then her son George and my daughter Ellen were born within two weeks of each other. We'd visit each other's houses for coffee, and sometimes she and her husband and Jim and I would go out for dinner on a Friday night. On these occasions, we talked about new movies, real estate, and, of course, our children.

But Cathy never told me that Benjamin had grown violent and physically abusive to his younger brother during the fall of 1984. Nor did she tell me about a game that Benjamin had begun playing that winter. The game, Butts and Penises, was a bizarre variation of Duck Duck Goose. The game so disturbed Cathy that she called her pediatrician and asked him about it. He told her it was typical for preschool boys to be sexually curious and to masturbate. When the behavior continued, Cathy called the doctor again. She mentioned that she might consult a psychiatrist. But the pediatrician said he thought it was unnecessary, and that the psychiatrist would tell her the same thing: it's a phase, ignore it, he'll get over it.

Initially, Cathy didn't even consider that Wee Care might be a possible cause for her son's deteriorating behavior. "None of us looked for it," she said later. "You found what was considered the best school around, you paid for it, and you thought everything would be okay. It boiled down to trust. We trusted the school completely."

But finally, midway through the school year, Cathy called Wee Care, described the behavior to Arlene Spector, and asked her if anything at school could be causing Benjamin to act that way. Arlene assured her that nothing out of the ordinary was going on at school. She asked Cathy if anything had changed at home that might explain Benjamin's behavior. It hadn't.

Cathy didn't discuss Benjamin's disturbing game with any of her friends, though.

"There comes a point when you're embarrassed," she said later. "You don't want people to think your kid is perverted." Cathy recalls that around the same time, Benjamin would go to the bathroom medicine chest and take out her box of tampons. When she asked him why, he told her that he "just felt like playing with them."

Although he had never had any problems sleeping, Benjamin grew fearful of going to bed, and he had nightmares. "Leave the light on," he begged his mother night after night. "Don't leave me," he would wail pitifully. "Don't go downstairs and leave me."

Cathy was perplexed and a little annoyed because Benjamin had never acted like that before. She also was puzzled by an incident that occurred one day when she went to pick Benjamin up from school in the afternoon a little earlier than usual.

She walked down the stairs and opened the door to the darkened nap room, where a dozen children were lying on their mats. Kelly, the only teacher in the room, was standing over Benjamin. When he saw his mother, Benjamin jumped up from his mat, rushed to greet her, and gave her such an enthusiastic embrace that he practically knocked her down.

When Kelly turned and saw Cathy, she gestured toward Benjamin and said, "You know, he's so sweet. When all the children are upset, he's the one that soothes them and calms them down. He's wonderful . . . did you know that?"

Cathy thanked her, hugged Benjamin, and then they left. She never thought about the incident again until months later.

That year, Benjamin grew increasingly anxious while getting ready for school in the morning. He insisted on getting there early so that he could "protect the girls." Benjamin's best friend, Henry Donnelly, made the same request of his father, Frank, who dropped him off at school in the morning. Privately, Frank and Cathy used to laugh about it. They thought it was kind of cute that their boys were being so chivalrous—macho, really—at their tender age.

Among the positions Cathy held in the community was a seat on Wee Care's Board of Directors. So along with other board members, she was notified in the beginning of May

47

by the board co-president of the allegations of sexual abuse.

Because Benjamin was a natural leader who enjoyed being in the middle of things, and because of all the behavioral changes she had noticed over the past several months, Cathy wondered if he might have been involved. She and Donald sat him down at the kitchen table and calmly asked if Kelly had ever done anything to hurt him or any of the other children at school. No, Benjamin insisted, kicking the leg of the table and refusing to look his parents in the eye. The longer they sat there, the harder he kicked and the more bad-tempered he became. Finally, Donald suggested that Cathy take George up and give him his bath so that he could talk to Benjamin alone. Donald had a trusting, open relationship with his son, and he felt confident that Benjamin wouldn't lie to him.

He was right. Although he appeared fearful and troubled, Benjamin told his father that Kelly had touched his penis with a spoon in the bathroom, and that she had locked him in a closet with another child. Cathy and Donald were stunned. Now Benjamin's behavior of the past few months was beginning to make sense.

A couple of days later, the Bairds took their son to speak to Detective George McGrath in the county prosecutor's office. Benjamin described how he and other boys had been victimized by Kelly in the bathroom and the nap room. He told Sara Sencer and George McGrath in separate interviews that Kelly had put a spoon under his penis.

When he was interviewed by Lou Fonolleras in June, Benjamin said Kelly held up his penis with a fork, pushed a fork under his scrotum, and rapped him across the penis with a wooden spoon. Benjamin also named other boys as Kelly's victims. Later on, when asked why he hadn't told anyone, Benjamin said he was afraid to tell because Kelly held a knife to his face and threatened to kill him and his parents if he did.

"Kelly said did I know what happened to little boys who

told," Benjamin said. "They got chopped up into itty-bitty pieces so their mother could never, ever find them."

Cathy felt numb. She couldn't even talk to any of her friends about it because other Wee Care parents had not yet been notified of the allegations of abuse.

Donald was even more devastated. In ten years of work, he had missed very little time due to sickness. Now he took off three days in a row and sat at home, unable to function. The following Sunday, Donald and Cathy took Benjamin to the Maplewood Police Department so that detectives there could videotape the little boy's statement. Henry Donnelly, Benjamin's best friend, had come along, too, because Benjamin had named Henry as another child Kelly had touched. So far, Henry wasn't talking.

It was a lovely warm spring afternoon, and Frank Donnelly had brought along a baseball bat so that afterward, they could all go to the park and play ball.

At the station, Benjamin carefully answered all Sara Sencer's questions. Then the video camera was turned on. But after taping Benjamin's interview the first time, the technician realized his equipment wasn't working and they had to do it all over again. This time, Benjamin's answers sounded rehearsed, as though he had been coached. The Bairds felt irritated, but they tried not to show it.

Next, it was Henry Donnelly's turn. But he appeared terrified, and was reluctant to respond to even the simplest questions about school. So Sara brought Benjamin back into the room, hoping that Henry would see that nothing bad had happened to his friend when he talked about Kelly.

But when Benjamin described for Sara how Kelly fondled the boys with spoons, Henry denied it.

Benjamin looked puzzled. "Yes, Henry, it did so happen," he said.

Henry turned his fearful face to his friend and said softly, "Benjamin, I said no."

At this point, Sara decided to intervene. "Okay, little boys," she said. "Just tell the truth."

Frank Donnelly, standing out in the hall listening, was outraged. He had had enough. It seemed to him like Sara was bullying his child into talking when the child was obviously petrified. Frank smashed the baseball bat over the staircase bannister, and began to scream obscenities at a startled Sara. "How dare you?" he shouted. "How dare you destroy what these boys have had, and what they have meant to each other over the past six months?"

He pulled his son out of the room and the two families left the police station. It took half an hour for his wife Mary and the Bairds to calm him down. Five-year-old Henry, who watched his distraught father lose his temper over incidents that the little boy perceived as having been his fault, was shaken. Although other Wee Care children later said that Kelly molested Henry, he remained reluctant to talk about what happened to him.

Exhausted, the two couples and their young sons drove back to the Bairds' house, where Cathy let Donald and the others out of the car. Then she went on to pick up their younger son at the baby-sitter's and buy some take-out food for their dinner. She felt too weary even to think about cooking. Mary Donnelly took the boys out to play on the swing set in the Bairds' backyard.

And suddenly, Donald's grief became too much for him to bear. He felt as though he were losing control, as if he might have a breakdown right there. He asked Frank to hold his pocket pen knife because he thought he was going to do something with it that he shouldn't. Then he went out and trashed the garage, throwing bicycles and scattering tools everywhere. He tore down the backyard fence he had just installed.

When Cathy got home, Donald was sitting at the table with the Donnellys, looking dazed.

"You've got to get me a doctor," Donald pleaded with her. "I'm losing my mind."

So Cathy called her internist, and told him how she and her husband had just learned that Benjamin had been sexually abused at his nursery school. As she began telling him about Donald, the doctor interrupted to ask her how Benjamin was doing. Donald grabbed the phone away and yelled into it, "Benjamin's okay but I'm losing my mind." Then he hurled the phone across the room.

The doctor prescribed a sedative, which Cathy went to pick up from the drugstore. She gave it to Donald, and he slept for seven hours. By the time Donald woke up, Cathy had telephoned his older brother in Washington, D.C. asking him to come for a couple of days. Cathy had never seen her normally calm and rational husband so upset before. Even after he calmed down, he seemed like a changed man.

Along with Joshua Peterson and Timmy Frankel, Benjamin testified before a grand jury in May. As he was leaving the grand jury room, he rolled his eyes at the twenty-three jurors and said, with a weird inflection in his voice, "I'm going to go outside and strangle my throat."

Back out in the waiting room, Benjamin told his parents about the last statement he had made to the jurors, adding, "I left them laughing." But Cathy knew that Benjamin didn't mean what he had said as a joke. Essentially, she believed, this was what Kelly had threatened to do to him if he told—cut his throat.

On May 24, the grand jury returned a six-count indictment against Kelly Michaels. And Sara Sencer hoped that this was the extent of the case.

"We kept trying to play it down," she said later. "We kept hoping it was a small isolated thing—boys being fondled at naptime. We weren't about to start interviewing all the kids because we didn't want to be accused of victim-hunting. It wasn't until Brian DeLuca told his mother about fellatio, cunnilingus, sticks and spoons and girls, that we knew we needed to talk to everyone in the school, or at least everyone in the nap room."

When Brian DeLuca had been interviewed by Lou Fonolleras, he seemed terrified. He told the investigator that he had seen other children being fondled by Kelly. He denied being a victim himself, but admitted he'd seen Kelly massage Joshua Peterson and Timmy Frankel's backs and buttocks. He also said Kelly inserted her index finger into their rectums, always prefacing the act by saying, "Let's play nurse, I'll take your temperature. . . . You feel warm."

When Lou asked Brian to draw pictures of his mother and father, he drew them with smiling mouths. But when Lou suggested he do a picture of Kelly, he drew her with a row of sharp teeth protruding from her mouth. When Lou interviewed Brian's teacher later, she recalled that in the past couple of months, Brian had drawn faces with jagged things in the mouth that he said were penises.

Lou Fonolleras also interviewed Brian's mother, Jane. She was concerned because Brian had been displaying a host of unusual behaviors in the past few months. In February, she had taken her son to the doctor because he had an irritated rectum. The doctor diagnosed it as a bacterial infection and prescribed Garamycin, but it kept recurring. In April, it disappeared.

Jane told Lou about the worrisome behavioral symptoms of the past several months. She said Brian seemed very anxious, and that he had begun walking around with his index finger stuck in his mouth—a new habit for him. Jane also recalled seeing Brian on one occasion with his hand under his pants. As he slid his finger in and out of his mouth, he said to his mother, "I feel warm . . . maybe you should take my temperature."

Brian might never have been able to say more, if an expert hadn't advised his mother how to help the frightened five-year-old open up. That expert was Montclair psychologist Susan Esquilin, who had attended a parents' meeting with Peggy Foster. At the time, Susan was a consultant to Newark Children's Hospital CORTS (Children of Rape Trauma Syndrome) program, which social worker Peggy Foster coordinated. When Cathy Baird later contacted Peggy for individual counseling, Peggy asked Susan to sit in on the discussion.

Not long afterward, Susan met with some of the parents of the early Wee Care victims. She felt it might be helpful for the parents to discuss ways of managing some of the behavior they were observing in their children.

At the meeting, Susan advised Jane not to question Brian, but just to let him know that if anything had happened that he was worried about, she was interested in hearing it. Susan also suggested that at bedtime, Jane read Brian a book called *No More Secrets*. The book has four vignettes about children who are molested, although none concerns a nursery-school teacher.

After his mother read him the book, Brian opened up and described in lucid detail a sordid litany of acts Kelly had performed on him. He also said he had been made to perform a variety of sexual acts on her. Brian asked his mother if he could talk to Lou Fonolleras again, and this time, he had a lot to say. Most significantly, he named little girls as his fellow victims. It was the first time investigators had heard that little girls were involved.

Brian told Lou that Kelly had inserted the handle of a wooden cooking spoon into his anus during naptime, and that she hit him on the penis and about his body with the same spoon.

Kelly sucked his penis, Brian said. And Brian had seen his teacher naked in the choir room. Brian said Kelly made the children remove all their clothes and pile up on top of her as she lay naked. He said Kelly directed the children to beat her about her naked body with a wooden spoon, and to fondle her pubic area with the spoon. He also told Lou that he had seen Kelly kiss and lick some of the little girls' vaginas.

For the first time, Lou was beginning to realize the grim magnitude of the case. Every interview turned up another victim. Children were corroborating one another's stories with alarming accuracy. It was the most heinous and extensive sexual-abuse case the young investigator had ever worked on. It was at this point that Lou began interviewing more of the Wee Care children. Wee Care, meanwhile, had closed indefinitely.

◼

I didn't know what was going on in the other victims' families at that point because I was so wrapped up in my own misery. I felt like I was coming unhinged, as though my life had been turned upside down. Summer, always my favorite season, seemed joyless and stifling. There seemed nothing to do but move mechanically through the days. I spent a lot of time recalling Hannah's strange behavior of the past six months, and then berating myself for not delving deeper to see why she had been acting the way she was. I blamed myself completely. If I had been a more careful and conscientious mother, it wouldn't have happened.

Before I became a mother, before I even had decided for sure that I wanted a child, there was one thing about parenthood that I feared. Not a fatal illness (though of course I wanted my child to be healthy). And not that my child would be dumb, or ugly, or unpopular. Instead, I worried that my kids would stop communicating with me when they became adolescents.

This fear of being shut out probably stemmed from watching what my own parents endured with us. As a teenager, I hadn't given them much grief—after all, how much trouble could you get into in an all-girls' Catholic high school? But many of my younger brothers and sisters had turbulent periods during adolescence when they alienated themselves completely from my parents.

It's difficult to believe it now, because they all get along so well with my mother and father. But for years they were hostile to my parents, rejecting their values and beliefs and love. They dropped out of school, ran away from home, refused to have anything to do with family life. They put my mother and father through such incredible hell that I sometimes marvel that my parents were strong enough to survive such rejection and hatred, stay married, keep on loving us all.

They did, of course, and now their children return the affection and want to spend time with our parents.

But the memories of those years stayed with me, and the thought of my own sweet, loving children growing into sullen, uncommunicative teenagers frightened me. Now, here the nightmare was unfolding in real life—years before it was supposed to. My daughter had shut me out, withheld a part of herself, stopped talking to me. Except instead of being a teenager, she was five. So far, on the surface at least, she seemed reasonably like herself.

Compared to some of the Wee Care children, Hannah had exhibited relatively few behavioral changes so far. If I had known then what she would be like in the coming months, I don't think I could have kept going. But she hadn't yet started with the tantrums, the inconsolable fits of weeping, the violent displays of aggression, and—perhaps worst of all—the pitiful lack of self-esteem. For us and the other children's parents, the nightmare was really only beginning.

Sara Sencer told me that another grand jury was planned for July, and asked if Hannah could testify. I wanted to do whatever I could to cooperate with the investigation, but I didn't think Hannah was going to be very forthcoming. She seemed reluctant to discuss any of this with Jim or me, and she'd given the detectives just a brief statement that could hardly be called graphic.

Still, I drove her down to the Essex County Courthouse one sweltering June afternoon so she could meet Sara. Sara's third-floor office was cluttered with old toys and books. I settled in to wait in a corner while Sara and Hannah talked in another room. When they came out twenty minutes later, Sara looked grim.

Hannah had told her that Kelly inserted a knife, fork, and spoon into her rectum and her vagina, and had forced her to participate in the nude pile-up game in the choir room.

Sara told me that if Hannah could tell a grand jury what happened to her, the upcoming indictment against Kelly would include twelve counts on my daughter alone. Of the counts, eight would be for aggravated sexual assault in the first degree.

I drove unseeingly home through the gritty Newark streets. My five-year-old daughter is about to describe to a grand jury how her nursery-school teacher sexually abused her, I thought. No matter how many times I told myself this, it didn't seem real.

I couldn't bear to look at my daughter, engrossed with the potato chips and Coke I had bought her in the courthouse snack bar. It was agonizing to know that Hannah had endured so much pain for so long without telling me. Even worse was her tacit unwillingness to confide in me, her mother and former confidante. I didn't know my child as well as I once thought.

C H A P T E R

■ ■ ■ ■ ■ ■ ■ ■ ■ ■

5

It happened almost a month before we found out Hannah had been sexually abused by Kelly Michaels. At the time, I didn't recognize it for what it was: a jarring preview of the violence and aggression that would come to characterize my daughter.

I was preoccupied that May night when I pulled into the driveway. Caroline, who was six-and-a-half, had stayed home from school that day with a fever, sore throat, and upset stomach. She seemed prone to tonsillitis that year, and I wondered if I should take her to the pediatrician that night. He knows I work and have a long commute, and is very cooperative about seeing my kids after regular office hours.

On that evening, I rushed in the front door and picked up Robert for a minute to cuddle before going upstairs. Caroline was lying on her twin bed in the room she shared with Hannah, reading. Hannah was playing dolls with Ellen, who was two and a half. I felt Caroline's forehead and, to my relief, it seemed cool, although I wanted to double check. I hugged the other two and went to wash up and get the thermometer.

Maria, our competent, ebullient Jamaican housekeeper, can make up a bed more expertly than a hospital nurse and she cooks tempting dishes whenever a child gets sick. But she cannot read a thermometer. Since Jim has never mastered the art of temperature-taking either, the job of monitoring the children's fever invariably falls to me.

I was washing up in the bathroom when Maria began screaming "Mrs. Crowley, Mrs. Crowley." She sounded hysterical. I felt the adrenaline begin to pump; something was terribly wrong.

Dripping soap and water, I opened the door. Maria didn't have to say any more. Ellen was lying on her back on the floor in the hall. She was very still, and her eyes were wide open, staring at nothing. My first thought was that she had somehow broken her neck and was dead.

Later, I realized that if her neck really had been broken, the next thing I did would have finished her off for sure. But at the time, I acted on impulse. I got down on my knees and picked up her limp, slight body in my arms. I shook her shoulders, shouting, "Ellen! Ellen!"

Time stood still. I wasn't aware that there was anyone else around. Ellen was all I could think about.

After what seemed like forever, although it couldn't really have been more than two or three minutes, she regained consciousness. But she still appeared stunned and disoriented.

Shaking, holding her tightly in my arms, I turned to look up at Maria. "What happened?" I asked weakly. Between her and Caroline, who had seen the entire incident from her bed, I was able to piece together the story: Ellen and Hannah had been playing by the open door of the bedroom Caroline and Hannah shared. Ellen took a toy that Hannah wanted, and Hannah went into a fit of rage. She shoved Ellen backward with all her might, so hard that when Ellen's head hit the edge of the door, she was knocked unconscious. Caroline and Maria were completely shocked, but Hannah seemed unperturbed by all the commotion.

There wasn't time then for me to think how uncharacteristic this violent act was for peaceable, affable Hannah. I went downstairs and called the volunteer rescue squad, and an ambulance arrived within minutes. At the same time, Jim pulled up in his car with my brother, Johnny. They, too, seemed nonplussed that a four-year-old could have knocked her sister out in a battle over a toy.

The medics shone a flashlight in Ellen's eyes to see if her pupils dilated properly, and they checked her reflexes and asked her some questions to see if she could respond. By now Ellen seemed aware of what was going on around her, and even a little puzzled to be the focus of so much attention. The medics wanted us to go to the hospital emergency room, and they strapped Ellen onto the stretcher in the back of the ambulance. I slid in next to her and held her hand.

I'd never been inside an ambulance before, and the wailing siren sounded distant. I felt a little as if the whole thing was a dream from which I would wake up soon. I squeezed Ellen's hand and smiled at her. Hopefully I looked calmer than I felt.

At the hospital, we waited for about an hour before she was examined by a doctor. Then we waited some more, until a technician was available who could do a skull X ray. Finally, the doctors told me Ellen had a mild concussion and that there was really no special treatment, other than to keep a close eye on her over the next twenty-four hours. They also said to wake her several times during the night to make sure she was responsive.

Jim drove out to the hospital to pick us up, and while we waited for him, the nurses fussed over Ellen and gave her a coloring book and some crayons. By now she was feeling more at home in the brightly lit, bustling emergency room and she wanted to get down and run around. But I wanted to hold her warm, wriggling body, and reassure myself that she was really alive and okay. Never before had I come so close to facing one of my children's mortality.

That night, I kept resetting my alarm clock to go off every two hours. Each time it shrilled, I would go switch on the light in Ellen's room and shake her gently awake in her crib. She always woke up quickly and seemed alert. Then I went in to Caroline to feel her forehead and make sure she was sleeping peacefully. But I lay awake almost all night, the image of Ellen's still form and her staring, unseeing eyes looming large every time I closed my eyes.

I wondered what I had said or done to make Hannah act the way she did. Maybe I just wasn't giving her as much time as she needed since going back to work, and this was a reaction. But I devoted most evenings to my children, reading stories, playing house, or just talking. Still, something about her lately disturbed me. There was a wantonness about her, a disregard for others' feelings, that hadn't been there before. It was nothing I could put my finger on. I resolved to spend even more time with the kids at night. And I tried to put the whole discomforting experience out of my mind.

On a Sunday afternoon a few weeks later, we drove into Brooklyn with all the children to have dinner at the home of some friends. Jane and Alfred have a boy Caroline's age and a girl who is a little younger than Ellen. On that day they had also invited our friends Bert and Genevieve, who have a boy Hannah's age. It was hot for the second of June, and Jane and Alfred's Cobble Hill brownstone was uncomfortably muggy. Alfred's avocation is cooking, and he had spent most of the day preparing a cold fish mousse appetizer, a roast, and an assortment of buttered and creamed vegetables.

The kitchen felt like it was about 120 degrees, and we left the men in the house to drink beer and tend to the dinner. Jane, Genevieve, and I sat outside on the steps of the stoop, chatting and keeping an eye on the kids. They ran up and down the sidewalk, played with tricycles and go-carts, or aimed streams of water at each other from squirt guns.

I was watching Hannah, who usually hung pretty close to her sisters when we visited people she hadn't seen in a while. That day, though, she seemed unusually boisterous and aggressive. If she wanted a riding toy, she simply pushed off whoever happened to be on it. One of the little boys was fairly passive and acquiesced to her demands with no argument. But Bert and Genevieve's son had the stocky build and quick temper of a rough-and-tumble street kid who didn't let anyone push him around.

When Hannah tried to knock him off his trike, he slugged her. I jumped up, ready to pull him off Hannah before he could bloody her nose. But then I stood still and stared in astonishment as my delicate-looking daughter proceeded to knock a child practically twice her size to the ground and begin yanking handfuls of his hair as hard as she could.

His mother moved forward before I was able to stop gaping. She separated the two of them and began to comfort her weeping son. I scolded Hannah and demanded that she apologize to the child. But though she complied, she looked for all the world as if she would do the same thing again if she got the chance.

The incident left everyone feeling tense, though no one talked about it. The fathers came out and sat around on the steps, but the earlier camaraderie had evaporated. Jane suggested that the mothers walk the kids over to the Burger King in Brooklyn Heights and buy them dinner. None of them would eat cold fish anyway, and they would be ravenous by the time Alfred had put the finishing touches on his feast.

All the way there, Hannah strutted ahead of us with the boys. I brought up the rear with Robert's stroller, and Genevieve and Jane walked in the middle with the three little girls. Gradually I became aware that Hannah was spouting vulgar language I had never heard her use at home, much to the delight of the two little boys. It was clearly audible, even with the distance that separated her from me, and I was embarrassed. I saw Jane and Genevieve exchange disapproving looks, but they weren't about to scold someone else's child.

I pushed the stroller faster to catch up with Hannah, and told her to stop that kind of talk immediately. She laughed raucously and skipped on ahead. At home later on, when I talked to Hannah and told her I didn't want to hear such language, she nodded sweetly. But I sensed that my disapproval didn't affect her.

I was puzzled. Where could she be learning this kind of talk? But perhaps, I rationalized, I hadn't heard the start of the conversation. The two other children must have taught her what to say. She was clearly out to impress the boys, acting flirtatious and show-offy the way a fifteen-year-old might come across with a guy she has a crush on. But not a five-year-old. Not Hannah. Again, I tried to push away the undefined flutterings of dread inside me.

If some of us Wee Care parents had compared notes back in the spring of 1985, we would have been surprised at the striking similarities in our children's behavior.

But we didn't. How do you tell someone you know only casually that your daughter knocked her sister unconscious? That she beat up a child twice her size? What mother would want her child to play with such a bully? A youngster's vulgar language and sexually oriented games aren't exactly topics for parental chitchat at the playground.

So we kept it to ourselves. We dealt with each incident as it occurred but never saw the big picture or related one incident to another. And we never knew until much later that our children were reacting to the degradation they were enduring at school in similar ways.

Some youngsters tried to tell their parents what was happening at school, but we didn't really hear them. One little girl reported to her mother that Kelly had hit her. But the mother knew that there was also a child at Wee Care named

Kelly, and she assumed her daughter meant that Kelly the child—not Kelly the teacher—had slapped her.

Another little girl told her mother she didn't like Kelly because Kelly made her do "hard work." The mother (and I'm sure I would have done the same thing) launched into a discussion on the importance and necessity of working hard at school and doing what the teacher says. Sexual abuse couldn't have been further from her mind. The idea of sexual abuse never occurred to me when Hannah repeatedly asked when she wouldn't have to take her nap at school anymore. And it never occurred to my sister Kathleen when her daughter Emily wanted to play "the Arlene game."

The winter before, my three-year-old niece Emily would sling a purse over her arm and slip on a pair of her mother's high heels. Pushing her doll carriage in front of her, she would approach her mother, who might be dressing for work, cooking dinner, or reading the newspaper.

"Is Arlene here?" Emily would ask, and Kathleen would always say no, not now. Kathleen figured Emily was playing a variation on the typical little-girl "house," and she didn't really pay much attention.

Then Emily told Lou Fonolleras on Friday, June 7, that she had been molested by Kelly. On the following Monday, as Kathleen was getting dressed for work, Emily appeared at her bedroom door, decked in high heels and carrying a purse.

"Knock, knock," she said. "Is Arlene here?"

"She's not here right now," Kathleen told her. "Why do you want to see Arlene?"

"I have to talk to her about something," Emily said.

"Well, Arlene isn't here right now. How about if you talk to me?"

"Kelly did bad things," Emily said sadly. "She hurt kids in their nap. She put things in their booties and all the kids were crying."

They tried to tell us, with their words and behavior. Some grew aggressive and violent. Others had nightmares.

Melissa Bethel began disrupting her family's mealtime ritual.

Melissa was four and a half years old in the fall of 1984, and she had sat up at the dinner table in a booster seat since she was old enough to feed herself. She was adept with a spoon and fork, and a hearty eater.

Her mother, Sharon, likes to cook and believes that families should sit down together for dinner. Each night Sharon would prepare a full-course meal, and she, Melissa, her husband Pete, and six-year-old Laura would gather around the big round table in their spacious kitchen. In nice weather, they sat on the deck overlooking the backyard. It was a pleasant, relaxed time when the girls talked about what they had done in school and knew they had their parents' undivided attention. Although Sharon and Pete didn't make table etiquette into a big issue, they gently corrected their daughters' manners during the meal. And their reprimands had paid off: the girls handled utensils properly and knew enough to sit up straight and chew their food quietly.

But that fall, Melissa stopped eating with tableware. Instead, she insisted on using her hands, scooping up handfuls of meat and vegetables and cramming them into her mouth. Even when Sharon served soup, Melissa would pull out the noodles with her fingers and stuff them into her mouth, leaving the broth untouched.

She became restless and hyperactive, refusing to sit at the table for more than a couple of minutes at a stretch. Instead, she climbed down from her booster seat and ran wildly about the kitchen, tirelessly charging around and around the butcher-block center work island while the rest of her family ate dinner. Sharon and Pete's attempts to get her to sit down were futile.

Melissa's nightmares began insidiously. In the beginning, they came maybe once a week and often were about monsters or oversized animals—big monkeys one night, big dogs on another. Sometimes she dreamed she was in very deep water and couldn't touch the bottom. She was always terrified and would wake up crying.

Sharon would go into her room and comfort her, then return to her own bed. But gradually the bad dreams got closer together until they occurred every night. Sharon was so exhausted from having her sleep broken that she often slept in Melissa's bed. Other nights, Melissa crawled into bed with her parents.

"It became like a joke," Sharon recalls. "Whose bed will I wake up in today?"

The nightmares never had a single theme that would enable Sharon to understand why her daughter woke up in terror. "I knew lots of kids had nightmares," she said. "I figured we had just hit a stage and it would pass."

Melissa had always been a shy, gentle child, so Sharon was surprised that fall when Arlene Spector wanted to discuss her daughter's aggressive behavior. Arlene said Melissa had taken to playing roughly with some of the more aggressive boys. She and Diane Costa, who was Melissa's teacher for the second year in a row, wondered if anything was going on at home to account for the aggression. Sharon said there wasn't.

Melissa's rowdy behavior at naptime was especially disruptive, according to the teachers. Perhaps she was outgrowing her need for an afternoon rest, they said. They wanted to put her upstairs in the Wee Care kindergarten two afternoons a week.

Sharon thought that was a wonderful idea, and Melissa was enthusiastic about it, too. She frequently asked her mother in the morning, "Mommy, will you tell me when it's kindergarten day?" Melissa didn't spend much time in the kindergarten, though, because things at the school were so disorganized that year that Diane Costa often forgot to send her.

That year Melissa and Laura used to chase each other through the house wildly, shouting "butts and penises" at the top of their lungs. Sharon yelled for them to stop it, saying she didn't want such talk in the house. She thought perhaps Laura had picked up some bathroom language in the first grade, although none of her six-year-old's friends ever talked like that. Sharon didn't connect Melissa's bathroom talk or aggressive behavior with the nightmares or the refusal to eat with tableware. In fact, Sharon's friends and sisters who witnessed Melissa's new pushiness told her it wasn't such a bad thing.

"She's finally coming into her own," they said. "She's pushing back, standing up for herself."

When Sharon learned about the allegations of sexual abuse at Wee Care, she went to the parents' meetings but never imagined Melissa might be involved. The idea that her daughter could have been sexually abused at school was so ludicrous, so totally out of sync with her life-style, that she doesn't remember considering it even for a second.

What she does remember—as clearly as she remembers learning that President Kennedy had been assassinated—is the June 5 phone call from Arlene Spector. Sharon hadn't gone to work that Wednesday because she had a stomach flu, and she spent much of the day running back and forth from her bed to the toilet. Pete came home early to be with her, and Sharon was just beginning to feel better when the telephone rang.

It was Arlene Spector on the other end of the line, asking the Bethels' permission for Melissa to be interviewed by the Division of Youth and Family Services investigator. Arlene explained that while Melissa wasn't directly involved in the abuse, she might have witnessed something. Arlene said she was sure the Bethels wouldn't want their daughter to go through life without having the chance to talk to someone about what she had seen.

Sharon wasn't sure what to do. She discussed it with Pete, and she called a close friend for advice. Pete thought they probably should at least let Melissa talk to DYFS. The friend felt that, since the Bethels had no reason to think Melissa was a victim, they should refuse.

In the end, Sharon wrote Arlene a note instructing her not to allow the DYFS investigator to speak to Melissa until she herself had a chance to question him. And the next day, Sharon drove to the school to meet Lou Fonolleras. She liked him right away, and could see he wasn't the kind of person who would frighten Melissa. So she gave her permission, and that night she told her daughter that the next day at school she would be talking to a man her mother had already met. He wanted to ask Melissa some questions, Sharon told her daughter, and it was okay for her to talk to him.

When Sharon arrived at Wee Care later that day, she forced herself to settle down in a corner of the staircase to wait until Lou was free. On the floor above her, she heard footsteps and voices. She couldn't help overhearing what one woman said to the other. "They found another child, and this time it was a girl," the woman said.

And suddenly, Melissa's behavior in the past six months made perfect sense to her mother. "When I heard the word 'girl,' that's when it all fit together for me," Sharon said. "Melissa's aggressiveness, the refusal to eat with tableware, the nightmares. Suddenly it all made perfect, horrible sense."

Struggling to stay calm, she walked into the office and sat down facing Lou. She was shocked at how thoroughly drained he looked. His shirt was open at the collar, his tie was askew, and he barely had any voice left. Sharon smiled at him, and determined to stay composed.

"You'll remember Melissa because she's got big blue eyes and she's always smiling and she talks to everyone," Sharon said.

Lou looked tired, and he didn't smile back. "I remember Melissa and she didn't want to talk to me," he said. "I finally took her on a tour of the school, and when we got to the choir room, she began to talk."

An articulate child and one of the older victims, Melissa was able to verbalize what younger children couldn't. Lou told Sharon that just the day before, he had interviewed a small boy who kept moving pieces of tableware around the table as if he were trying to tell Lou something. But he wasn't verbal enough to make Lou understand. But Melissa explained to Lou that Kelly had put forks, spoons, and knives on the floor. She then took off her clothes and had the children undress, and they all piled up on top of the utensils, Melissa said. Lou asked her if it hurt, or if she was scared. But from what Melissa said, it appeared that it was almost like a game. Everyone wanted to be on the top of the stack.

Not all the illicit activities had an element of play in them, though, the child said. Kelly also had inserted a knife into the girl's vagina, and Melissa had seen other children being penetrated as well.

Sharon felt like she was in shock when she left Lou's office that day. She and Pete sat numbly at their kitchen table that evening. At some point, Sharon—who that afternoon had seen the names of other suspected victims on a pad in Lou's office—talked to me. She was the one from whom I first learned that Hannah may have been molested.

During the evening, they had a visit from Traci MacKenna, a Wee Care parent whom Sharon had just met that day. The three of them talked a little, and the women cried. There was so much to absorb, so much in their daughters' behavior to look back on and reexamine. They marveled that they hadn't seen the signs sooner.

Four-year-old Tiffany Newton used to wrap her arms around her mother and kiss her from behind. She would kiss her mother through her legs, and then up her front. She would wrap her legs around her mother's neck, pushing her crotch toward her mother's face. She always wanted to kiss with her tongue. Often she would come up and lick her mother's face and arms.

"I thought it was pretty strange," said Fran Newton, a nurse. "But she would say she was being a cat."

Fran's mother noticed and disapproved of the licking games. Sensing this, Fran tried to make Tiffany stop. But her daughter was remarkably uninhibited, and the licking and tongue kissing would start again soon after the reprimand was delivered.

Other strange behaviors that the pert little blond four-year-old displayed wouldn't make sense to her mother until June. In the meantime, Fran could only wonder why her daughter began refusing to go to the toilet at school. By the time the child climbed into the car at night to go home, she would be practically wetting her pants. Her mother told Tiffany that she could hurt herself by holding it in and asked why she didn't go to the toilet at school. To which Tiffany replied, "Because I'm shy."

One day shortly before Christmas, when her mother arrived at school to pick her up in the late afternoon, Tiffany was nowhere to be found. The aides told Fran that Tiffany's grandmother had picked her up. There was nothing unusual about that, because Fran's mother worked in the area and occasionally picked Tiffany up from school. So Fran just went on home. But when she got there, Tiffany wasn't there; Fran's mother had not picked her up. A frightened Fran rushed back to the school, where she found Tiffany playing in the gym with the other children who stayed late. She never did tell her mother where she had been, and none of the aides seemed to know either.

■

In terms of the sheer number of Wee Care children involved in a single incident, Michele Schwartz's birthday party in the late spring was particularly alarming. The guests included most of her Wee Care class as well as assorted youngsters from the neighborhood. While Michele was opening her gifts in the living room and the parents who had stayed to help were watching, a group of Wee Care children went off to play on the sun porch.

When a neighbor and Michele's aunt happened to glance onto the sun porch shortly after, they were shocked by what they saw. Wee Care child Rachel Goldstein was lying on the floor on her back with her pants down. A classmate, Keith Parsons, was inserting an instrument from a child's doctor kit into her rectum. For the two adults, though, the most startling aspect of the whole scenario was not the inappropriate behavior of the two youngsters. It was the attitude of the onlookers. None of the Wee Care children appeared to think there was anything out of the ordinary in what they were witnessing. It was as if this was a routine activity they saw every day.

The two women called a halt to the activity and Keith's mother arrived to pick up her son. She was visibly embarrassed, and the two left shortly.

When the neighbor told Claudia Schwartz about the incident, the two women agreed that it was a typical preschoolers' game of doctor. But the neighbor, though she didn't say so to Claudia at the time, thought it was remarkably odd.

Pulling her pants down in front of her classmates was just one of the strange things three-year-old Rachel did that year. Her mother, Soma, works as a banker in Manhattan and the family's live-in housekeeper or a neighbor usually picked Rachel up from school. The child attended Wee Care three mornings a week from 9 A.M. to 1 P.M. Kelly was her teacher.

Rachel is the quintessential little girl, extremely careful about her clothes and very neat in her personal habits. She had been completely toilet-trained at age two, so when she suddenly began to wet her bed every night, Soma was concerned and took her to the doctor. On three separate visits the doctor examined her and did urine cultures, but found no evidence of infection. He attributed her reddened vaginal area to the frequent bed-wetting.

Rachel, normally an insouciant, easygoing child, had begun to throw tantrums that year. And she grew very clingy to her mother, repeatedly asking her, "Do you love me? Do you love me?" She started waking up in the middle of the night and going into her parents' bed, and was nervous about going to bed at night.

"Because she was my first child, a lot of the strange behavior—the clinginess, the tantrums—was explained away," Soma said. "I also had a newborn baby at home, and I thought perhaps this was a reaction to him."

There was no new baby at Jodie Minetti's house during the 1984–85 school year. But her personality changed so drastically during that period that her parents felt as if they were living with a different daughter.

Jodie has suffered from a seizure disorder since infancy, and, hence, is on medication. She is a cuddly, round-faced only child who is adored by her father and her mother.

Both saw changes in Jodie that year. She began to exhibit very sophisticated sexual behavior. "It was almost as though I had to throw her into a cold shower to calm her down," her mother said.

Jodie insisted on wearing her Dr. Denton pajamas (with the feet in them) to school every day under her clothes. The first few times, her mother tried to take them off her, but it turned into a wrestling match. Finally, Julie told her she could wear the pajamas if she wanted to, but said the other children probably would laugh at her.

"I thought at the time it was quirky, but adorable," Julie said. "I thought to myself, she's just exercising her right to wear what she wants to wear."

Months later, Julie interpreted her daughter's insistence about wearing her nightclothes to school much differently: "She felt it was protection from Kelly," Julie said. "She felt more secure wearing them."

Since age three, the child had seen a speech pathologist

for a minor speech disorder. Three days a week, her mother picked her up forty-five minutes early from Wee Care to take her to her appointment. Jodie's therapy was progressing nicely, but in the late fall of 1984, her disorder went from mild to moderate to severe. It became difficult to listen to her. She stuttered so badly it was like listening to a broken record; you wanted to just smack it and set it back.

The speech pathologist reassured Julie that while many children stutter, they do grow out of it. She said that stress frequently contributes to stuttering in a child, and she told Julie to try to keep the stress level down in the home.

Julie was puzzled. She and her husband got along well, they both had fulfilling, enjoyable jobs, and they had more than their share of friends and relatives close by. What stress? she wondered.

As the year went on, the stuttering got much worse. By the start of 1985, it was terrible. Julie felt as if the therapist blamed her and her husband. She used to come back from her daughter's appointments and say to her husband, "You have to try not to take so many phone calls. We have to try to sit down and eat more meals together as a family." Yet no matter what they did, the stuttering grew increasingly severe and noticeable.

Then in January, Jodie stayed home from school for an entire week because she was ill. And the stuttering stopped. It didn't just improve, it ceased completely. "It was dramatic," Julie said. "I thought it stopped because I was indulging Jodie, lying on the couch and watching TV with her. I never thought the stuttering was because of school. I thought it was all my fault because I went to work."

When Jodie returned to Wee Care, the severe stuttering began again. It lasted until that spring, when it disappeared —four days after Kelly Michaels left Wee Care.

Jodie was also among the many Wee Care children who had stopped eating peanut butter sometime that winter. She didn't like baloney or tunafish, so Julie asked what she

72

wanted to take to school for lunch. Jodie always requested the same thing: a butter sandwich.

"Every day from then on, she ate a plain butter sandwich for lunch," Julie recalled. "And I remember thinking to myself, she's going to have hardening of the arteries from eating all that cholesterol."

Hannah, who scarcely knew Jodie, also stopped eating peanut butter quite suddenly around February of that year. She didn't want to take it for lunch anymore, she disliked it on crackers, and she even lost her taste for homemade peanut butter cookies.

I'd read enough of Dr. Spock and Penelope Leach to know that kids go through phases where they turn against a formerly loved food. As proof, I had Caroline, the world's pickiest eater. One day, she could eat three hot dogs at a sitting. A week later, hot dogs for dinner would elicit wails of protest. I'd even written articles for my newspaper on the care and feeding of finicky kids. So I took Hannah's refusal to eat peanut butter as a typical childhood phase.

Michele Schwartz, who was in Kelly's class, stopped eating peanut butter at the same time. Like the rest of us, her mother, Claudia, wasn't concerned. And Benjamin Baird had always been a good eater, so when he stopped eating peanut butter, his mother didn't worry. She fixed cold cuts and figured that sooner or later, he'd start liking peanut butter again.

In the summer of 1985, it became painfully clear why our kids had lost their taste for peanut butter. At school, the children told investigators, Kelly had spread it on their genitals and then licked it off. She also spread it on her own breasts, stomach, and vagina, and had the children lick it off.

By that summer, too, enough children had told investigators about Kelly's threats so that the nightmares many of her victims had been experiencing became explainable. Hannah didn't have sleep disturbances until later on. But other children kept their exhausted parents up night after night that preceding winter. The kids woke up in the middle of the night, sleep walked, and had night terrors.

Shortly after my niece Emily began attending Wee Care in November of 1984, she began having nightmares. The pattern was the same, night after endless night. My sister would put her to bed only to have her wake up, screaming and terrified, and insist on going into her mother's bed. If Kathleen tried to put her back in her own room, Emily became hysterical. Soon she slept in Kathleen's bed every night. And although the dreams obviously terrified her, she never was able to describe them to my sister.

Casey MacKenna refused to go to bed that winter unless someone was in her room with her. Her mother, Traci, would put her to bed in her own room and stay with her until she fell asleep. Then Traci would go back downstairs. But invariably, when she went back upstairs, Casey would be asleep at the head of the second-floor staircase.

I hardly knew Traci back then. Even if I had, we might never have mentioned to each other that both our four-year-olds wanted to move away from South Orange. I'd overheard Hannah that winter asking my father the same question over and over. Snuggling up close to him on the couch when he came to visit, she would look up at him and ask gravely, "Grandpa, when are we ever going to move?"

My father, who helped rear all of us, thought it odd that a four-year-old would want to move away from home. But he never expressed his feelings to me about this, and since Hannah was never insistent, he didn't pursue the subject with her.

But Casey was much more persistent. She begged and badgered her mother to let the family move away. She told Traci their house was too small, that she didn't like the neighborhood. When it became apparent that her mother wasn't about to go house-hunting, Casey asked if they could paint the house. The house was pale yellow at the time, and all the other houses on the street were white. Only later Traci learned that Casey wanted her house to look like all the others so that Kelly wouldn't know which one she lived in.

Of the constellation of symptoms that our children displayed in the months prior to discovery, perhaps the most universal was a dislike of going to school and, more specifically, an aversion to naptime. Nap assignments weren't random. Kelly had the same youngsters each day, and among her charges was Jodie Minetti.

Jodie Minetti would get up in the morning and whine a litany of excuses for why she didn't want to go to school: a headache, a stuffy nose, a hurt knee. Her mother, Julie, figured lots of children probably didn't want to go to school, and she cheerfully ignored Jodie's morning maladies and took her anyway. Once they got there, Jodie seemed okay, as long as her mother didn't linger at the playground talking to other parents. Julie soon learned that the most painless way to get Jodie to school was to drop her off and leave very quickly.

Jodie began to tell her mother that she didn't want to nap at school. Julie assumed that she meant she didn't want to sleep at school. At her daughter's request, each day she used to write on Jodie's lunch bag, "If Jodie doesn't want to eat her lunch, she doesn't have to. If she doesn't want to take a nap, she doesn't have to."

"I thought that she just wasn't tired and that instead of closing her eyes, she just wanted to read a book quietly," Julie said.

But one day Jodie appeared so agitated about naptime that her mother took her daughter up to Arlene's office and said, "Jodie wants me to tell you that if she doesn't want to take a nap, she doesn't have to. Is it okay if she just reads a book instead?"

Arlene assured her that it was, and Julie told her daughter to thank Arlene. Jodie looked at Arlene and blew her a kiss. On her way back down the stairs, Julie turned and rolled her eyes at Arlene as if to say, "Oh, these kids."

Months later, just thinking about that incident made Julie feel guilty—if only she had probed deeper.

Like Claudia Schwartz and Julie Minetti, Marge Farrell had worked outside the home since becoming a mother. Billy was three and Linda was starting kindergarten when Marge began to look at nursery schools for him. A trusted friend raved about Wee Care to Marge, so she went to see it for herself.

"It came highly recommended," she said. "It was my first exposure to nursery school but it looked fine to me. All the schools I had looked at up until that point either were co-ops, where the parents had to work on certain days, or they didn't have long enough hours."

Four-year-old Billy started at Wee Care in the fall of 1984, and soon began to balk at being driven to school. But Wee Care was his first experience in day care (previously he'd been cared for by a neighbor while his mother worked) and Marge thought he would adjust.

Marge, who works as a buyer for a major department store, drove a station wagon. When she drove into the Wee Care parking lot with Billy in the morning, he invariably crawled way into the back and begged his mother not to make him get out. Every morning she had to drag him out of the car and into the building.

When the weather was too cold for the children to be at the playground, those who arrived early would go to the gymnasium and be watched over by one or two teachers. Balls, assorted toys, and climbing equipment kept them occupied until 9 A.M., when the group would be broken down into classes and the day's structured activities would begin.

Because Billy got to school at eight thirty, he went to the gym. But instead of joining the other youngsters in play, he would press his face up against the window that faced onto the parking lot to watch his mother leave. Hoping to coax a smile onto his small, forlorn face, Marge would stand outside for a few minutes and make a variety of funny faces.

Even though it never cheered him up, she made it part of her daily routine in hopes that her efforts might distract him from feeling so miserable.

There were other signs that something was wrong. Billy refused to take his beloved baby blanket to school for nap-time, and he begged Marge not to make him take his nap there. Brenda, an aide, told Marge that every day Billy would hold out as long as possible in the nap room and finally fall asleep from utter exhaustion. When Marge arrived at the end of the day to pick him up, he was always furious with her. He stalked angrily past her into the car, where he would sit with his thumb in his mouth. Because he had started refusing to go to the bathroom at school, by the time he arrived home he would bolt for the toilet.

Billy insisted on wearing his heavy, cumbersome work boots to school every day, even though they were difficult to get on and off. Marge recalls that one day in November, her son arrived home with his spaceships underwear on inside out. She figured he must have had an accident and that the teacher had changed his pants. He wouldn't tell her what had happened.

The worst part for Marge was leaving Billy at school in the morning. Sometimes as she drove to work, she was in tears herself. It got so that she began to dread Sunday nights because she knew that soon the painful morning ritual would begin. Once, her husband William took Billy to school for her. That night he asked his wife, "How do you do this every day? How can you stand the look on his face when you leave?"

In March of 1985, Marge accompanied William on a three-day business trip to San Diego. Her teen-aged step-son Stephen was to take Billy to school in the morning and pick him up at night. But the child cried and carried on terribly when Stephen tried to drive him there. Billy, crouched in the back of the station wagon, muttered repeatedly, "I hope you get lost. . . . I hope you don't take me to school."

So Stephen kept him home all three days. When Marge got back, she was angry with Billy, who she felt had unfairly manipulated his half-brother. She scolded him, saying, "Just because I'm not here doesn't mean that you can get away with things."

Another day, a neighbor drove Billy to Wee Care because Marge had to go to work early. Billy gave her a hard time, pleading with her not to take him to school. She finally kept him home all day with her and her own children. Later, the neighbor told Marge, "I just couldn't do that to someone else's child."

In December of 1984, Arlene Spector called Marge at work to tell her Billy was sick and that she should pick him up. When Marge got to the school, Billy was sitting all by himself in the third-floor bathroom, sobbing hysterically and holding a filthy garbage can that Arlene had given him in case he needed to vomit.

"I was furious with Arlene," Marge said. "I didn't take the time to go and yell at her then because I thought I should take Billy home. I was so unassertive back then."

When she got her son home and attempted to take his temperature, he got hysterical and began to scream and sob. But once she gave up trying to put the thermometer in his rectum, Billy calmed down and went about his play. Marge wondered whether he was really sick, or if he had just wanted to go home.

Marge didn't know any of the other Wee Care mothers very well, so she never discussed her son's behavior with anyone but her husband. And although she used to ask Billy what he disliked about school, he would never say.

Marge was deeply troubled by the changes in her child, who had metamorphized over the course of the school year from an easygoing little boy into an angry, hostile introvert.

Marge learned in May about the allegations of sexual abuse at Wee Care, and she wondered whether her own son might be involved. Perhaps this was why he had had such a tough year. But Billy wasn't even in Kelly's class.

Unlike some Wee Care parents, Marge at least knew who Kelly was. For a three-week period in the winter when Marge had to be at the department store early, she'd asked permission to drop Billy off at school at eight o'clock. Kelly was the only teacher there that early, and very few other youngsters were there, either. Marge would take him down to the classroom, where Kelly was usually talking softly on the phone.

"She would have a furtive look on her face," Marge says. "Billy would take one look at her and start to scream and yell. I physically had to peel him off me every day for those three weeks. I would leave and my guts would be in knots. But he wouldn't tell me what was wrong."

Then on the night of Friday, June 7, as she sat watching "Dallas," Marge got a telephone call from Jane DeLuca, Brian's mother. She knew Jane slightly because Brian and Billy had played together occasionally in the previous months. Now Jane told Marge that Brian had been molested at school by Kelly, and that it was clear that other children were involved.

"Suddenly it all clicked," Marge recalls. "The behavior changes, the tough time we'd had with him all year. It all made sense. I thought, oh, God, I hope he wasn't involved. But I think I knew right then that he was."

Three days later, Billy talked to Lou Fonolleras. The child denied that he was a victim, but when the female anatomically correct doll was presented, he reacted violently, punching the doll and throwing it around the room. When he saw the silverware on the table before him, he seemed fearful and apprehensive.

A week later, he told his mother he wanted to talk to Lou and "see those dolls again." But in Lou's presence, he grew quiet, anxious, and unwilling to talk. Over the next couple of weeks, though, Marge came to understand why he had acted the way he had. What her son described to her was lurid and sickening, and she had to hide her shock from him.

Billy said that Kelly made him pinch and slap his class-mates, and that she had inserted a knife into his rectum. He had been forced to climb on Kelly's naked body, press himself against her, and suck her nipples, he said. Billy also reported to his mother that Kelly made Brian poke her all over her naked body with a fork, and that she forced Benjamin Baird to strike her with a spoon. Billy inserted a knife into Kelly's rectum, he told his mother, and he kissed her vagina. Once Kelly allowed the children to hit her on the legs, Billy said.

"We were glad we had the chance to hurt her back," he told his mother.

Why hadn't he told this to anyone sooner? Because if he did, Billy told his mother, Kelly would "throw him into the street and run him over."

In Billy's case, threats kept him quiet. In my case, there were no threats, and yet, years earlier, I hadn't told my parents either.

C H A P T E R

■ ■ ■ ■ ■ ■ ■ ■ ■ ■

6

I didn't tell them, and to this day I don't know exactly why. Was I afraid they would be angry or—even worse—hurt? Did I think they wouldn't believe me? It's something no parent wants to believe, and yet I can't imagine having doubted Hannah, even for an instant. I don't know if that's in spite of, or because of, what happened to me.

I was eight years old when my great-uncle Barney began to molest my younger sisters and me. He and my great-aunt Anna lived in Michigan, but once or twice a year they visited us in New Jersey. Staying at our house for a couple of weeks at a time afforded Barney plenty of opportunities to climb into bed with us, and the pattern continued for several years. My sisters and I didn't talk about it to each other, and we didn't tell my parents. (Hannah didn't tell us either, of course, and yet my own childhood experience—having kept my sexual abuse from my parents—didn't make it any easier to accept that my little girl had kept her secret from me.)

Barney was my mother's uncle; he was married to Anna, her father's sister. In stature, the pair were like Jack Spratt and his wife—Barney tall, lean to the point of gauntness, and rather stooped. Anna was short, stout, and big-bosomed. Barney wore buttery-soft flannel shirts and thick wire-rimmed glasses that made him look owlish. He smelled of a sweet shaving cologne and butterscotch candy.

Anna was a buxom, cheerful woman who gabbed incessantly and laughed loudly and often. She laughed just as easily at herself as at others, but beneath that sunny, affable exterior was a dominating, straitlaced prude who frowned on liquor, cigarettes, and for all I know, marital sex. I've often wondered if the reason Barney and Anna never had any children was because they never had intercourse.

In any case, they were both terribly fond of all their greatnieces and -nephews. When my father switched jobs and we moved to New Jersey from Michigan in 1959, Barney and Anna came out ahead of my mother and us to help ready the rented house in South Orange. We children were quite disgruntled because our airplane flight was on Halloween night so we missed out on trick-or-treating. Never mind that we were leaving all our relatives and friends hundreds of miles away, or that we would all have to start in a new school. We just wanted Halloween candy.

And we got it, too. When—due to bad weather and delayed connecting flights—we finally arrived in New Jersey around midnight, Barney and Anna had bags of candy corn, lollipops, chocolate bars, and black licorice twists waiting for us.

Though they were already in their mid-sixties, they didn't seem to mind making the fourteen-hour drive from Michigan to New Jersey to see us. Anna loved to cook, and spent hours in the kitchen making us pies, layer cakes, and all sorts of cookies. Barney was a handyman who once installed a new bathroom in our house. They both were devoted to my parents, who joyously welcomed visitors from back home despite caring for seven children under age eight.

When Barney and Anna visited, my parents had the

chance to go out at night, something they couldn't afford to do otherwise. It was when Barney baby-sat for us that the abuse first began. Whenever he had the chance, he would creep into bed with one of us. He would put his fingers into my vagina and guide my hands down under the covers until they cupped his limp, flaccid penis. Then he instructed me to rub and stroke it. Oddly, I don't remember that he ever ejaculated.

Looking back, it seemed as if this ritual took place frequently, although I don't see how it could have happened every night since my parents didn't go out that often. Although it almost always happened in bed at night, sometimes Barney managed to get one of us alone in the basement, where he spent a lot of time puttering among the tools and hardware.

I was too old for naps, but some of my little sisters were still put to bed in the afternoon. Barney would follow them into the bedroom, telling my parents he was going to kiss so-and-so good night before her nap. One of my sisters remembers that Barney often kissed her on the vagina. Two can recall being molested in the basement of Barney's house. He got this opportunity only on the infrequent summer trips my family made back to Michigan, where we often stayed with my aunt Ruth. Sometimes she dropped us at Barney and Anna's to play croquet while she ran errands.

But Barney took Jana and Kathleen one at a time out to his garage and molested them in there. When they would ask where Anna was, Barney said that Anna was taking a nap. Nothing was ever mentioned to Aunt Ruth when she came to pick us up, nor did we protest to her when she suggested taking us to Barney and Anna's for a visit.

It was a secret we girls kept for several years, until I was eleven or twelve and Mary was nine or ten. Mary had a quick temper and a mind of her own, and she wouldn't do anything she didn't want to without the world hearing about it. I was surprised Barney even had the nerve to touch her. Prompted by a letter from Barney and Anna in which they announced another visit, Mary and I finally discussed the situation with each other, how much we hated what Barney did to us, and how ashamed and guilty we felt. I don't remember what words we used to describe our feelings, but we decided that I, as the oldest, should be the one to tell the priest in confession.

There were four priests in our parish and one of them, tall, dark-haired Father Gibson, was my favorite. He seemed gentle and understanding, not someone who would yell at me for the terrible things I had permitted. It would be embarrassing to describe to a priest what had happened to us, to speak words that I knew but never used. But thanks to the anonymity offered by the darkened confessional with its one-way screen, the priest wouldn't even know who I was.

The next time my mother took us to church to make a confession, I recited the usual prayer, "Bless me, Father, for I have sinned. My last confession was two weeks ago." Then I quickly blurted out what had been eating at me for so long—that my sisters and I were being degraded by my uncle, that we were allowing it to happen.

Father Gibson was wonderful. He didn't scream or shout, but gently told me that I should tell my mother about it. This seemed like a terrible penance, much worse than the enormous number of Hail Marys and Our Fathers I'd been expecting. I told my sister Mary that if she wanted me to tell our mother, she would have to come with me. We waited until my mother was alone in the laundry room, surrounded by orderly piles of folded clothing and where the hum of the washer and dryer would soften the harshness of our disclosure.

Although my mother was horror-struck by our news, she reacted calmly. (I think I would have been screaming.) I'm sure inside my mother must have felt the same nausea and disbelief that I experienced when Lou Fonolleras first told me about Hannah. Yet both of us managed to remain poker-faced—outwardly, at least. To her credit, she believed us right from the start. There was never any question that we might be making it up for attention. But a few days later, when she called her brother in Michigan who had young children to warn him about Barney, so he could protect his own daughters, he told her angrily that we must be lying.

My mother told my father, and the two of them told Anna about it shortly after she arrived for their visit. Anna believed it, probably in part because it wasn't the first accusation. While I was working on this book, my mother filled me in on a little background. It seems that a neighbor on the quiet street where my aunt and uncle lived had hinted to Anna some years earlier that Barney, a great favorite who passed out treats to the neighborhood youngsters, had done something to her children. But aside from forbidding her children from visiting Barney anymore, she never did anything about it.

My aunt and uncle were childless themselves, and my mother doesn't know why. Perhaps Anna couldn't have children, or maybe she knew about Barney's aberrant tendencies early on and decided not to risk anything with a child of her own.

At any rate, my parents, their emotions in a jumble, never did confront Barney. They believed us and were deeply shocked by what he had done, and yet they loved Barney, wanted to protect him and not ruin his life. Their solution was simply never to give him the opportunity to be alone with any of us. They didn't leave him and Anna to baby-sit with us at night anymore, and when he suggested he would go in and kiss one of my sisters good night before she fell asleep in her nap, my mother accompanied him and stood watching with grave eyes till he left the room. It took just a couple of days for Barney to figure out that my parents were on to him, though he never mentioned it.

That was as far as my parents took it. They didn't press charges against my uncle, and my sisters and I didn't go into therapy. My parents didn't discuss what had happened with any of us. I never even knew if my mother had told my father, or how she had stopped the abuse, until I started to write this book. Then I asked my mother, and she told me.

My other sisters and I never discussed our abuse by Uncle Barney until we grew up. My sister Mary is a lawyer now. For a time she worked as an assistant district attorney, prosecuting child molesters. She used to tell me about her cases, and one topic led to another. Before long, we were talking about the degradation we had endured twenty-five years earlier under the same roof, and never shared.

After Hannah and Emily were molested, my sister Kathleen and I began to talk about Barney and how much of it we remembered. I hadn't thought consciously of my uncle in years. What he did to me was buried under many other layers, and there was no reason for it to surface. But within weeks of finding out that Hannah had been molested, the experience rushed, unbidden, back into my consciousness. What amazes me is that my sisters and I still remember it so vividly and that still, after all these years, it makes me feel dirty and used. And, realizing how clearly I remember what happened to me, I know, sadly, there's not a chance Hannah won't carry her memories with her for a lifetime.

■

Kelly Michaels was arrested in June 1985 and charged with six counts of child sexual abuse. She spent most of that summer in the Essex County Jail Annex in Caldwell, New Jersey.

Meanwhile, her young victims were in a prison of their own devising, held in bondage by a host of confusing and conflicting emotions. For months they had acceded to Kelly's commands, played along with her games, and complied with her explicit directions not to tell anyone.

That part wasn't hard at first. Why should they let a grown-up in on any of this? When it all got started, back in the fall, it was kind of fun. Kelly was a virtuoso at inventing naughty games, the kind no other grown-up would ever play, that's for sure.

And the most amazing part of it was that an adult—a teacher, no less, someone Mom and Dad had told them to obey—not only sanctioned the games, but masterminded them.

Of course, not all the things Kelly did were fun. She stuck knives and forks and spoons into private parts of the body where it hurt. She got angry and she hit and punched. She made kids hurt each other.

But they couldn't tell their parents. Kelly said not to. Besides, deep down, they knew what they were doing was wrong.

By the time the children wanted—needed, really—to tell their parents about the bizarre goings-on at school, it was too late. They were a part of it. They were every bit as responsible as Kelly. They were ashamed. Mom and Dad would be angry if they knew. Then, just when it seemed as if this would go on for the rest of their lives, the grown-ups found out about it. Mom and Dad somehow learned about Kelly. The parents said Kelly was bad. They said she was in jail. And the kids figured that meant they were bad, too. No use pretending they weren't. Maybe they would have to go to jail, too.

Of course, if Mom and Dad really cared, then why hadn't they picked up on these signals sooner? They must have known before, because parents know everything.

It was enough to make our children furious at us.

Sadness and tension hung over our house that summer. Hannah began to regress in her behavioral habits almost immediately after disclosing that she had been abused. She wanted me to dress her, feed her, put on her shoes, hold her on my lap, and wipe her after she went to the bathroom. She grew very depressed and withdrawn, sitting by herself in a corner for long periods and sucking dejectedly on her

87

thumb. Nothing—affection, sympathy, attempts at games or stories—could distract her from turning inward.

When we were invited to a barbecue at the home of friends, all the other neighbor children there raced in and out of the sprinkler, played Red Rover and tag, and stuffed themselves with corn-on-the-cob and hamburgers. Hannah dragged a reclining chair to the far side of the lawn, as far away from everyone as she could get. Then she huddled up in a little ball, stuck her thumb in her mouth, and wept quietly. Both Jim and I went over and tried to talk her out of it, but it was no use. She couldn't tell me what was wrong, and she refused to be consoled.

Hannah grew increasingly fearful that I was going to die. If we left the children for a couple of hours in the evening to go out to a restaurant, she cried nonstop the entire time we were gone, sobbing to Maria that "Mommy is going to die." Maria is like a second mother to the kids and they are all perfectly comfortable with her. But that summer it got to the point where Jim and I simply stopped going out together at all. I simply couldn't bear the sound of Hannah's frantic pleas as we were leaving, or the pathetic sight of her tear-splotched face when we got home.

But in terms of Jim's and my relationship, the decision not to go out together probably was disastrous. Our occasional nights out were the only chance we had to talk and catch up on each other's lives, because at home there was never any time. Our private dinners were a way to keep the lines of communication open. Without the chance to talk to each other, except over the heads of the kids at the dinner table, we began to pull apart.

However, that was just one factor in the gradual deterioration of our relationship. We had different needs that summer. He needed a calm, rational wife who was able to accept his need *not* to talk about Wee Care. He didn't need someone who seemed on the brink of a nervous breakdown, which I was. I probably could have used a psychiatrist. At the very least, I needed someone to sympathize and commiserate. But when I perched on the edge of our bed at night, ready to let go to someone, having held back the flood of tears until the kids were asleep, Jim was uncommunicative. He didn't want to hear me berate myself, worry about Hannah's future, vent my anger at Kelly, Arlene Spector, and the world in general.

Usually, Jim would lie stiffly on his side of the bed, holding up the newspaper almost like a barrier between us. If he didn't have his head buried in the paper, he would have the TV remote control button in his hand. Flicking from one channel to the next, over and over, he'd seem interested in whatever flashed on the screen. Even the most tedious commercials appeared to fascinate him. By midnight, Jim would turn out the light on his side of the bed and burrow, back to me, under the covers. If I happened to be talking on the phone, as I often was by that point, he'd growl at me to use the downstairs extension so he could get some sleep.

But I hardly ever seemed to sleep that summer. Depression, rage, and guilt were the only emotions I was capable of feeling. Each morning I left home and began driving north on the Garden State Parkway toward my office. Before long, I would be viewing the highway through a wall of water as tears washed my makeup into unsightly streaks. I was determined that the kids not see me so upset, so I had to cry alone in the car or after they were in bed.

In mid-June, on the advice of Lou Fonolleras, I took Hannah to the pediatrician to be examined for physical evidence of sexual abuse. We walked into the office and the receptionist asked crisply, "And what is Hannah here for today, Mrs. Crowley?"

I wished I could give the same routine answers as the other bored-looking mothers lounging in the waiting room, who were flipping through *American Baby* or *Parents Magazine*. An annual checkup. A booster shot for summer camp. An ear infection. Chicken pox.

Instead, I leaned forward just a little bit and lowered my voice. "She's here for an internal exam because she may have been abused sexually at her nursery school," I said, determined not to let my voice break.

The receptionist's shocked look was harder to take than if she had been brusque about it. The nurse who ushered us solicitously into an examining room had deep sympathy etched on her face.

Hannah was extremely agitated because, of course, she had never had a pelvic examination before. The doctor tried to be patient and gentle as he explained what he was doing. But Hannah cried and shrank away from his touch. I held her hand and my breath, hoping the doctor would reassure me that at least it appeared outwardly that everything was normal. But after Hannah had hopped down from the table, dressed, and gone out to play in the waiting room, he took me into the office and told me what I had been dreading to hear.

"There is no evidence of acute sexual abuse, such as vaginal irritation or redness," he said. "But her hymen is patent."

Patent?

"It's open," he explained. "Now, that isn't conclusive. Sometimes the hymen can be open for other reasons—a fall, an accident, sometimes a child can even be born that way." The shock I felt was nearly eclipsed by pure rage and hatred for Kelly. Here it was, then, physical evidence. A doctor had confirmed what I pretty much already knew.

Like the other pediatricians who examined the Wee Care victims, ours didn't have much experience with treating sexual-abuse victims. Not that he wasn't genuinely concerned. But for the first time in the four years we had been going to him, his advice to me rang false. Make as little of this as possible, he urged, and then Hannah will do the same.

I could see it from his point of view. He was used to dealing with childhood's more obvious tragedies—severe burns, leukemia, the multiple, bloody injuries sustained in automobile accidents. Outwardly, Hannah seemed perfectly normal, and I'm sure he thought he was being kind, giving me guidance that would sustain me through what he perceived as a relatively minor crisis.

But I wouldn't be consoled. Driving to work later that morning, I felt such rage in me as I had never felt before. Kelly Michaels had violated my daughter. Hannah's sexual innocence was lost forever, and nothing I could do would ever bring it back. I have never wanted to harm someone physically in all my adult life, but I fantasized that day about killing Kelly. If she had been in front of me, I would have scratched her face and put my hands around her plump white neck and squeezed and squeezed. Never before had I felt such intense hatred for another human being. It amazed me. And frightened me a little.

As the weeks passed, I couldn't think of anything else but the fact that my daughter had been sexually abused. One perfect, cool June morning just a few days after the awful visit with Hannah's pediatrician, I drove to the South Street Seaport in lower Manhattan to write a feature story for my newspaper on the new shops and restaurants there. But I could barely drag myself through the narrow streets. Groups of schoolchildren on end-of-the-year class outings only brought fresh tears of pain.

A couple of days later, I accompanied Caroline's first-grade class on a trip to a local arboretum. Caroline had looked forward to it for weeks because it was the first time I would be the "helping mother" at a school function. She seemed oblivious to my black mood, and for that I was grateful. But I couldn't keep my eyes off the little six-year-old girls in her class, who merrily sang songs at the top of their lungs on the bus. They were so happy and carefree as they raced along the paths in the woods, giggling and calling out to one another.

Their parents had been able to protect them from harm.

But I had failed my child, and now she was suffering because of me.

"Get hold of yourself," Jim scolded as we sat facing each other over a restaurant table in late June, a few weeks before our decision not to go out and leave Hannah at night anymore.

I'd been trying to explain to him why I was so depressed; he didn't seem to understand at all. "Thirty children in the whole world get molested at their day-care center, and my kid has to be one of them," I said bitterly. "There are millions of kids out there. Why did it have to happen to Hannah?"

"Look," he said patiently. "It could have been much worse. She could have been maimed or murdered. She could have been raped. Her mutilated body could have been found in a field. She isn't dying of cancer."

"It doesn't matter," I said, starting to cry again. I didn't care that I wouldn't let myself be comforted by him.

"Go in the bathroom and fix your face," Jim said, losing patience. "People are starting to look at us."

I obediently left the table and retreated to the rest room, where I splashed cold water on my face and tried to rein in my emotions. Then we left the restaurant, leaving behind two untouched steaks.

Though he didn't show it visibly most of the time, I knew Jim was as depressed as I was. One night, when I felt unable to face anyone, he attended one of the parents' meetings at the preschool. Later, both my sister and the Bairds told me how my husband, whom I had never seen shed a tear in twelve years of marriage, had broken down and begun crying when he asked a question of the moderator.

I don't even recall Kathleen or the Bairds saying what his question was—but I ached for my husband, who was so afraid to display emotion over things that were causing him a lot of pain.

I remembered how he had refused to cry or show his grief when his older sister Christine had died seven years earlier, at the age of thirty. She was living in California at the time, unhappily married. On a trip back to the East Coast just months before her death, Christine had begun to see a psychiatrist. She was very depressed, and Jim's parents begged her to remain with them at their upstate New York home. But Chris flew back to San Francisco, and within a matter of months, hung herself from the showerhead in the bathroom.

If this had happened to one of my siblings, I would have been out of my mind with grief, and would no doubt have showed it. But I never saw Jim shed a tear. He was polite and attentive to his parents and brothers and sisters, and he took charge of the funeral arrangements. To Jim fell the task of digging a grave on his parents' farm and burying the urn that contained his sister's ashes—his parents were simply unable to function. Jim was their support and comfort, and yet I don't think he ever cried, or really talked to them about his sister and what it felt like to lose her.

We'd only been married for four years at the time and I remember being amazed at how calm he stayed, not getting hysterical, as I would have. It took me years to realize that he was just as grief-stricken as I would have been, that he only showed it differently.

Jim always remembers to call his mother on Christine's birthday. When my oldest daughter was born, he asked that her middle name be Christine. On the infrequent occasions when he talks to our children about his sister (usually her name comes up when they see her in a family picture and ask about her), he refers to her as "your aunt Chris."

Just as he didn't discuss Chris with me, my husband never talked to me about breaking down at the Wee Care meeting, and I didn't mention the incident to him. It seemed important to him that he be able—outwardly at least—to maintain a semblance of invulnerability. Women are allowed, even expected, to be vulnerable. But in a man it's a sign of weakness, a threat to his very masculinity. So Jim kept his feelings locked inside. And I, feeling rebuffed, began to turn away from him and to get what I needed elsewhere.

What I needed was to talk about Wee Care ad nauseam.

My mother, my brothers and sisters, my closest friends at work were all sympathetic and willing to listen to me. But the only people who truly understood what it felt like were the other victims' mothers. Only they felt those same feelings of powerlessness, the sense of loss, the self-destructive guilt.

Julie Minetti remembers that summer as one of the lowest times in her life. Like so many of the rest of us, she didn't believe at first that Jodie had been involved in the bizarre sexual abuse at school. She, too, felt that it could only happen to someone else's child.

A brief incident involving her daughter a year or so earlier kept coming back to Julie when she heard about the allegations of sexual abuse. It reinforced the confidence she felt that her daughter would rebuff anyone who tried to abuse her.

When Jodie was three, the Minettis took her to Atlantic City when they went to watch Muhammad Ali. As they walked through the hotel lobby, with Julie carrying Jodie in her arms, they saw the boxing star coming toward them, surrounded by bodyguards and hordes of well-wishers. Muhammad Ali stopped when he saw Jodie, and reached out to greet her. But Jodie just looked him right in the eye and said, "I hate you," before turning her face to her mother.

"That little incident stuck in my mind and I convinced myself that Jodie would tell anybody anything," Julie said. "My husband and I said to each other, if she could tell Muhammad Ali she hates him, of course she could say no to a teacher who tried to touch her.

"Little did I understand back then that sexual abuse isn't a one-time thing where a stranger is going to grab your child in the bathroom and the kid is going to scream no," Julie said. "We had no idea back then how sexual abuse works. The time involved, the game playing, the escalating, the whole relationship that it involves."

Jodie, interviewed by Lou Fonolleras on June 11, said Kelly had inserted a knife and fork into her vagina. She spoke of being hit on the genitals and on her body with a large wooden spoon by Kelly. Later she described how she and other children had been forced to "pile up" on a naked Kelly and how she had watched Kelly sit at the piano in the nude and play "Jingle Bells." And she told how she and Kelly had performed cunnilingus on each other.

It wasn't until after her daughter's initial interview with Lou Fonolleras that Julie believed the unbelievable. Like the rest of us, she began recalling all her child's odd behaviors of the past months, fitting the pieces of the puzzle together.

Julie felt devastated that her only child had been so horribly molested. Although once she had thought nothing could ever be worse than finding out about Jodie's seizure disorder, this was worse.

Julie readily admits that she is a person who likes to be in control. And with her daughter's seizures, she was able to be. She could make sure her daughter took her medicine, and take her to her appointments with the pediatrician and the speech therapist. But the knowledge that her daughter had been sexually abused left her feeling impotent. "At least with the seizures I realized it was out of my hands, that she was in the care of the best doctors," Julie said. "Wee Care was worse because someone took away my right to protect my child, and did it under my very nose for so long. So initially, I really lost it."

She would sit in the backyard with her mother, unable to stop crying. Her mother said, "Julie, stop it. You're scaring me. I've never seen you like this."

The anger she felt was directed mainly at the school's director, Arlene Spector. "Kelly I could just write off as a sicko, a stoned wacko, a bona fide lunatic," Julie said. "But Arlene was in charge of the school. If she had been there when she should have been, she would have known what was going on."

■

Cathy Baird felt like she of all people should have known what was going on with her son, Benjamin. He had already been sexually abused the year before—by Chris, a teen-aged boy the Bairds hired to baby-sit for him on Friday nights.

Chris's mother had cared for Benjamin as an infant, while Cathy was still working as a teacher. Chris's whole family, who lived down the street from the Bairds, adored Benjamin. There was even a framed picture of him in their living room. Cathy trusted Chris completely.

Donald's work week was very demanding, and by Friday night he felt drained and in need of physical exercise. Since he and Cathy were both watching their weight, they played racketball on Friday nights. Chris would come over around seven o'clock and Cathy and Donald would go for a game of racketball. Afterward, they returned home to shower, change, and go out for a quick bite. They were always home before midnight.

Early one Saturday morning, Benjamin came in and sat down on his parents' bed before they were up.

"So how was Chris last night?" asked Cathy, just to make conversation.

"He made all kinds of creamy white stuff come out of his penis for me," said Benjamin casually. His parents looked at him and then at each other in disbelief.

"He what? Are you sure?"

Benjamin told them that the night before, Chris took him into the bathroom, locked the door, and masturbated in front of him. Cathy was able to establish that this had happened more than once, and that Chris may have touched Benjamin as well. But she doesn't think Benjamin even knew what was going on, and, in retrospect anyway, the acts were fairly benign.

Cathy and Donald didn't press charges against the baby-sitter. She talked to Chris's mother, who promised to have her son see a psychologist. And Cathy wrote an anonymous letter to all Wee Care parents about the experience and the importance of choosing a baby-sitter carefully.

"It even had a line in there like, parents spend more time choosing peanut butter than they do choosing a baby-sitter," Cathy said. "I thought I did everything right choosing Wee Care."

When she found out Benjamin had been molested again, she felt doubly betrayed. Because she also believed initially that many Wee Care parents blamed the school's Board of Directors for what had gone on, Cathy—a member of the board—didn't feel as if she could talk to other mothers. She was isolated and alone, and Benjamin's behavior that summer wasn't making her feel any better.

He had terrible nightmares. He acted even more abusively toward his infant brother, and he was aggressive around other children. With his parents he was impetuous, demanding, and incorrigible. In desperation, Cathy chose a psychiatrist and Benjamin began making weekly visits to him. At the same time, he began talking more freely with his mother about all the things Kelly had done to him and forced him to do to her.

He would say, "Kelly did this," and then pull down his pants in front of his mother. He told Cathy that he and another little girl at the school, Suzi Holmes, had to lie on top of each other. As he told Cathy this, he stretched out face down on top of her and started grinding his hips into hers. She made him stop it. She was trying so hard to be patient with him.

Benjamin told his mother that when Suzi Holmes wouldn't do what Kelly wanted her to, Kelly threatened to hurt her. But Benjamin said, "Don't hurt her. Hurt me instead."

"He was such a caring child before Kelly," Cathy said. "I think he used up all his caring for a lifetime. Sometimes he's helpful, but he's just not sweet the way he was. That's gone, and there's no getting it back, no matter how much therapy they have."

Cathy felt as if she was falling apart. She turned to food as consolation and began to put on weight rapidly. Within a few months' time, Cathy had gained forty-five pounds. She looked and felt terrible.

Once Billy Farrell revealed what had happened to him at school, his behavior deteriorated further than it had the previous winter. It was as if now that his parents knew what he had endured, he felt justified in venting his anger on them for not recognizing and responding to his cries for help. He hadn't used words to make them aware of the pain and degradation he was enduring. But he no doubt felt as if they should have known from his actions.

Billy grew increasingly angry and sullen that summer, and he was especially furious with Marge. He called her a bitch to her face, and one morning she woke up to find him standing over the bed, staring at her. When he saw that she was awake, he wordlessly spit in her face.

One day he came into the house from playing and told his mother he wanted to tie her up. He looped a belt around her neck, tied up her feet with rope, and put sweat bands over her eyes and mouth. Then he said, "If you tell, you're going to be thrown into the street and run over by a car."

Another day he told his mother to lie on the bed on her side. "Now we're going to stick the sword in you," he told her.

After a couple of such episodes, his mother called a halt to Billy's games. She told him, "If you want to talk about what happened at school, okay, but I'm not going to let you do this to me."

It was a trying time for Marge, who already felt tremendously guilty for what she saw as her own inability to prevent her son from being molested. "Billy would take me by surprise and I'd try to think what to do," she said. "I would try to think how to respond, how to talk to him. I wanted to ask the right questions. Sometimes I just burst out crying. It was like he was dropping into another personality."

The personalities of the other Wee Care victims were undergoing changes that were every bit as disturbing. Our children had been hurt and traumatized, and we were seeing the consequences. It was a dark side of childhood that, fortunately, most parents don't ever have to witness.

Claudia Schwartz is a strikingly pretty, dark-haired woman with an optimistic outlook on life and a streak of the perfectionist in her. Her husband, Peter, is a slight, slender man with horn-rimmed glasses and thick curly blond hair. They are devoted to each other and to their daughter, Michele.

When the Schwartzes first heard about the allegations of sexual abuse at the preschool, they never dreamed their tall, slender four-year-old could possibly be involved. The Schwartzes were in Florida for a vacation when the first parents' meeting was held at Wee Care in May. They might have forgotten all about the whole thing when they returned, but before long other Wee Care acquaintances filled them in on the ever-widening scandal. By early June, it was general knowledge that more than one child was involved, and parents were growing anxious about their own children.

Still, Peter and Claudia never considered that Michele might be a part of all this. Very early on, some parents believed that the pupils in Kelly's own class had been spared. They felt this way because initially, many children in Kelly's class hadn't been as forthcoming as some other youngsters about what Kelly had done to them. (This might have been coincidence, or maybe it was because Kelly's pupils were age three—less able than four-year-olds to verbalize what had happened.)

At any rate, since Michele was in Kelly's class, the Schwartzes were more than happy to latch onto this theory. But more and more children were being named as victims. Some were in Kelly's class. Some were good friends of Michele's.

In mid-June, Michele readily talked to Lou Fonolleras about what Kelly had done to her. She told how her former teacher had beaten her on her breasts, belly, and genitals with a wooden spoon, and punched her in the mouth. Michele recalled having to strike Kelly on her vagina and belly with the wooden spoon, and she said Kelly had inserted a fork and spoon into her vagina. Kelly also had kissed her on the mouth, anus, and vagina, the little girl said. Michele seemed relieved and happy to learn that Kelly was in jail.

Claudia was shocked and numb. "I was extremely upset, but I didn't want Michele to see me so upset," Claudia said. "They had told us that just as important as what happened is how you react to what happened. I was terribly distraught and very emotional. But I was determined to preserve the status quo and keep things as normal as possible."

Claudia Schwartz works as a personnel manager for a Fortune 500 corporation, and she is competent at what she does. But that summer, she was unable to concentrate on the job.

"As a manager, I wasn't very good," Claudia said. "Nothing seemed terribly relevant and it was hard to concentrate. I would see people coming into my office and I could tell by their expressions that they could see something wasn't right with me. I couldn't think in terms of the future because I could barely make it through day to day."

Peter agreed. "I would just lapse and start thinking about it," he said. "I was preoccupied, although it didn't totally affect my work."

Michele became uncharacteristically temperamental that summer, and she threw tantrums that grew more prolonged and violent as the weeks went by. Always a good sleeper, she began wanting to sleep on the living-room sofa, and she had nightmares.

After the Wee Care preschool closed in June of 1985 (and the toddler center was reorganized with a new staff under a different name), Claudia hired a series of baby-sitters to take care of her daughter while she and Peter were at work. But Michele's moods were so dark and explosive that no baby-sitter lasted long. The Schwartzes enrolled Michele in a local summer camp while they tried to figure out day-care arrangements for the fall.

Claudia took Michele to the pediatrician for an internal examination, and he tried to console her by telling her sexual abuse isn't the worst thing in the world. "I'm not saying that what Michele went through was pleasant, because it wasn't," she remembers him saying. "But there are much worse things. She wasn't raped. Nobody maimed her. She wasn't killed. For that matter, she's not retarded. These are tragedies. Michele will bounce back. Kids are resilient. What we're dealing with is not a tragedy."

The pediatrician wasn't the first person to make such a comment. Throughout the Wee Care ordeal, the observation that our children hadn't been raped was often offered by well-meaning observers who meant to be comforting. But it was little consolation at the time. Besides, we felt as if our children *had* been raped.

Claudia felt a horror such as she had never known. She found Michele's up-and-down mood swings and her constant clinginess frustrating to deal with. Also upsetting for Claudia was her daughter's overt sexual behavior.

"I remember at one point she was putting her finger into her rectum," Claudia said. "That to me was the ultimate, the most horrifying. I couldn't handle that at all."

Oliver Madison was one of the few Chinese children at Wee Care that year. He was in Hannah's class, although the two weren't particularly close and never saw each other outside of school. Because he is stout and tall for his age, Oliver looks older than the other youngsters. His stern countenance and big stature could frighten a smaller child who didn't know him well enough to realize that he is as gentle and sweet as a puppy.

Diane Madison, his mother, had no idea that her child was being used as a bully to help Kelly sexually abuse his classmates. Nor did she know that Oliver himself was a victim. She would first find this out, not from her son or from the investigators, but at a parents' meeting at the school in June.

This meeting was held the week after I learned about Hannah, and it was the first one I felt emotionally strong enough to attend. The school's parking lot was packed. I remember standing with Jim outside on that warm evening and waiting for the doors to be opened. My eyes were red from crying in the car, and I was surprised to see that a lot of the other parents looked as if they had been crying, too.

We all sat in an upstairs meeting room and listened to psychologist Susan Esquilin give us some suggestions for coping with our children. It was the first time I had ever met Susan, who is short and plump, and has curly dark hair—in looks, a quintessential Mrs. Piggle Wiggle of the popular children's book series.

But Mrs. Piggle Wiggle is an amiable, grandmotherly spinster who dispenses fanciful, funny cures to anxious parents whose children won't eat healthy meals, take a bath, or clean their room. Susan is a child psychologist specializing in sexual abuse. She has a calm, reassuring manner. That night, I listened carefully as she began to outline what I felt was sound, helpful advice to a beleaguered and besieged crowd of parents. She spoke of the importance of not putting words into the child's mouth, and of not coddling the children. Some victims' parents had begun to baby their kids, giving them whatever they wanted as if this could somehow make up for what they had been through. Susan maintained that discipline still was important, and that parents needed to keep a firm upper hand.

Not all the parents who were there that night knew for sure that their children had been victims. Diane Madison, sitting across the room from me, raised her hand and said that apparently her child had been one of the lucky ones who had escaped. Several parents looked at her in surprise and said that Oliver had been named as a victim by their children.

Diane, who had come to the meeting mainly because she felt obliged to go to all school functions, until that point had played the role of an onlooker. She was a single parent on a tight budget, and she had worked ever since her son was born.

A friend of her mother's told her about Wee Care, and Oliver began attending the toddler center when he was two. He moved over to the preschool when he was four. She felt good about her choice of schools, for Oliver had adjusted smoothly. But he grew aggressive with other children and clingy to his mother the year Kelly was at Wee Care. His mother noticed that occasionally he didn't eat his lunch, but figured he had been playing hard on those days and didn't have time to eat.

She never figured sexual abuse. Now, at the meeting, she crumpled in her chair, weeping. I could feel the silent sympathy of the other parents go out to her, and someone sitting nearby leaned over to comfort her.

After that meeting, Diane got in touch with the school and said she needed Oliver to be interviewed. Apparently the investigators were so backed up by then that no one had contacted her yet.

But in two interviews with Detective Richard Mastrangelo, Oliver provided an even more complete and vivid picture of what had gone on in the secrecy of unused rooms. The child said he saw Kelly defecate on the floor. She urinated on the floor, on him, and on other children, and she hit him about the genitals with a wooden spoon, he said. During one interview, Oliver observed, "Girls don't have a penis, they have blood."

When invited to name the body parts on a doll, he pointed carefully. "This is the head, these are the shoulders, this is the waist, and this . . . [pointing to the doll's vagina] is the blood."

Asked if he had seen blood coming out of somewhere, he told the investigator he had seen blood coming out of Kelly's vagina.

That summer, Oliver began to wet his bed occasionally and to play very aggressively with other children. He was rough and pushed and shoved other children around. He was "like an engine running constantly," his mother said. "A lot of energy but not going anywhere."

He began to have difficulty sleeping, and he had to have a lamp on in his room. Oliver and Diane live with her parents. Oliver is very close to his grandparents, and his grandfather is almost like a father to him. That summer the child was fearful that something was going to happen to "Poppa." Whenever he was away from home, he insisted that his mother call home and make sure his grandparents were all right.

"Please call home, Mom," he would say repeatedly. "I just have to make sure they're okay."

His behavior got so out of hand that Diane's mother suggested she put him in therapy. For the first few visits with a psychologist, he refused to talk at all. He just sat, in silence, and played with the toys, but not the way most youngsters do. Instead, he tied them up, blindfolded them, or undressed them. He used string or tape to bind up all his playthings—trucks, dolls, teddy bears, and G.I. Joe figures.

Diane was having a tough time herself that summer. She could not come to terms with the fact that someone had violated her child, who had shared her bedroom since he was born. "I felt like it was my fault," she said. "If I hadn't been working, if I had been there more often, if I had come by more often, if I had noticed what was going on, then this wouldn't have happened.

"I took up drinking for a while and then I said, whoa, Lord, let's hang in there. Oliver and you are the only ones. If I go cuckoo, who's he going to have? So I had to snap out of it really quick."

She did a lot of housecleaning that summer. She painted her son's room, stripped wallpaper off the walls, and scrubbed windows. To keep busy was one way to keep sane, she reasoned.

I felt the same way. But what also gave me a sense of purpose was to engage in activities that were connected to the case. By then we all knew there was going to be a criminal case. It helped focus my energies to take Hannah down to the courthouse in Newark several times to meet Sara Sencer and see the grand jury room so that Hannah would feel more comfortable testifying. And then, my line of reasoning went, Kelly might be convicted and put in prison for life.

It helped to go to the meetings at the school because I was around other parents who were suffering just as I was. At one of these gatherings, Susan Esquilin suggested our children might benefit from small group-therapy sessions. I was enthusiastic because it seemed as if nothing I could do or say would make Hannah feel better.

Susan felt that these groups would meet several goals. They would allow the children to see their classmates and be reassured that all the children were safe and healthy. They would address certain psychological issues Susan felt may have been raised by the abuse. They would engage the children in normal preschool games and songs that may have been involved in the abuse to "neutralize" them. Finally, the groups would give Susan the chance to observe the children and be able to recommend to their parents whether further therapy was necessary.

The children were broken down into groups of about five or six, and five parent-child sessions were planned for July and August in various homes. Susan decided to make them parent-child because many of the youngsters were so clingy they wouldn't separate from their parents anyway. Also, having the parents there would give Susan the chance to model for them some helpful ways of dealing with the children.

Susan mentioned Kelly only once, at the start of the first session, when she told the kids that the meetings were being held because of some of the things they said had happened at Wee Care with Kelly. Other than that, none of the adults ever mentioned Kelly in the group-therapy sessions.

In some of the sessions, the children sang songs like "Old McDonald Had a Farm" and played games like Duck Duck Goose. Kelly had made up sexual versions of these, and the idea was to make the children comfortable with them again. Susan read them Maurice Sendak's *Where the Wild Things Are*, and they discussed how the child in the story controlled the monsters in his dream and how the children might be able to control the monsters in theirs.

They talked about body parts and the functions of various body parts, and Susan read a book about how a baby is made. She encouraged the children to look at the pictures and ask questions. Then there were relaxation exercises, games, songs, and refreshments.

At the final session, held at my parents' house in Maplewood on a muggy Friday morning, Susan's student helper used hand puppets to tell a story about a little bear whose mother goes off and leaves him with a baby-sitter. While she is gone, the bear gets hungry and wants some honey, but the baby-sitter is an otter and doesn't know where to find honey. The bear is very upset, because he is hungry and can't get the food he likes. The student then asked the children to each make up an ending for the story.

Hannah's ending was simple and sounded reasonable to

me: the little bear should get a new baby-sitter. Susan later told me that this was a healthy conclusion. "It shows a kind of flexibility, the notion that one doesn't have to accept this and live without eating honey," she said.

The aim of the next exercise was to help children understand that there is both good and bad in all people. The kids were asked to draw a picture of someone who does good things, and then to draw a picture of someone who does bad things. Most children drew their mothers the first time and Kelly the second time. Then the children were asked to think of something bad that the good person they drew does. The kids' answers were predictable: they said sometimes their mothers got angry with them or yelled at them.

Then Susan turned to the pictures of the bad people, asking if they ever did anything good. I was sitting at the rear of the living room, keeping an eye on the coffeepot through the kitchen door, and Hannah couldn't see me. In fact, she may have forgotten I was there at all. Otherwise, I doubt she ever would have said what she did next.

Hannah looked at her picture of Kelly, and then said that a "good" thing that Kelly used to do was to play games. "She played the jail game with us," Hannah told Susan. "We chased her around, and if we caught her we got to put her in jail. It was fun."

But Kelly also did things that were bad, Hannah continued, unbidden. "Kelly pooped in her pants," giggled my five-year-old daughter, who had steadfastly maintained to me that nothing out of the ordinary had ever happened at school. "She made pee-pee on the floor in the gym and it dribbled all over the floor. When she cleaned it up she put the towels in the metal garbage can."

I was so amazed by this revelation that I simply sat there in silence. I had heard earlier that summer that Kelly had made some of the children eat and play with urine and feces. Kelly also had made cakes out of feces, I was told.

At the time, I found this scenario so revolting that I

almost didn't believe it. And of course I never inquired of Hannah if she was involved in any of this. Once again, I just assumed she wasn't. Now here she sat, telling a psychologist she barely knew more of the sordid details of the past school year. It was just one more indication of how little my daughter confided in me these days. She was growing apart from me. As much as I longed to be able to, I could never unlock the terrible secrets she held in her little head.

C H A P T E R

■ ■ ■ ■ ■ ■ ■ ■ ■ ■ ■

7

When I didn't believe that Kelly had forced her three- and four-year-old charges to drink urine and play with feces, I wasn't alone. None of the parents automatically assumed their own children were involved in any of the sordid activities that took place at Wee Care. On the contrary, as each unsettling disclosure surfaced, we hoped and prayed our youngsters had been spared.

Susan Esquilin had a lot of contact with many of the troubled families that summer. She described this common reaction among the parents in a report she prepared for the prosecutors:

> At each new revelation, the parents seemed to hope that whatever was now emerging had not happened to their child. . . . Far from believing that their child was a victim of each alleged abuse, initially each set of parents tended to deny that this could have occurred to their child. All the parents were astounded that this could have gone on without their child having in-

formed them as, in their eyes, this called into question the nature of the relationship they had with their child.

And through it all Wee Care director Arlene Spector, whose mandate was to preserve order and sanity at the school, was coordinating the children's interviews with Lou, taking calls from tearful, angry parents, trying to keep her day-care center from going down the tubes.

Not one of the parents recognized what was happening to the children, though there were occasional signs that something was amiss. For instance, once that winter, when Wee Care parent Diane Madison was changing four-year-old Oliver's clothes, she noticed a few speckles of blood on his underwear. She assumed he had made a hard stool, and thought no more about it.

"You wouldn't click on something like child abuse, not in a place like Maplewood or South Orange," Diane said. "It never dawned on me, and Oliver didn't mention anything to me, of course."

Diane still isn't sure she could have prevented her child's victimization. "To this day I don't know what I could have done differently," she said. "We sent them to what we thought was the best day-care center, and for the amount of money, it certainly should have been. And still I'll think to myself, something should have clicked when I noticed those blood spots on his underwear."

In November of 1984, a five-year-old girl named Shana McFee left Wee Care because her parents had recently divorced and she was going to live with her mother in a town forty-five minutes away. Shana and Hannah had been great friends for the previous two years, and Hannah was sad to see her leave. Shana came over to our house for a farewell lunch one Friday while I was at home.

She and Hannah sat at the kitchen table, shouting "Penis!" and "Vagina!" at the top of their lungs and laughing uncontrollably at their wittiness. Maria, who had only been with us for two months, looked thoroughly disapproving.

She pursed her lips as she went about her chores and muttered several times that she was glad the little girl was moving away.

I was shocked at the bawdy talk, and wondered whether it was Shana's reaction to the recent divorce. Perhaps she was trying to get her parents' attention by using vulgar language. In any case, I wasn't sorry to see her move either.

Shana's departure was significant for two reasons. For one thing, it may have helped investigators pinpoint how early the abuse at Wee Care had begun. Months after leaving the school, Shana had dreams of sweeping urine and feces off the stairs at school. Since she had left Wee Care in November, it seemed not unlikely that Kelly had started with her illicit activities almost immediately after she was hired in September.

The other significance of Shana's departure had a more immediate impact on our family because of the vacancy it created at the Wee Care preschool. That spot was filled by my three-year-old niece Emily. When she was an infant, her father cared for her while Kathleen worked. Then Kathleen and Wayne got divorced, Wayne got a job, and eventually both my mother and I urged Kathleen to consider Wee Care. We pointed out how Caroline and Hannah had thrived there, and said it would do Emily good to be in a learning environment with children her age. True, it would cost a lot. But Wee Care had a scholarship fund, and we figured my sister, a single parent with a relatively small income, would qualify for financial assistance.

When Kathleen had first applied to Wee Care that fall, there were no openings. But when Shana McFee left, Arlene called Kathleen to say that Emily could start immediately. My sister was thrilled.

Emily loved her teacher, a motherly, competent woman named Joan Higgins. But outgoing Emily seemed quiet and reticent around the other kids. Still, Kathleen figured it would just take her awhile to adjust to a day-care center.

When Emily had been at the school for about a month

and a half, she had a black eye when my sister arrived to pick her up one night. Kathleen asked her about it, but Emily was vague. She said someone had thrown something at her. Kathleen thought maybe she had gotten kicked by another child's foot when they were playing on the climbers in the gym.

It was the end of the day and only a couple of aides were still there. None of them knew how Emily's eye had been blackened. Kathleen was concerned, but not overly. Emily had just turned three a few months earlier. Maybe she wasn't verbal enough yet to express what had happened to her. Wee Care was Kathleen's first experience with a day-care center. She figured kids occasionally got banged up by the other kids. No sense making a big deal out of it.

Kathleen probably would have taken it up with either Emily's teacher or Arlene, but the incident happened on the last day before the Christmas break. Kathleen took the next two weeks off from work. By the time Emily started school in January, her eye was back to normal and Kathleen didn't pursue it. Looking back, though, my sister suspects it was Kelly who blackened Emily's eye.

When Emily started at Wee Care, she had long hair—my sister had never cut it. It framed her cherubic, round face and then curled softly down her back. In February of that year, Emily did something that was so unlike her, my sister was flabbergasted. She gobbed an entire jar of Vaseline all over her hair. When Kathleen found her, Emily's hair was hanging down her back in long, greasy tresses. It was so oily that if you touched it, your finger came away shiny with Vaseline. No matter how many times Kathleen washed Emily's hair, she couldn't get the Vaseline out.

My sister was getting married that month, and Kathleen was mortified that her daughter would have to go to the wedding looking as if her hair hadn't been washed in months. She took Emily to the local beauty parlor and asked if they could somehow wash the Vaseline out. They told Kathleen the only way to get it out was with lighter fluid, and my sister wasn't about to risk that. So, on the day of the wedding, my sister put Emily's hair into a French braid to make the greasiness less obvious. And gradually, over the next couple of months, the Vaseline washed out.

"I found out much later from Emily that Kelly had pulled her hair a lot," Kathleen said. "I think Emily put the Vaseline in her hair so Kelly wouldn't touch her head. I believe the hair-pulling was why Emily went through this whole phase with her dolls, too."

That year, Emily had a lot of She-Ra dolls, with long flowing hair. Emily began insisting that Kathleen take a pair of scissors and cut their hair off. She also wanted this treatment for all her baby dolls. Kathleen, of course, never stumbled on the fact that some hurtful goings-on at school were causing her daughter's aversion to long hair.

The school Kathleen had chosen with such care for her daughter had turned out to be a nightmarish place where children got hurt and humiliated. And yet it had been so highly praised by people whose judgment she trusted. Kathleen felt angry and betrayed. I felt guilty for recommending the center to my sister in the first place, and, in some illogical way, at least partly responsible for Emily's victimization.

But how were we to know? And can parents prevent their children from being sexually abused? Months after we'd found out about Hannah, I asked Susan Esquilin what we should have done differently.

The child who cries when dropped off at his day-care center isn't necessarily being molested, she said. Many children do resist going to school at first, but then settle down. But when a child who appears to have made a satisfactory adjustment to school suddenly balks at going, the parent should make every effort to determine why the child dislikes school.

But the bottom line, Susan told me, is that parents simply

113

can't be one hundred percent sure their child isn't being molested. For one thing, it is the nature of preschoolers to communicate unclearly, to tell things in bits and pieces.

"To get an idea of what I mean, have your three-year-old watch a TV show you haven't seen—have your husband screen it first—and then ask the child to tell you what he saw," Susan suggested. "You'll get bits and pieces of it, but you're not going to get a sequence of events from beginning to end that is going to make much sense to you. And a TV show, unlike sexual abuse, is neutral, nonconflictual. The child is not trying to hide anything."

Happily, there are steps parents can take to minimize the possibility of sexual abuse, Susan said. Start sex education —though not necessarily sexual abuse education—at a very early age, like one year old.

When parents label a toddler's body parts for him (or her), they're likely to skip the trunk entirely and point out everything but the genitalia. The first time most parents mention the genitalia is during toilet training, and then they communicate that these parts are dirty or embarrassing, Susan said.

Many parents also become upset by seeing their child masturbate. If a baby as young as eight or nine months old puts his or her hand on his or her genitals, the parent automatically removes it. So at an early age, the child receives his parents' nonverbal message about sexuality— "there's something wrong with it, and it's not an area that I can talk about easily."

Susan doesn't advocate allowing nursery school–aged children to masturbate in front of others. Once a child has reached eighteen months or two years old and is being taught what kinds of behavior are acceptable, he or she should be told not to touch his or her genitals except when alone.

Meanwhile, to establish an ease of communication from a young age, label *all* body parts for your child. It doesn't matter whether you use adult or baby words. What's important is that children have words for their genitals that they have learned in a nonconflictual way.

Susan also recommends that, beginning at about age three, the child be read preschool sex education books—not necessarily those that deal with sexual abuse or contraception—but those that explain the differences between male and female bodies, and where babies come from.

"Usually there is a mention somewhere of a penis being put inside a vagina, but I have to tell you that except with children who have been abused, I don't think that information takes," Susan said. "It goes in one ear and out the other. What kids that age are most interested in are the differences in the male and female bodies, and that the baby grows in the mother's body and comes out through the mother's vagina. The actual concept of a penis going into a vagina seems so bizarre that it doesn't take until age seven or eight."

If a child has names for his genitals and someone tries to touch him in these areas, the child will feel more comfortable raising the subject with a parent, Susan explained. The child will reason: Mommy knows that people have penises and vaginas, Mommy has told me about this and even told me what people do with their penises and vaginas. So I can tell Mommy about something that happened with *my* penis or vagina.

There's another whole area in which parents need to educate their children, Susan feels. Besides teaching a child about sex, parents should teach their children from a fairly early age that not everything other adults do is right. "I know a lot of people would disagree with me," she said. "There are people in school systems who are enraged when a parent criticizes a teacher. They think it's bad parenting to criticize a teacher's actions. But I believe if you think a teacher did something wrong, it is absolutely imperative that you let your child know you think this.

"We constantly present a united front to children—the world of adults at large—and often assume that adult behavior is right. And so the child gets the message from the parent, and I think it comes very early, that other adults can do no wrong."

If a child doesn't like a baby-sitter and can't say why, get another baby-sitter if possible, Susan said. If your youngster doesn't like a teacher, don't dismiss it as nothing.

"It's not always easy to get the story and I'm not saying it is," Susan said. "Many adults drop out of a class in college because they don't like a particular teacher, even though they may not be able to verbalize why. Children's likes and dislikes should at least merit a parent's attention."

Susan feels day care must become a societal responsibility. She is in favor of on-site facilities in the workplace that are open to parents and staffed by trained, professional, well-paid, and valued teachers. "We have tremendous numbers of women entering the work force and no one thinks about what is happening to their children," she said.

Susan encourages parents of children in nursery schools and day-care centers to hold regular parents' meetings to discuss common problems that the parents are having with the children. If it turns out that a significant number of youngsters don't want to take naps, someone ought to be looking into what's going on at naptime.

We didn't hold such parents' meetings at Wee Care. And for all the time and energy I'd spent checking out day-care centers before choosing Wee Care, I didn't know things at the school were starting to slip that year. It's still hard to pinpoint exactly when the supervision and the quality of the care began to deteriorate.

One significant factor was a change in the center's administration. When Caroline and Hannah started Wee Care, Arlene Spector and another woman, who had founded Wee Care together years earlier, co-directed both centers. Their offices were at the preschool. But when they began having disagreements, it was decided that Arlene would stay in Maplewood to run the preschool while her colleague went to South Orange to administer the toddler center.

It was this other day-care administrator who had so impressed me when my two older daughters first started attending Wee Care in 1980. She seemed to care so much about the children, and she would pitch in and teach a class herself when a teacher was absent. Arlene, on the other hand, seemed to have little contact with the children. She kept pretty much to herself in her third-floor office, and some of the children didn't even know who she was. One teacher recalled that Arlene "never checked on the teachers."

In the fall of 1984, Arlene may have just been getting bored with the child-care field. One day that winter, she called to ask if I thought the current American passion for croissants would continue to build, or if it had peaked. She'd been thinking of going into the business of buying croissant dough, she said, and then selling it to bakeries and restaurants to bake and market as their own "homemade" croissants. She'd already been around and tasted some of the doughs on the market, she said. But she valued my opinion on food trends and wanted to know if I thought it would be a lucrative field for her to get into.

I sat on the bed, nursing Robert, with the telephone receiver tucked between my ear and shoulder while we chatted for perhaps fifteen minutes about the pros and cons of her proposal. In the end, she was still undecided about whether to go forward with her plan, and I was puzzled over her wanting out of the day-care profession. Since Arlene was rarely at the school when I arrived in the morning and had left by the time I picked up Hannah, I didn't realize she wasn't really involved with the children very often.

In the early spring of 1985, shortly before I returned to my job after being on maternity leave, I took Caroline, Hannah, and Ellen into Manhattan for a day of sight-seeing. On the train that morning, we met Arlene and her teen-aged daughter. Arlene told me they were going shopping for a prom dress for her daughter, and I remember noting that she wasn't at the preschool that day.

My sister Kathleen got the feeling that Arlene was rarely at Wee Care. Kathleen had applied for financial aid to help pay Emily's tuition, but the school hadn't bothered to let her know whether or not she qualified for a scholarship. Kathleen began to receive letters from Wee Care's treasurer, asking why her tuition hadn't been paid. Repeatedly, Kathleen called the preschool to ask Arlene what was going on, and every time she called, she was told that Arlene wasn't in that day. Kathleen began to feel increasingly annoyed. Was Arlene ever there? she wondered.

Around the same time that Arlene became the sole director of the preschool, Wee Care lost its educational director, a wonderfully creative, competent professional who was respected by all the parents and loved by the children. Her duties were split among the other staff members; no replacement was hired.

We learned later that Wee Care was very short-staffed in the 1984–85 school year. The Board of Directors was having a tough time finding aides, and at times there simply were not enough aides for every teacher to have one. Like other day-care centers, Wee Care had trouble attracting workers willing to put up with the low pay, long hours, and often tedious work.

The staff shortage was reflected in the lack of supervision at the school. One aide called supervision that year "the pits, there's no other way to describe it." Another said, "Often we were shorthanded. . . . There was very little supervision at Wee Care."

In the fall of 1984, a young woman named Elizabeth Frank was hired as a teacher. From the day she started, she didn't feel comfortable at Wee Care. After she had been working at the preschool just a few weeks, Miss Frank was surprised to be asked to lock up at night.

"They placed too much trust in you," she said. "There

118

weren't enough people. They hired me pretty much on the spot and left me alone with the children. It wasn't that I couldn't be trusted. It was that they trusted me."

Beth Frank resigned October 18, 1984 to accept a job in the public school system. Her departure created an opening for the three-year-old class teacher. That vacancy was filled by Kelly Michaels, an aide with less than a month's experience.

Kelly had been a theater major at Seton Hill College in Greensburg, Pennsylvania, where she took some photography courses and acted in and directed more than a dozen plays. More than anything, she wanted to be an actress. In the summer of 1984, a few credits short of her undergraduate degree, Kelly accepted a college classmate's offer to share an apartment in a run-down neighborhood in East Orange, New Jersey. Broadway it wasn't, but it was within an easy commute of Manhattan. Kelly figured she'd get a job to make ends meet. And then she'd pursue her dream of going on the stage.

When the twenty-two-year-old Pittsburgh native walked into Arlene Spector's office, she seemed like an ideal candidate to teach preschoolers. She said she'd baby-sat before, and that she had studied piano for ten years. And she was almost a college graduate. Kelly impressed Arlene as being very creative—a fine person to introduce the children to photography and the dramatic arts. Kelly was hired and began her new job as an aide on September 26, 1984.

There were a few things about herself that Kelly didn't tell Arlene—like the fact that she'd been very depressed during her last year of college. Or that in a photography class, when the students were assigned to take pictures of something beautiful, Kelly had shot a whole series of toilets.

One summer while she was in college, Kelly said on a résumé, she had a job as a mother's helper. Her duties were to help dress and feed a nine-year-old boy. A nine-year-old

119

boy who needed to be dressed and fed? Later, that struck me as rather odd.

Kelly didn't look like the kind of menacing person you'd suspect of being a child molester. She was young, well-spoken, and attractive in a fresh, Irish way. She had a creamy white complexion, short curly dark hair, and a sturdy build that tended to plumpness. She wore jeans or casual corduroy pants paired with sweaters, and sometimes bandannas around her neck.

"If you lined up all the teachers from Wee Care and said, which one is a child abuser, I would have picked her last," Julie Minetti said. "I remember being so surprised to find out it was Kelly who was referred to in that first letter from the Wee Care Board of Directors. I'd always thought of her as a person who was neither here nor there, but certainly not as a child molester. I thought a young, hip dresser wouldn't be a child molester. Kelly had a Dorothy Hamill haircut back then. I pictured a child abuser as a loner who's out of touch with reality and who dresses like they're from outer space."

That fall, Sharon Bethel, whose four-year-old daughter was one of Kelly's victims, attended a get-acquainted night at Wee Care. Because she arrived late and the place was filled with parents and teachers, she had to stand off to one side. But she heard Arlene introduce Kelly as "our marvelous Kelly" and she saw Kelly blush and smile. Arlene went on to describe Kelly's devotion to the children, and how she came in early (at 7:45 A.M.) and stayed until 6 P.M.

A couple behind Sharon were shaking their heads and looking at Kelly with a mixture of admiration and sympathy.

"How could she keep those hours?" one asked.

"Because she needs the money," whispered the other.

Kelly so impressed Arlene with her apparent dedication to the youngsters that when an opening for a teacher of the three-year-old class became available in October, the decision was made to promote Kelly even though she'd been at

Wee Care only a few weeks. And having her own class meant lots more responsibility—and more opportunities for Kelly to be alone with the children.

If the aide was busy in the tiny third-floor kitchen cutting up fruit for snacks, or if she took some children off to the bathroom, Kelly was alone with the children. And if enough opportunities didn't come up naturally, Kelly was a master at creating them. Co-workers remember Kelly volunteering to take groups of children to the bathroom, for instance. She would say, "That's all right. Don't worry about it; I'll do it," one teacher recalled.

One aide who worked at the school from February to June 1985 said Kelly was alone with the children in the gym for thirty minutes a day and during lunch and naptime.

In the gym once, Jodie Minetti complained to her teacher, Joan Higgins, that she was very tired. Joan told Kelly to take Jodie downstairs and let her rest. No one but Kelly and Jodie will ever know for sure what happened down there in the nap room. Later, Jodie told investigators that Kelly had performed cunnilingus on her. She didn't know the date, of course. But she said it happened in the nap room, when the lights were on and she was alone with Kelly.

In any case, Kelly told Joan that Jodie had simply fallen asleep as soon as they reached the classroom. Joan told Jodie's mother about the incident when she came to pick up her daughter. Although Jodie hadn't had a seizure in months, Julie took her straight to the hospital to have her blood levels checked. Perhaps the medication needed adjusting.

Oddly, Jodie told her mother she had had a seizure and didn't object to having her blood drawn, which she usually hated. But Jodie later confided in her grandmother that she hadn't had a seizure at all, and the blood test confirmed this.

Other teachers thought Kelly was a little strange, though they kept these thoughts to themselves. Later, they would say she seemed "spaced out" at times. She was disorganized and a little messy, they said, and occasionally she smelled as if she hadn't taken a shower.

Then there was the disconcerting way Kelly would sometimes just dance away from her co-workers in the middle of a conversation. They would be talking along about something and suddenly Kelly would extend her arms like an oversized ballerina and waltz off.

One teacher remembers a discussion between herself and another staff member in October, soon after Kelly's arrival. The two had been talking about how the hiring process at Wee Care was rather loose when Kelly turned around and asked, "How do they know I'm not some kind of child molester?"

One aide said that Kelly usually didn't talk with her co-workers. But once Kelly came up to the aide as she was conversing with a co-worker and asked if they had noticed whether her zipper was down. They both said no.

"Good," Kelly is said to have replied. "Because it would have been embarrassing since I'm not wearing any underwear."

Kelly regularly received afternoon phone calls at the school from a man. Some parents thought she was talking to her boyfriend, but it may have been her father. One co-worker recalls overhearing Kelly on the telephone saying, "I love you, Daddy," or "I know you love me, Daddy." Afterward, Kelly sometimes appeared upset.

As the 1984–85 school year wore on, none of Kelly's young charges openly professed any dislike of her. But neither were they effusive in their fondness for her. Once when Traci MacKenna was driving Casey to school, they passed Kelly walking up the hill from the Maplewood train station toward Wee Care.

"Oh look, there's Kelly," Traci said. "Should we pick her up and give her a ride?"

"No. Let her walk," said Casey, staring straight ahead.

Another morning, Diane Madison did stop the car to give

Kelly a ride up the hill. Oliver sat quiet and expressionless in the back seat and avoided looking at her.

For most of that year, Kelly was in charge of the first nap period from 1 to 1:45 P.M. An aide who relieved Kelly for the second nap period recalls that the children in Kelly's nap class were frequently awake. She often rubbed the children's backs, sometimes under their shirts, former co-workers later recalled. One aide remembers walking into the nap room once and noticing that Emily was completely undressed.

The aide may have figured that the child had had a toilet accident, and that Kelly was helping her change her clothes.

Ginny Williams, whose four-year-old daughter Miriam was in Kelly's nap class, occasionally picked up her daughter early, on her way home from work. Sometimes she heard the children crying in the nap room. Ginny, who didn't remember any crying the year before, even mentioned it to some teachers.

"Oh, the kids are just overtired," she was told. "They're just settling down."

A young college student, who had worked at Wee Care the preceding year as part of her high school senior-class community service project, was asked by Arlene to come work during winter vacation in the 1984–85 school year. "She was very, very short-staffed," said the aide, who went to work the same day the director called her. "The first thing I remember was that the kids were awake . . . a good majority of them, and I had a lot of problems getting them to sleep [at naptime]."

This behavior contrasted sharply to her experience the preceding spring, when the children slept. She recalled that when the divider between the art room and the nap room was closed, she couldn't hear a sound from the children.

The young woman returned to the school to teach briefly in the spring after Kelly had left Wee Care. She noticed then that the children were once again sleeping during naptime.

Once, teacher Joan Higgins forgot a book in the nap room and went back to get it during the first nap period. When she opened the door, "There was Kelly, leaning over one of the children. I can still see her face. There was hair coming down. It was a very wild look." Joan apologized to Kelly for interrupting her class and left.

Joan also noticed that utensils were missing from the school. "Things you put back one day were not in the same spot the next day," she said. "Knives were never there when I'd go back the next day." Joan, who used plastic knives to spread peanut butter on crackers at snacktime, finally began hiding a knife behind a bookshelf.

Kelly sometimes chatted with Elaine Norton, who had a three-year-old daughter at the school. One day in April, Elaine noticed that Kelly didn't seem like herself. Elaine mentioned to Arlene that Kelly seemed withdrawn, and Arlene said, "She's been depressed lately, but try to talk to her."

So when Elaine saw Kelly later, she asked, "Is everything okay?"

"I have to leave early today," Kelly told her. "I'm going to the doctor. I'm bleeding from the rectum—a lot."

"Maybe you have colitis," Elaine said.

"Well, something like that," Kelly responded.

By the spring, Kelly must have realized that she better leave Wee Care before one of her victims enlightened the authorities.

Her roommate helped Kelly land another job. The roommate was a supervisor at a school in Newark, which provided volunteers to help out at a day-care center in East Orange. Through her job, she heard about an opening at the Community Day Nursery in East Orange, and she recommended Kelly. On April 12, 1985, Steffi Lorman, the center's education supervisor, interviewed Kelly for an hour and a half. Kelly impressed her as a bright, articulate young woman.

On the application form, Ms. Lorman told Kelly to write that she had graduated from college when Kelly told her she was only one class short. Kelly listed her roommate and some college professors as references, but none of her references were ever contacted. Nor did the East Orange day-care center ever call Wee Care to check on Kelly's performance, because it was not the school's practice to call the facility where a prospective employee was still working.

Ms. Lorman, no doubt short-staffed herself, offered Kelly the job. In a letter to Ms. Lorman dated April 22, Kelly accepted the job at the Community Day Nursery. Because of the investigation into allegations of sexual abuse against her, she would only last at her new job for four-and-a-half days. (A shocked Steffi Lorman later couldn't remember whether Kelly quit or was fired.)

Meanwhile, Kelly tendered her resignation to Arlene Spector on April 15. She told the director she was leaving for personal reasons. Arlene was annoyed that Kelly only gave two weeks' notice because teachers were asked to give a month's. But Kelly was adamant about leaving in two weeks. Her last day at Wee Care was April 26, just four days before Joshua Peterson told his pediatrician's nurse about Kelly taking his temperature rectally at school.

At Wee Care, no clear explanation was provided to the parents about why Kelly was leaving so suddenly. Many were puzzled by her hasty departure.

"It was sort of unclear why she was leaving," said Soma Goldstein. "My impression was that someone was ill in her family and she had to go. I told her I was sorry to see her leave."

On her last day at the school, Kelly didn't make a big point of saying good-bye to the children. There wasn't any farewell party. Co-workers recall, though, that Kelly crooned a Bob Dylan song that day. The song was entitled "It's All Over Now, Baby Blue."

C H A P T E R

8

The earliest newspaper articles about Kelly Michaels were so small and easy to miss that none of us would have believed back then the sensational coverage her case would ultimately receive. Two years from the first indictment, though, her face was a familiar sight on the six o'clock news, and the story received daily coverage from the Associated Press, United Press International, and the local papers. The headlines were splashier, the stories longer, and Kelly's picture was on Page One.

That fall, while Kelly's attorneys dickered over strategy, the Wee Care children went back to school. The kids who had been four the year before started kindergarten at various schools, while the younger set, the three-year-olds, had another year of nursery school in front of them. Many continued to experience behavioral problems and to see therapists.

Hannah was lucky enough to get the same kindergarten teacher Caroline had two years earlier. She was a no-nonsense, middle-aged veteran of the public school system who had little use for troublemakers. She was warm and tender, though, and Caroline had flourished in her class-room. She was always telling me clever things her teacher had said or done, and by the end of that year, was reading on a first-grade level.

Hannah seemed to like kindergarten well enough, and she was soon reading in a primer. She joined the Brownies and she lost her first tooth. Although she did just fine in school, she was also growing increasingly restive and violent at home, and she was more aggressive than ever in her play.

In the kitchen one day while I cut up vegetables for a salad, Hannah snatched up a heavy chef's knife, brandished it, and then almost absentmindedly started jamming it into the wooden breadboard. After several tries, she managed to bury the tip of its blade in the wood so that the knife stood erect on the board. She laughed raucously when I told her to stop it, and skipped away.

She tore through the house with what seemed to be a permanent chip on her shoulder, slamming doors, shoving people out of her way, screeching like a fishwife at the slightest provocation.

Much of her anger was directed at me. Before, if I told her she couldn't have second helpings of dessert or that it was bedtime, she might whine or else just sigh loudly and accept the decision. Now, any time she was crossed in the most minor way, she would scream "I hate you! I hate you!" as loudly as she could before running upstairs to her room and slamming the door.

She spent a good deal of her time sitting in a corner with her thumb in her mouth, staring at nothing in particular. It broke my heart to see her so despondent. When she smiled, it was only with her mouth. Her eyes were flat and no longer sparkled the way they once had. She seemed to have lost her former verve, and the sunshine was gone from her personality.

Ellen, who was now three, and Robert, not yet a year old, watched solemnly when Hannah threw tantrums. Ellen grew more subdued than usual when Hannah flew into one of her rages, and Robert's expression in his high chair was grave. He was placid, chubby, and uncomplaining, such a good baby right from the start that it was easy to divert my attention from him to Hannah. Then I felt guilty about it.

When I should have been cuddling Robert to sleep at night, I was sitting on the edge of Hannah's bed, trying to get her to stop weeping. I let Maria give Robert his bath and take him to the park, and it was she who heard his first words and saw him take his first steps.

One good thing to come out of all this was that Jim began to take care of Robert more and grew much closer to him than he had been to any of our daughters. I had been so intent on being the perfect, conscientious mother before Wee Care that without meaning to, I'd edged Jim out. I'd always been there for the girls, so much so that I think Jim sometimes felt that he wasn't needed, that he didn't have much of a parental role to play. But then we found out about Hannah, and Jim, seeing that I was distracted much of the time, quietly began to fill in for me with Robert. He took the baby with him everywhere he could, and spoiled him with toys. But Robert needed this, and I didn't criticize Jim for bringing home trucks and footballs for the baby.

If Ellen and Robert back then were young enough to remain untroubled by Hannah's state of mind, seven-year-old Caroline was more aware of the upheaval in the household. I hadn't intended to tell her that Hannah had been sexually abused, but she soon wanted to know where her sister was going when she went to group therapy or down to the courthouse. And Caroline wondered what took her father and me out to so many meetings in the evening.

I finally told her, reluctantly, that Hannah had been hurt at school, and when she pressed me for details I quietly explained that Kelly had touched Hannah in her private parts with spoons and forks. Caroline looked as if she didn't believe me.

"That's sick!" she exclaimed. And then didn't ask about

it anymore. Caroline had left the preschool long before Kelly arrived, and her Wee Care experience had been a positive one. It was incomprehensible to her that something so bizarre could have taken place there. And maybe there was some denial on her part, too. She simply didn't want to believe this could have happened to her sister.

Caroline and Hannah are as different as two sisters can be, not just in looks—the older dark and exotic looking, the other fair and fragile—but in temperament. Caroline the perfectionist is shy, somewhat serious, and her own toughest critic. Hannah is extroverted, giggly, relaxed about things to the point of sloppiness, and the quintessential ham who is always ready to jump up and perform. Caroline would never let anyone see her dance, but Hannah has only to hear music she likes to start sashaying around the room.

Different as they are, though, my two older daughters have always been close. They're twenty-one months apart, just as my sister Mary and I are. And so far, anyway, they're best friends just like my sister and me. When Hannah grew violent and unhappy that year, it saddened Caroline. And I think she also felt a little jealous of Hannah as the months wore on and Hannah got so much attention.

My own sisters and brothers were terribly concerned about what had happened to Hannah. To make it up to her, they took her to Gruning's for ice cream and bought her new Care Bears and clothes for her Cabbage Patch doll. Caroline endured this without comment for the most part, but several times she asked me why Hannah got so many new things even when it wasn't her birthday. It did seem rather unfair, especially in light of Hannah's unpleasant behavior to everyone around her.

By late fall, Hannah was so difficult to control I sometimes felt I couldn't manage her on my own anymore. She flew into frequent rages, and got upset about every small frustration. She took no pride in herself or her appearance, and criticized her own work.

I called Susan Esquilin, who suggested I bring Hannah in for individual therapy. So we began making the half-hour drive to the therapist's Montclair office every Friday. We'd leave home at five and return about seven o'clock. I would always make dinner in advance so the others could eat before we got home.

Hannah constantly expressed to Susan that she was "bad," but she couldn't verbalize what was bad about her. Though she allowed Susan to engage her in play activities, she was very tense. Hannah didn't like herself anymore. She wished that her hair and eyes were a different color. She thought she was too thin, then too fat.

Hannah hates car rides, so to distract her on the way to and from Susan's office I taught her different Christmas carols or we sang songs she already knew. She has always loved to sing and has a clear, bell-like voice. But that year, she sulked and fretted, saying her voice was ugly. She insisted I had a prettier voice, and that she sounded terrible when she sang. Nothing I said would change her mind.

When I mentioned this to Susan, she told me to ask Hannah what her voice would have to sound like in order to sound good. Hannah didn't have any answer to this question. Fortunately, it was around this time that her school had try-outs for the chorus, which was made up of about two dozen children who could carry a tune. Hannah was chosen.

"You see, Hannah?" I said, hugging her. "You really do have a beautiful voice. And I'm not the only one who thinks so."

The ongoing strain began taking its toll on me. I had terrible stomachaches every day and chugged Maalox right out of the bottle every few hours to keep from doubling over in pain. I kept one large bottle of the chalky-tasting antacid in my desk drawer at work, and one in the linen closet at home. I constantly felt exhausted, but at night, the only way I could get to sleep was by drinking a couple of glasses of wine. I felt as if I was no longer in control.

So when Susan Esquilin told me she was planning a series of support meetings in her office for a small group of parents, I decided to go, even though it meant making the hour-long drive to and from Montclair twice on Fridays instead of once.

The sessions would be held four Friday nights beginning in October. I asked Jim to go, but he didn't want to. Since her husband also had opted not to attend, Sharon Bethel and I drove over to Montclair together. Jim finally attended one session with me, but he was so obviously uncomfortable that I didn't ask him to go back.

A lopsided male-female ratio was evident at these sessions, which generally were attended by about six women but only one or two men. Like my husband, many of the Wee Care fathers tended to avoid discussing the Wee Care tragedy, and to bury their feelings about it beneath thick layers of indifference or disinterest.

Susan said this boiled down to the fathers' feelings of vulnerability. "No one likes to feel vulnerable," she explained. "Women experience it as terrifying, although it doesn't threaten their sense of femaleness. Men, on the other hand, feel that their maleness is heavily dependent upon *not* feeling vulnerable. It brings into question their masculinity. For the fathers, the simple fact that this happened to their children is a big threat. It makes them feel as if they weren't man enough to take care of their family. And that's a big threat to most fathers. So their way of coping is not to let themselves think about it."

Women, on the other hand, traditionally feel more vulnerable about their bodies anyway. Our coping mechanisms are different: traumas like rape and abuse are horrifying to contemplate, and yet we consciously permit ourselves to think about them.

Susan moderated the group sessions, where we talked about how we were helping the kids cope and how we ourselves were faring. She was so supportive and comforting, and she was obviously very affected by what all of us were going through. Once I was startled to realize that she had tears in her eyes.

Susan said I didn't have to hide from Hannah my sadness over what had happened to her. So when we were in the car together one day I hugged my daughter and told her, "You know, I feel really bad about what Kelly did to you, too."

"I know," she told me in a voice that meant she didn't want to discuss it anymore.

At the last session, I asked Susan if the hurt would ever go away. I was so weary of carrying around this enormous burden of guilt and grief.

Susan compared the depression we were experiencing to the feeling of loss when someone close to you dies. "At first, the intensity of the feeling is enormous," she said. "But as time goes on, you're not only thinking about that. You're involved with other things in your life and you think about it less frequently. When you think of it, you're still sad, of course, but it doesn't evoke the same intensity as when it first happened."

When I got back from these meetings, I tried to tell Jim about them. But he just didn't want to hear; he couldn't understand why anyone would want to sit around and talk about something sad. He threw himself into his work, staying later and later at his office. He hadn't told any of his colleagues about Hannah, so he could go to work and not be pressed into thinking about the whole unpleasant affair.

For months Jim didn't even tell his parents about Hannah. Finally, he mentioned it to his mother on the phone one day as offhandedly as if he were telling her about one of our children losing a baby tooth. My mother-in-law took her cue from him and downplayed the whole thing to me whenever we talked on the phone. She and my father-in-law live a five-hour drive away from us, so we don't see as much of them as we do of my parents. Jim's sisters and brothers, spread out all over the country, visit infrequently. I knew they knew about Hannah, though, because I asked Jim if he had told them. Yet whenever I saw one of them and tried to discuss Hannah, they changed the subject.

I decided that avoidance of unpleasant subjects ran in my husband's family. It irked me, and I felt annoyed with Jim much of the time. When the two of us talked, we tried to keep on neutral topics. Except hardly anything seemed to be neutral grounds for us anymore. We bickered constantly, and I was easy to provoke. If Jim turned up from work half an hour late, I got angry. And yet one Friday when he arrived home early, I flew into a rage at him for that.

"If I'd known you were coming home early, *you* could have taken Hannah to Susan's today," I shouted. "Why does it always have to be me who takes her? She's your daughter, too."

One Saturday morning, I came in from an errand to find that he had already given the kids their lunch. This was highly unusual—ordinarily when Jim baby-sat, he simply took all the kids down to his basement workroom, where he busied himself with small chores until I got home. They could be cranky and practically flying off the walls from hunger, but it would never occur to him to feed them.

On this day, instead of offering encouragement and praise to my husband for getting lunch, I screamed at him for not using up the cold cuts and for making them peanut-butter-and-jelly sandwiches instead. I was impossible to please, and he began to seem withdrawn and disinterested in pleasing me.

In December 1985, two indictments alleging 229 counts against Kelly were handed down in Essex County Superior Court. Along with a lot of other Wee Care parents, I went to court on a Friday morning for Kelly's arraignment. I hadn't seen her since the previous spring, and much as I dreaded the sight of her, I was curious if there was anything ominous in her appearance that I had missed before.

We all stood outside Judge William Harth's eighth-floor courtroom, waiting for Kelly to arrive. When she got off the elevator and began walking briskly past us, her eyes fixed firmly ahead, I couldn't stop the tears from welling up. How could this one person have caused so much pain for so many, I wondered. Why would one seemingly normal young woman subject so many trusting preschoolers to such sadistic, degrading acts?

My sister Kathleen and some of the other mothers surrounded me immediately, and sort of herded me off into a corner while I clenched my teeth and fought for control.

"Sara doesn't want any displays of emotion," Kathleen whispered. "The defense is going to try to paint us as a bunch of hysterical parents, and she doesn't want to give them any ammunition."

I knew she was right. As we moved into the courtroom, I got a grip on myself and we all listened in silence as Kelly pleaded not guilty. No bail was set, and she was taken off to jail. I found myself hoping she would have to spend Christmas in prison, and then I was shocked at myself for hating another person enough to think this.

That night, the Wee Care story was big news. Every TV channel I switched to was reporting the story, and Kelly's picture appeared over and over. I sat on the floor in front of the television in our bedroom, tears streaming down my face. It was bad enough to know in your own heart how gruesome it was that your child had been molested. But to hear it validated and hammered home by grim-faced television announcers seemed just too much to bear.

The next day, a Saturday, the phone rang early at our house. It was my brother Johnny, who has been like a second father to our kids since his baby-sitting stint. I figured he was calling to say he'd seen the story in the paper, and to offer his sympathy. Instead, Johnny told me that he had been in a car accident earlier that morning on his way to work. He was at the hospital emergency room.

"Are you okay? What happened?" I asked him, feeling like I couldn't take much more bad news without cracking up. He'd broken ribs and possibly ruptured his spleen, he told me. Johnny's voice broke as he asked me to call my parents and tell them. I hadn't seen my younger brother cry since he was a little boy. I promised to go to the hospital as soon as I got the older girls home from their ballet class.

I spent much of that weekend with Johnny, who was kept in the hospital for observation. Blood kept showing up in his urine, and the doctors weren't sure why. He was depressed, and I tried to distract him with books and different things to eat. Hannah, who loves Johnny, didn't seem all that concerned when I told the girls about his accident.

And Monday morning, when Maria returned to work and I started describing Johnny's accident to her, Hannah's reaction was so atypical it sent chills through my body.

"Johnny, Johnny, Johnny, all the caring's for Johnny," she shrilled harshly. "Doesn't anybody around here care about *me* anymore? Big deal if Johnny got in an accident!" And she slid down out of her chair and skipped from the kitchen, leaving an untouched bowl of Cheerios and two open-mouthed women behind her.

Was this really my daughter talking? Was this the same child who used to cry if she imagined my feelings were hurt when she didn't like something I cooked for dinner? The little girl who made elaborate get-well cards every time someone in the family had the sniffles? I wasn't the only Wee Care mother who felt as if she were viewing a scenario out of *The Exorcist*. A stranger lived in our house, and there was no reaching out to her because she rebuffed every attempt at cuddling and kindness.

■

I took the following Tuesday off from work and the three girls and I rode the train into Manhattan to see the Santa

Claus at Macy's. We left early, hoping to beat the holiday crowds. It was a clear, crisp morning and I read to them all the way in to Thirty-fourth Street. In Macy's, we had about a forty-five minute wait to chat with Santa Claus, but the time went by quickly because there were so many gorgeous decorations to view along the way.

The girls were enthralled by it all; for them the Macy's display was like a mini–Disney World filled with mechanical elves and reindeer, twinkling lights, and Christmas trees laden with bows and baubles. They sat on Santa's lap and I paid an exorbitant price for a silly Polaroid picture. Afterward, we stopped in the toy department and they exclaimed over the giant stuffed animals, life-sized baby dolls, and fascinating mechanized toys.

Finally, around noontime, we took a cab over to the *Newsweek* building on Madison Avenue to meet my friend Kate for lunch. She and I had worked together before she joined *Newsweek* as a senior editor, and she always loved getting together with my kids. On this day, we walked to one restaurant to get pizza and then to another for giant, chocolate-dipped chocolate-chip cookies. The girls were in seventh heaven.

I felt almost happy for the first time in months. Johnny was out of the hospital with nothing worse than broken ribs, so that worry was gone. I love Manhattan, which was home for seven years and will always be my favorite city. I thrive on the quick-paced mood and the people, all so different from one another. I could stroll through the crowds for hours. New Yorkers may have a reputation for being rude, loudmouthed, and aggressive, but I find them endearing and unique. Just being in the city buoys me up and gives me energy.

Christmas—one of my favorite times of year—was in the air. Wherever you looked, there were street-corner Santas ringing bells; gaily decked store windows beckoning shoppers; and sidewalk peddlers hawking roasted chestnuts, hot dogs, and giant pretzels. Even the business executives seemed to have succumbed to the holiday spirit. There wasn't the usual impatient lunch-hour stampede along the avenues, when people are in such a hurry they'll do everything short of knocking you down to get a few steps in front of you.

That day the pace seemed almost leisurely. I allowed myself to relax and just take it all in. As we headed over to Rockefeller Center to see the giant Christmas tree, Kate slowed down slightly so the girls were in front of us on the sidewalk.

"It's a good thing you took off today," she said in a low voice, looking grim. "Have you seen the paper yet?"

I hadn't. We'd been so busy that I hadn't even bothered that morning to pick up the newspaper I worked for. Now my heart started racing. On the way home, I stopped and bought a paper, taking care to fold it so Hannah wouldn't see the Page One photograph of Kelly in which she seemed to me to be sneering.

Depression washed over me in waves again. There was no escaping this. Judging from the in-depth article on the latest charges, it was apparent that the enterprising reporter at my paper had actually gone down to the prosecutor's office and read the indictments. Thus she was able to detail the sadistic acts in her story, which appeared on Page One.

> Indictments against Margaret Kelly Michaels, 23, include charges that she made children drink urine, made a child lick peanut butter off her toe, and played Jingle Bells and Rudolph the Red-Nosed Reindeer on the piano for them while she was nude. The indictments also allege dozens of occasions when Ms. Michaels molested naked boys and girls, ages 3 to 6, and forced them to touch her. Many of the assault charges relate incidents involving spoons, forks, and knives.

I was grateful that I hadn't been at work that day to sense the silent sympathy among the reporters who knew Hannah was a Wee Care victim. I had told only a few colleagues. But newspaper people are paid to probe and snoop, and we love to trade stories. I knew how quickly and efficiently gossip spread through the newsroom. I imagined myself as the object of my co-workers' pity, and it was an unfamiliar, distasteful role.

I wasn't used to being in such a vulnerable position. At work I was accustomed to being in charge, a supermom with more children than anyone else and a heavy workload in the features department. Other women regarded me as a role model. Now I felt as if everyone at the paper thought I'd failed my child. I, who had so blithely given others advice on child care, couldn't even accomplish something as basic as protecting my own daughter from sexual abuse.

Probably far fewer reporters than I imagined knew of my involvement with the Wee Care case. They had their own problems, and better things to do than watch to see if I would break down under the strain. But I was paranoid and distrustful, and I walked around the office feeling isolated from all but a few close friends.

To make matters worse, just before Christmas, a friend and colleague whom I'd confided in almost from the day I found out about Hannah was assigned to cover the Wee Care story. Jack had recently been reassigned from the paper's features section to news side, and in December he was told to cover the local courts. His beat included the Wee Care case.

Jack had no say in whether or not to accept the assignment, and he felt as bad, if not worse, than I did about it. The father of two young children, he'd been deeply affected by the Wee Care victims' ordeal. His desk was next to mine in the newsroom, and he often asked me how Hannah was doing and scolded me for not taking better care of myself through the crisis. He looked miserable the day he told me he would be covering the case.

For me it was as if he had suddenly become the enemy, as though he'd turned overnight from confidante to prying outsider. The judge had ordered the press not to disclose the identities of any of the victims or their families, so I knew he wouldn't use names in his articles. But irrationally, I wondered if he would try to incorporate into his stories any of what we had discussed in the past six months.

None of my suspicions was ever borne out, and in the end it was immensely helpful to me for Jack to cover the story. He was as interested and nearly as consumed by it as I was, and he could talk for hours with me about any aspect of the case. Theorizing a motive for Kelly's actions. Speculating over why none of the victims had told for so long. Dissecting the actions of the attorneys at the pretrial hearings. Worrying over symptoms the children were exhibiting. Agonizing about their future.

He was the perfect remedy for my consuming need to talk about Wee Care, and we spent hours over lunch or on the telephone.

I got through Christmas somehow. As if to make it up to my kids for being such a neglectful mother, I went way overboard buying toys and games. Hannah wants another Cabbage Patch doll? No problem. I'd stand in line for hours to buy one because it was something concrete that I could do. It meant I had the ability to make her happy, see her smile again, simply by plunking down X number of dollars for an overpriced toy. It was a way for me to regain my power.

Impulsively, I suggested to Jim that we have a post-Christmas party. It would take my mind off Wee Care and keep me busy. And it would be a way to let everyone know that we had weathered the crisis and were back in circulation again. Jim, who loves to entertain, was all for it. I set the date (a Sunday afternoon at the end of December), called friends, told everyone to bring their kids. I made two punches, one nonalcoholic, and the easiest dip and appetizer recipes I could find in my cookbooks.

The girls valiantly pitched in to cut out and decorate more Christmas cookies so we'd have plenty of sweets on hand for their friends, though I think at that point they were tired of holiday baking and eating.

On the day of the party, the weather cooperated and sunlight streamed through the house all afternoon. The punch disappeared so fast I had to go out and hastily spice up some more cold cider, and the guests exclaimed over the food and mingled well.

Having the party had been a good idea, I thought, as I helped find various children's boots and coats as guests prepared to leave. I had to start putting Wee Care behind me and to get on with my life.

My exuberance, however, was short-lived. My friend Kate lingered after everyone else had left. Finally, she came up to me as I was clearing dishes and nervously said she had to tell me something. *"Newsweek* wants a story on Wee Care and they want me to do it," she blurted out finally, looking thoroughly uncomfortable.

I felt even worse than I had when Jack told me he was covering the case for my paper. *Newsweek?* So then another two million people would know what we were going through? I could just see the sensational cover story it would make. And Kate—as a close, personal friend of mine privy to so much inside information—would do a fine, in-depth story sure to make every parent in America hug their child closer and thank God nothing like this ever happened in *their* family.

"Why do you have to do it?" I asked her, not really knowing what to say. "Was it your idea? How did they even find out about the story?"

Kate said it hadn't been her idea, but that as an editor on the magazine's national desk and a resident of New Jersey, where the case was unfolding, she had been assigned to the story.

Suddenly, the party no longer mattered. I felt uncomfortable as we said good-bye, and I went back into the kitchen to call my mother. She had never met Kate, and immediately voiced her suspicion that my friend must have turned the magazine on to the story herself. I didn't want to believe that. That night I slept poorly again. And the next morning, I called Kate and asked her to see if she could get *Newsweek* to kill the story. Within an hour, she called me back. The magazine had agreed not to do the article. Kate and I never talked about it again, and I don't think *Newsweek* ever did print anything about the Wee Care case.

The parents' support group met for the last session two weeks before Christmas, and because Jim had a late meeting at his office, my parents baby-sat. I felt almost panicky at the thought of no further contact with the few people I was really able to relate to. Perhaps this is the way smokers or drinkers who are trying to quit feel when they're suddenly left without the solace and company of fellow addicts.

I asked Susan whether we could all get together again after the holidays, and she proposed trying to meet again in six weeks. None of the others seemed to feel my acute need for more sessions. I thought maybe I was just taking longer to bounce back than the others. But they were suffering as much as I was.

Benjamin Baird was so hyperactive in his kindergarten class that fall that his teacher considered putting him in a special-education class. He continued to see his therapist weekly, but was rambunctious and abusive with his little brother George.

The incidents at Wee Care were still very much on his mind. He began refusing to eat peaches because of their red centers.

"I'm not eating anything with blood on it anymore," he told Cathy.

The Bairds had begun to suspect that George had a learning disability, and they wondered if Benjamin might be part of the reason. Then one day, Donald came home from work and told Cathy he was being promoted—and transferred to California. Cathy was devastated. Her family and friends all live on the East Coast, and she couldn't imagine pulling up her roots and moving three thousand miles away—especially not with the burden she now carried around in her heart. She would have no one to talk to if they moved.

"You can't do this to me," she told her husband. "I just can't take another change. My support, everything is here."

But if Donald didn't accept the promotion and move, his career would be stalled indefinitely. He had to go. When Cathy called to tell me they were leaving, I was heartsick. We'd grown used to talking on the phone a couple of times a week, and the conversations made us both feel better.

But their house sold quickly and they bought a beautiful new home with a swimming pool in Los Angeles. The day before they left, I went over to say good-bye and return some of George's baby clothes Cathy had loaned me for Robert. We hugged each other, promising to stay in touch.

The Bairds had a terrible time when they first got to the West Coast. George had simply stopped talking at all when Donald left New Jersey in the summer to look for a house in California. Once they moved, he didn't speak for months, although by now he was three years old. His parents decided to have him evaluated by a team of specialists. He was in the hospital for a month, and the Bairds weren't allowed to see him at all for the first two weeks. Initially, the doctors thought George might be autistic. They finally decided on a different diagnosis, one that meant he had assorted learning disabilities. They felt that Benjamin was the cause of some of George's troubles.

"It was frustrating for George not to be able to commu-

142

nicate with a brother who was always abusing him," Cathy said. "Benjamin would kick him, punch him, hit him. George still is not grade-appropriate—partly from Benjamin abusing him."

Soon after they moved, Benjamin told Cathy he needed a "special friend." Cathy found a new therapist and Benjamin began making weekly visits. But he missed his Wee Care friends terribly, and it took him a long time to grow accustomed to his new school. Once he tried to tell one of the children in his new neighborhood about Wee Care.

"You know what?" Benjamin said to the little boy on the way to soccer practice. "There was a bad teacher where I used to go to school."

Benjamin started to elaborate, but the other child looked at him as though he were speaking in another language. He couldn't relate to what Benjamin was telling him at all, and Benjamin got embarrassed.

"Benjamin wanted to share, but the kid made fun of him," Cathy said. "So then Benjamin said, never mind, it wasn't really that big of a deal."

Cathy found herself depressed much of the time and unable to talk to anyone about it. Donald was patient and willing to listen, but he refused to indulge his own feelings by showing emotion over what had happened to his son.

Cathy would say, "I can't handle it," and Donald would respond, "I've handled it. I'm better now."

"No, you haven't," Cathy told him. "You're a liar."

Their parish had a special children's Mass at which all the youngsters were invited to go up on the altar so they could watch the service. But Benjamin refused to go to church.

"Kelly did things to the kids in the choir room with choir robes and crucifixes," Cathy said. "I think that's why Benjamin just couldn't bear to go to church. I would say to Donald, I can tell when he gets a certain look on his face that he's thinking about her. Don't force him to go."

Cathy was sad, too, because she felt Benjamin would never be the same child again. "Children are the sum total of all their experiences, and no matter how much therapy they have and no matter how hard we try, we can't take these experiences away from them," she said. "I look at Benjamin and he's not the same child. That hurts."

■

Soma Goldstein also endured tremendous emotional distress in the months after learning four-year-old Rachel had been sexually abused by Kelly at age three. She watched her little blond daughter change from an easygoing, amiable little girl into a frightened, clingy child who wet the bed and wasn't interested in making friends. Soma herself grew so ill by that fall that she wondered if she might have cancer. And marital problems developed for the Goldsteins.

Soma is a take-charge person who, when confronted with a problem, meets it head on and deals with it right then. That first summer, she took Rachel to the pediatrician and arranged for her daughter to see a therapist. But what Soma worried about was the future, because she felt Rachel would face problems as she matured. And Soma's lack of control over this, her inability to do anything about it now, frightened this formerly confident mother.

Soma recalls a strange conversation she had with Rachel just a few days before the first letter went out from the Wee Care board informing parents about the allegations of sexual abuse. Soma had been feeling for some time that Rachel was too friendly to strangers, and she bought the book, *It's OK to Say No*.

When she finished reading the story, for no special reason, she asked her daughter, "Have you ever seen anyone else's private parts?"

"Yes," Rachel said casually. "At school I saw Dennis Hammer and Adam Cohen's tushies."

The puzzled Goldsteins thought their daughter was just talking nonsense. But Soma did call Dennis's mother to ask her if she knew anything about this. The mother, who also had two older boys, made light of it and didn't seem concerned. Soma let the whole thing slip out of her mind. Until the letter arrived several days later.

When Rachel finally spoke with Susan Esquilin, she had some interesting things to tell. Kelly led the children in a strange version of Bingo, said Rachel. In Kelly's game, the children would pretend to be puppies and they would lick each other and Kelly's naked bodies. Rachel demonstrated how Kelly played "Old McDonald Had a Farm" using hand puppets to bite the children's genitals.

"My daughter was like a wild animal in Susan's office," Soma said. "It was horrible. I'll never forget that day in my life. Rachel generally tended to be calm, mellow, and gentle. Certainly not hyper. Yet all of a sudden, it was like it was not my child I was seeing. It was like *The Exorcist,* you know? It's your child and yet it's not behaving like your child."

A few days later, Rachel talked to Sara Sencer in the prosecutor's office. She graphically described how she herself had been victimized. She said Kelly had inserted a fork into her vagina. She said she saw another classmate's penis and "tushie." She told Sara that she had to lick jelly off Kelly's vagina.

"Who made the jelly?" Sara asked her.

"Kelly did," Rachel said.

"Where did Kelly get the jelly?"

"From her," said Rachel.

"From where?" asked Sara.

"There," Rachel replied, pointing to her vagina. Rachel thus became one of the earliest of many children to describe seeing Kelly's menstrual blood.

A devastated Soma recalls: "Then I knew she hadn't been just a witness. Until that day, I didn't think it had happened to my child."

Immediately after her interview with the prosecutor, Rachel began to wet her bed nearly every night. (Three years later, she was still wetting the bed five out of seven nights.)

Rachel grew increasingly weepy, clingy to her mother, and fearful.

Soma wanted her daughter to testify before the grand jury if she was able to. Over the Fourth of July weekend, the Goldstein family—David, Soma, Rachel, and baby Ted—drove down to the Essex County Courthouse so Rachel could speak to the prosecutors. Rachel seemed frightened, even though she knew from her parents that Kelly was in prison. (Kelly had threatened to turn Rachel into a monster if she told about the incidents at school, the child said.) At the courthouse, Rachel expressed a desire to see the jail. She seemed to need reassurance that the bars were strong enough that even Kelly couldn't escape.

Soma doesn't know how she got through the summer. She took to her bed, getting out only to care for Rachel and Ted. David, unable to cope with her depression, began spending more and more time away from the house. He often telephoned her to say he had to work late. Suddenly, he had lots of business dinners and pressing engagements. Soma, too wrapped up in her own grief to think of anything else, passively and unquestioningly accepted his newly hectic schedule.

By the end of the summer, things were no better. Soma, wondering if she might be having a nervous breakdown, sank into deeper and deeper gloom. She felt terribly guilty and unable to realize that there was no way she could have known about or prevented the abuse.

That fall Rachel started at a new nursery school, but she didn't like being with the other pupils. She hung around her teacher at school and her mother at home. Maybe she just needed the comfort and security offered by adults. Or perhaps she had come to distrust other children her age. In the Wee Care case, all the children were in a sense co-perpetrators, forced by Kelly to hurt and degrade each other. Small wonder that some of them came to distrust other youngsters.

Then Soma got sick. She had severe diarrhea every day

146

for six weeks that fall, and no medicine made it stop. She visited a couple of physicians and finally landed in the office of a gastroenterologist, who asked if she was under severe stress. Soma said she was. To rule out a physiological problem, the doctor ordered various tests, some of them painful. No medical cause ever was found, and eventually she became better.

In October, David came home one night and told Soma he wasn't happy with their marriage anymore. Soma knew she should respond with wifely concern and try to work things out, but she felt so drained emotionally she just couldn't bring herself to make the effort. The couple went away for a weekend to the Concord Hotel in the Catskills to talk things out, but both avoided speaking of Wee Care and the heinous acts Kelly Michaels had performed on their only daughter.

"David just denied it," Soma said. "Rachel was his prize, and he just couldn't handle the whole Wee Care thing. He started staying away. He was out more and more and I just couldn't deal with that. I was so out of it myself. David would come home and the kids and I would be sleeping. And I just didn't think about it, the fact that he suddenly had all these business dinners."

On Christmas Eve, Soma's housekeeper—no doubt fed up with the constant gloom and tension in the household— told Soma she was quitting. And David came home from work and told his wife that he was having an affair and was leaving Soma.

Soma, who had celebrated her eleventh wedding anniversary with him the previous summer, felt as if the bottom were falling out of her world. "Basically, I was always a very happy, contented person," she said. "My husband and I come from similar backgrounds and we never had fights about how to raise the children. He made a nice income and we never really had money problems. We weren't rich, but we had enough money that we didn't have arguments about money. I was—I thought I was—happily married. We had our problems. But I think that Wee Care caused our eventual separation.

"What hurt me the most," she said, "was that someone did this to my child, that they hurt her in this way and that I couldn't take it back."

■

Traci MacKenna, who was studying for her bachelor's degree in family and child studies, took the summer off that year. She spent a lot of time with five-year-old Casey.

Casey had vivid memories of how Kelly had hurt her friends and made them hurt each other. She remembered seeing her friend Emily hurt and bleeding in the choir room. She watched Kelly use a wooden spoon to beat little boys on their penises and girls on their vulvas, Casey said. As the summer wore on, additional glimpses of her Wee Care experiences emerged. Casey said Kelly had made a birthday cake and flushed it down the toilet. Later, Casey told assistant prosecutors Sara Sencer and Glenn Goldberg that the cake was made of feces.

So agitated and preoccupied with Wee Care was the little girl that her mother suggested she write a book about her experiences. With Traci's help, she wrote three little pamphlets: "Kelly hurt us at Wee Care. She hit us and pinched us," read one book. "She made us take off our clothes. Kelly went to the bathroom in front of us. She put knives and forks in our 'ginas.'"

Kelly had threatened to hurt Casey with a knife and to kill her mother if she told. The five-year-old was visibly terrified that Kelly would follow through on this grim promise. That summer she was fearful and timid, never seeming to relax or let down her guard. Even when the family was vacationing in North Carolina, Casey was convinced that Kelly could track them down. On a camping trip, she begged her mother to lock the car so Kelly couldn't find them.

Every day, Casey raised the subject of Kelly, asking constantly if her former teacher would always be in jail. She seemed especially concerned that Kelly might hurt Suzi, Casey's older sister. Traci took Casey to the Maplewood police station so she could see how strong the bars were on the jail there. But until her adult cousin, who stands six feet, six inches and weighs 275 pounds, demonstrated that he couldn't escape from the cell, Casey didn't seem reassured.

Because she had so many fears, her mother arranged for her to start seeing a therapist. Casey often insisted on sitting on her mother's lap during these sessions. If Traci left for the bathroom, Casey became agitated and distracted until she returned.

Traci walked around that summer feeling as if she was going to lose it at any minute. "I am having anxiety attacks almost constantly now," she wrote in her diary. "I feel like I am going to completely panic. I am so afraid I don't know what to do. My heart pounds, my stomach is in such knots, and my mind goes off in a million directions."

As the opening day of kindergarten drew near, Casey seemed excited about going to a new school but she repeatedly asked her mother, "Do you think anyone is going to hurt me there?" Only the fact that her older sister Suzi had attended kindergarten at the same school and had promised Casey it was a safe place, allayed her anxiety.

She was reluctant to separate from her mother on the first day, but Traci managed to disentangle herself and leave without Casey making a scene. But the little girl continued to be preoccupied by her Wee Care experiences that fall, and to verbalize them to a horrified Traci. Once when the two were riding home after dropping Suzi off at her karate class, Casey began telling her mother how they had to "poop" and "pee" on the floor at Wee Care.

"What I don't understand," Traci said, "is how you cleaned it up."

"With paper towels," Casey said without hesitation.

Asked where they put the paper towels, Casey promptly replied, "in the garbage can."

"But Casey, didn't it smell?"

"No," Casey said patiently, as if she were talking to a simpleton. "The garbage can had a top."

By that October, Casey refused to sleep alone again, and she hated being in her own room because she thought Kelly might look in the windows. One day in November, she wanted to explain to her mother the difference between the star game and the pile-up game. She ran upstairs to get her and Suzi's Care Bear stuffed animals. She piled them on top of each other in a crisscross fashion and explained that this was the star game, and that the children had no clothes on when they played it. Then she rearranged her toys, piling them in a different way. But Traci still didn't understand the difference.

"They were different games," Casey insisted.

Traci felt light-headed. On the one hand, it seemed so implausible that something like this could have gone on with no other Wee Care staff members knowing. On the other hand, Casey was so sure of what she was saying that her mother knew she couldn't make it up.

Theirs was a subdued Christmas, and Kelly's presence hung like an invisible shroud in the house. On Christmas Eve, Casey asked her mother if Kelly would be in jail for Christmas, and if Santa would bring her presents. Traci, who was growing weary of the constant talk of Kelly, told her daughter she didn't know if Santa would bring anything for Kelly or not.

"If she ever gets good, Santa will bring her presents," Casey said.

Traci told her daughter that someday they both would go to court and tell the judge what Kelly did so that she would stay in jail and not be able to hurt other children. Traci asked Casey what she was going to tell the judge.

"Kelly hit us and pinched us and piled us up," Casey said quickly. "She put forks and knives in my vagina."

Trying to appear outwardly calm, Traci said soothingly, "I wonder what you were feeling then."

"Sad and mad—very mad," replied her daughter.

Shortly after Christmas, Melissa Bethel and her older sister Laura came to visit the MacKenna home. Laura Bethel and Suzi MacKenna were almost the same age, and the two older girls began discussing teachers they liked at their schools.

Then the subject changed to bad teachers. Melissa began to talk about how Kelly had made the children urinate and defecate on the floor. She said the girls had to clean up one side and the boys had to clean up the other side, and that there was a wall of blocks in between.

Casey got angry. "I don't want to talk about Wee Care," she shouted, and someone changed the subject.

The entire winter vacation was hard for Traci. Casey acted crazy much of the time, running through the house, yelling, and then crying for long periods. Sometimes she woke up and started right in singing "Jingle Bells" or "Old McDonald Had a Farm." Traci asked if she had learned the songs in kindergarten.

"You know who taught me," Casey shouted. "Kelly."

One day she fell and came downstairs to Traci, crying and holding her crotch. "I hurt myself there," she wept piteously. "And it reminds me of when Kelly hurt me."

Traci felt as if she were at her wit's end. They talked about pain, and how it was nice to have someone hold you when you hurt. Although Casey seemed to feel a bit better, she was very withdrawn for the rest of the afternoon.

"My heart feels torn from my body," Traci wrote in her diary. "When will the pain cease for this baby?"

C H A P T E R
■ ■ ■ ■ ■ ■ ■ ■ ■ ■

9

Winter is my least favorite season—it's so cold, grim, and unpredictable. But December is such a busy month that, for me anyway, winter's arrival doesn't really penetrate until late January. Then I take comfort in the fact that February is mercifully short, and March—though it doesn't feel any better outside—at least sounds like spring is in the foreseeable future.

The winter after we found out about Hannah (1985–86) got off to a rough start. There was the unfortunate holiday party at which Kate had hinted at a *Newsweek* story on Wee Care. And that Christmas Eve, Jim was uncharacteristically snappish with the kids, barking at Caroline when she didn't like a sweater from his mother until she rushed off to her room in tears.

Jim snarled at Hannah and Ellen for talking and fooling around at the late afternoon Christmas Eve Mass we traditionally attend as a family. Later that night, he seemed not even to be aware of the three girls as they sang carols under the lighted tree and passed out fudge and cups of hot cocoa

—a Christmas tradition in deference to our family of chocoholics.

By the time the kids went to bed that night, I was so weary I could barely drag the wrapped presents out of their attic hiding place and pile them in front of the tree. And despite my attempt to be lighthearted the next day, Jim was gloomy and uncommunicative when we went to dinner at my parents' house.

Then came January. Six months had passed since we'd first learned that our daughter was a victim of sexual abuse, and the bleak weather matched my mood perfectly. Like Casey MacKenna, I was unable to shake off the pain—sharp and persistent as a toothache—and get on with life. My chest felt so tight most of the time it was hard to swallow, and I had periodic numbness in my arms and legs. But, of course, I tried not to show my black mood around the kids or at work.

Hannah didn't ever directly broach the subject of Wee Care with me, but she used to back into what was obviously a painful subject to discuss. She kept coming back to it, the way your tongue returns over and over a canker sore in your mouth.

One morning at breakfast, she asked why Ellen didn't have to take a nap at her nursery school. The previous fall, I had enrolled Ellen in a small, cooperative preschool program held in a local church three mornings a week. Parents were required to work as an assistant to the teacher one morning a month.

I arranged a car pool with another mother even though it meant getting to work late a couple of days a week, and juggled my schedule so I could work the one session a month. It didn't endear me to my editors, but I'd resolved this was the only type of nursery school I would ever allow a child of mine to attend again. I just didn't trust anyone anymore; behind every baby-sitter and teacher lurked a potential molester.

I hadn't known Hannah was even aware of the hours

Ellen attended school. But I sat down with her that morning and explained that Ellen went to a nursery school, not a day-care center like Wee Care where parents could take their children for an entire day.

Looking woebegone, Hannah reminded me that she had to take naps when she was in nursery school. I cheerfully explained that all schools are different, and that Ellen had a nap at home instead. "Well," she scowled finally. "Naptime at Wee Care was dreadful."

Hannah still seemed preoccupied by the notion that she was "bad." One Friday afternoon as we drove to Susan Esquilin's office for Hannah's weekly appointment, she asked me if she would go to hell. Shocked, I assured her that she would never go to hell and that only people who do very, very bad things, such as kill other people, go to hell.

"Is Kelly going to hell?" she asked me.

"I don't know, honey," I told her, suddenly wishing I was a psychologist so I would know the right thing to say. "I guess it depends on the good things and the bad things Kelly does in her life. And if she's sorry for the bad things, then I'm sure God won't make her go to hell."

"All the things Kelly did weren't bad," Hannah volunteered. "Some of the games were good. When we played the jail game and chased her around the gym and put her in jail, that was fun."

By the time she was five and a half, Hannah's self-esteem had ebbed to a new low. One day she stood dejectedly in the driveway as her sisters played kickball in the yard. She sucked her thumb and shook her head sadly when I asked what was wrong. I suspected she was probably thinking about what she called "all the yucky, dreadful things that happened at Wee Care."

Finally, she picked up a piece of chalk and started scrawling letters on the cement. She called to me, "How do you spell appreciate?" When I went over to her a few minutes later, she had printed on the driveway, "Nobody appreciates me."

In therapy, Susan and Hannah didn't simply sit around and talk about Wee Care. Instead, Susan tried to clarify Hannah's sexual confusions and get her to address her feelings about herself. Hannah was guarded on the subject of Wee Care, but every so often some aspect of her preschool experience would slip out unsolicited.

Once, Susan drew a line on a piece of paper to represent an ugly-pretty dimension. When she asked Hannah what she should put at the pretty end, Hannah told her to make the beach, the water, and the sun. Then Susan asked what she should put at the ugly end. Hannah said she should draw "poo" and "pee." At that point, the therapist noticed that Hannah was masturbating anxiously.

"You know, some kids think poo and pee are fun," Susan observed.

"Well, then, they're disgusting," Hannah answered. "And Kelly is more disgusting because she touched it."

Once Hannah drew Susan a picture of Kelly urinating on the floor, and then a second picture of Kelly pouring urine from a spoon into a garbage pail.

Another time, Hannah was playing with some puppets in Susan's office. The two were pretending that one of the puppets, a pig, had been at Wee Care. Picking up the pig, Hannah stated, "I'm a pig." Then she handed the puppet to Susan and said, "Pigs stink. They eat slops." When Susan asked Hannah what the worst stink of all was, Hannah answered, "Doo doo."

Holding the pig, Susan invited a fully clothed male anatomically correct doll to play "pig" with her. Hannah picked up a female doll and removed its clothes. She made the doll roll in the "slops" and "do pee pee and doo doo in the slops." Hannah then observed that the doll would "bleed because she pees so hard." During this conversation, Hannah kept inserting her finger into the doll's vagina.

Another day, Hannah and Susan played the "Thinking, Feeling, and Doing Game," a therapeutic board game in which participants take turns answering questions printed on cards. When Hannah picked a card that asked whether she had ever been afraid to tell her parents something, she said she had been afraid to tell her father about being touched by Kelly because she thought he would spank her.

Later in that same session, the two played "police" with the toy police helmet and plastic handcuffs Susan keeps in her office. Hannah was the policeman. She told Susan to steal something, and then arrested her. She instructed Susan to touch a child's private parts, and arrested her again.

But when Susan was arrested, she denied touching the child. Hannah insisted that she had seen Susan do it. Then she asked the psychologist angrily, "How do you think the kids feel?"

"I wasn't hurting them," Susan said. "I was just having fun."

"No," Hannah told her. "They were scared."

Susan suggested that I come alone one Friday so we could discuss Hannah's progress in therapy. But when we sat down, Susan asked me how I was feeling. She wanted to know what was the hardest part of the whole Wee Care ordeal for me to accept.

"That I didn't prevent it from happening," I said, my eyes filling easily with tears.

"But why do you think you could have prevented it?" Susan asked quietly. "I don't think there was any way you could have known what was going on."

"I should have known," I said wearily. It was my fault, I knew it was my fault, and nothing anyone said would dissuade me from this position. Exhausted, I sank deeper into the leather couch in her office. I looked around the cheerful, plant-filled room, at the games piled high in her closet, the baskets of stickers and lollipops and sugarless bubble gum she handed out to her small patients at the end of a session. Whoever thought my five-year-old daughter would need to see a shrink, I thought.

I could tell from the way Susan was talking that she was

worried about me. "What are you doing to make yourself feel better through all of this?" she asked me, a look of concern on her face.

"Nothing, really." The thought of trying to allay my own depression had never occurred to me before. I was too wrapped up in attempting to turn Hannah's world right side up again. Impatiently, I changed the subject to Hannah. Susan felt that my daughter had a poor self-image, which is common in sexually abused children. We talked about some ways to make Hannah feel more positive about herself.

But just two weeks later, Hannah's self-esteem plunged even lower. Suddenly, we had a brand-new crisis to deal with.

It was a snowy Saturday in February, the day after Valentine's Day, and Jim had taken Caroline and Hannah sledding while Ellen and Robert napped. After they left, I chatted on the phone with my sister, who was visiting my parents' house.

I had an article to write, and after we said good-bye I settled down with a mug of coffee and my portable computer. Then I heard the car pull into the driveway and Caroline shrieking. She sounded scared, and at first I thought she'd gotten a bloody nose. I jumped up and ran to the front door. But Caroline wasn't hurt. She was babbling hysterically that something had happened to Hannah. I ran out to the car, where Jim was just opening the back of the station wagon. Inside, Hannah was curled up, sobbing quietly. Her right leg was twisted at an odd angle. She was obviously in tremendous pain.

Two years earlier, when we were sharing a summer vacation house in Maine with my sister and her husband, three-year-old Hannah had fallen off a couch in the living room and gashed the back of her pigtailed head on the edge of a coffee table. In the initial few minutes after it happened, pandemonium reigned. Hannah was screaming, there seemed to be blood everywhere, and the adults rushed around in a panic.

Except me. I was the model of calmness. I soothed Hannah, got the number of the nearest hospital, and phoned ahead to let the emergency room know we were coming (a good idea in rural Maine, where there isn't always a physician on duty).

I held her on my lap all the way to the hospital, sopping up blood with the towels I'd thought to throw in the car. And I held her hands and spoke softly to her while she was being wrapped in an immobilizing "papoose," having her hair shaved, and getting five stitches put in her head. Calm, collected, the model mother.

One indication of how much my mental state had deteriorated since Wee Care was my reaction when I saw Hannah crying in the car that February day. I shrieked at Jim to tell me what had happened. Apparently Caroline and Hannah had been trudging back up the hill, pulling their sleds, when a bigger child on one of those metal saucers that you can't steer came careening down the slope toward them. Jim, standing at the foot of the hill, shouted at Hannah to get out of the way but she didn't hear him. The boy plowed into her, his flying saucer smashing into her right calf.

I turned on Jim and began blaming him for the accident. "What's the matter with you that you can't just take them to the park for an hour without having them get hurt?" I yelled. "It's all your fault. Why did you let them go up the hill by themselves? It's just one thing after another. With everything else, Hannah really needed this."

I was so angry I didn't even feel cold without a coat. I stalked into the house and called the rescue squad, and within minutes, an ambulance had pulled up. The attendants loaded a whimpering Hannah onto a stretcher and strapped her into the bed. I sat next to her in the ambulance and held her hand on the way to the hospital. She had a huge gash on her temple, didn't seem responsive, and was breathing erratically. Every so often she would take in a great gulp of air, tilt her head to the side, and roll her eyes back in her head. I was so frightened I could hardly speak.

"Do you think she's going into a coma?" I whispered to the attendant. "Look at the way she's breathing." Every gruesome coma story I'd ever heard came into my mind.

"She may just be in shock and hyperventilating from the pain," one of them told me, but I heard him phoning ahead to the hospital that the patient had a possible head injury, and I started praying. Please, God, don't let her die. Please, God, I'll accept what you've given me to bear without complaining any more.

We waited a long time in a small examining room at the hospital. Hannah shivered and said she felt like she was going to throw up, but gradually her breathing returned to normal and her vision seemed more focused. A doctor examined her, and then we waited a long time for an X ray. Even after they told me her leg was broken, we had to wait another hour before the orthopedist showed up to set it.

By now I had calmed down enough to comfort Hannah. I kept phoning Jim to tell him what was going on. He sounded miserable, and I think after my earlier tirade, was beginning to believe the accident really was all his fault. My sister and her husband came out to the hospital, and I called my parents a few times to keep them informed.

The shot of Demerol they gave Hannah to lessen the pain made her nauseated and she kept throwing up. Finally, her right leg was immobilized in a heavy plaster cast that extended from her toes halfway up her hip. She sucked her thumb and looked thoroughly miserable as we waited for Jim to come and pick us up.

He carried her into the house and deposited her on a couch in the living room, where my parents and a couple of my sisters and brothers were waiting with the other three children. Caroline, Ellen, and Robert were impressed with the cast, but Hannah turned her face away and wouldn't talk to anyone.

Jim was silent that night after we had put the kids to bed.

159

As he usually did on a Saturday night, he went off to the bagel bakery near midnight to buy the Sunday paper early. But when he got home, instead of dividing the sections between us on the bed and asking if I wanted a glass of wine, he poured himself a large tumbler of Scotch and went down to the living room to read.

I didn't apologize for losing my temper earlier that day, and he offered no explanation for why the two girls had been sledding on a section of the hill reserved for older children. Before Wee Care, when Jim and I fought, we always ended up discussing it that night after we'd each had a chance to cool down. But in the past few months, we seemed constantly so angry at each other that the only way to live under the same roof without exploding was to keep out of each other's way.

I've always felt that marital battles were best fought behind closed doors, away from the children. And in spite of the subsurface hostility between the two of us, we managed to maintain an air of civility around the kids most of the time. In a way, open confrontation might have been healthier than the ongoing cold war because it would have meant facing issues. Instead, we were unfailingly polite and terribly distant with each other.

I fixed myself a mug of hot vanilla milk that night and sat in bed by myself, reading the paper. The next day, I woke up feeling flu-ish and achey all over. I figured it was just from the strain of the previous day, and tried to ignore it. Hannah had to be carried everywhere, and while she was light, the cast was heavy and cumbersome. My back ached by evening, and Hannah continued to vomit.

Initially, I wrote my malaise off to a common flu. But by the end of that week, I felt no better at all. I took Hannah to the orthopedist's office, and then on to the hospital's physical therapy department to be fitted with crutches and taught how to use them. By the time I had carried her halfway across the hospital parking lot in a freezing rain, I felt completely drained of energy.

The crutches were frustrating for a five-year-old to master, but Hannah gamely struggled with them until she was able to get around the house. She went up and down the stairs on her rear end. I called the school and described Hannah's accident to the principal, who assumed at first that she would miss the next eight weeks of classes. But we finally worked out an arrangement that on the days when I or a friend couldn't pick her up, she could ride the small school bus that transported the district's handicapped children. I was glad she wouldn't have to miss any more school, and Hannah seemed to brighten at the thought of returning to kindergarten.

But she hated her cast. She said it made her look ugly, and she wouldn't let anyone sign it. When she went to the pediatrician one Saturday morning with a stomach virus, she begged Jim to carry her in a blanket so none of the other children would see her cast.

"I don't understand it," the nurse said, shaking her head. "Most kids are excited when they have a cast. They like the attention, and they like it when their friends sign it."

When Hannah began her weekly visits to Susan again, the therapist felt the broken leg had set her back in her treatment. Her self-esteem was even lower than it had been. She looked woebegone, and—no matter how many puzzles and books her doting aunts and uncles brought to distract her—she was bored.

And I not only wasn't getting better, I actually felt worse than when I first got sick. I stayed home from work for two weeks, dosing myself with orange juice, cough drops, and over-the-counter cold preparations. Finally I dragged myself to the doctor, who thought I had the flu. When I had been sick for three weeks, I called a colleague at my newspaper whose husband is an infectious-disease specialist. He did blood tests and said he would get back to me in a week with the results. Meanwhile, he suggested I try going back to work part-time.

I was ready to try anything at that point. But I could

barely manage to sit upright at my desk, much less write or edit a story. My throat was sore, my body ached, and I felt nauseous much of the time. I was beginning to wonder if I had leukemia.

One morning at the end of March, the doctor called me at work. "Well, I think I've got your answer for you!" he said jubilantly, as if he was a detective who had just solved a tough case. "You've got mono!"

Mono? Wasn't that what college students came down with when they pushed themselves too hard at exam time? Something you got when you were a teen-ager? Surely I couldn't have mono at my age—thirty-four!

But the doctor assured me that all my blood tests pointed to a diagnosis of infectious mononucleosis. He said it was unusual to contract mono after age thirty-five, and that it's a much lengthier and serious illness in an adult than a teenager. "It's not unusual for someone in your age group to be out of work for four or five months," he told me cheerfully. "And there is really no treatment for it other than rest. It just has to run its course."

I stayed home from work for the next ten weeks, lying in bed or on the couch. Gradually, the nausea subsided and the sore throat cleared up, but the unbearable fatigue persisted. I was so tired I couldn't even walk around the block.

Maria took over more and more of the household duties, and on the weekends, Jim cared for the kids. I was depressed, listless, and enervated. I went back to work at the end of April but still lacked the stamina to make it through a whole day without rest periods. By the end of the day, I was so cranky from exhaustion I could barely read to the kids and get them into bed.

And I continued to puzzle over why I, of all people, would come down with mono. I, who didn't smoke, drink excessively, or take any drugs. Who did I catch it from? Would I ever get better?

The more I read about mono—and I devoured every article or book I could get my hands on—the clearer it became why I had succumbed to illness. I'd been under severe stress for eight months before I got sick, ever since the awful Friday I found out my daughter was a sexual-abuse victim.

Some of the recent literature about mono was particularly alarming because it talked about a chronic form of the disease. Victims of this so-called chronic fatigue syndrome just don't bounce back, and can stay ill for years. At first I didn't think this would happen to me, but by the summer I was beginning to wonder.

One hot July night while Jim was at work and all four kids seemed to be miserable and wailing about something, I burst into tears. "This is hell," I sobbed to no one in particular as I stood washing dishes and feeling sorry for myself. "This is the worst illness to have when you have little kids. I just can't go on like this."

For the first time, I actually contemplated what it would be like to commit suicide. Sure, everyone would miss me for a while, but in the long run maybe it would be better for all concerned. Wouldn't it be better, I reasoned, for my children to remember me as a loving, caring mother than as an exhausted, burned-out shrew who did nothing but cry or be angry?

Jim tried to be understanding and sympathetic, but I was so hopelessly depressed that his patience wore thin. One night, I was crying so hard he suggested we go for a ride, just the two of us. We sat in the car in the supermarket parking lot for a long time, and he listened to me rave on about how awful I felt and how miserable life was.

"Stop feeling so sorry for yourself," he told me finally. "Just listen to what you sound like. If you're tired, then rest. And be glad you don't have some awful, painful disease. But if you're this depressed, you really should be on an antidepressant."

My family worried about me. My mother and sisters baby-sat for the kids on the weekends whenever they could. My father brought over big batches of his rice pudding, chili-macaroni, and applesauce, and he would frequently turn up with pizza for dinner so I wouldn't have to cook. My two elderly aunts, who lived together a couple of blocks away, also cooked dinner occasionally and ran errands for me.

Grateful as I was for all their kindness, I didn't fit comfortably into the role of invalid. As the oldest in a large family, I've always been the one others relied upon and looked up to, and it was a position I relished and excelled at. I'd been a second mother to the youngest seven in the family, feeding and caring for them since infancy. I kept up their baby books, ran their birthday parties, and nagged them about their homework. Even after they were grown up, they continued to confide in me, lean on me, and come to me in a crisis.

Now, suddenly, their oldest sister was a weepy, burned-out basket case. They were genuinely concerned and wanted to help me. But it was hard for me to be gracious about accepting their help.

In July, my family talked me into going to Michigan for a couple of weeks to visit my sister Jana, who was seven months pregnant with her first baby. A younger sister, Bonnie, a student at the University of Maine at the time, left her summer job early so she could live at our house and help Jim and Maria with the kids. And various brothers and sisters volunteered to drop by and take the children to the pool or the park in my absence.

I didn't want to go. I'd never left my children overnight before, and I couldn't imagine being away from them for two days, let alone two weeks. In the end, though, my family won out. They persuaded me that two weeks of complete rest might be just the thing to knock the virus out of my system.

And I did have a wonderful visit with Jana. She'd lived in Michigan for nearly ten years, so we hadn't seen each other much. Spending time with her was relaxing—she and her husband are gentle and serene but have a well-honed sense of humor. We watched movies on their VCR, went out for brunch and rich desserts, played Trivial Pursuit, and just talked for hours.

I took naps, helped Jana practice her Lamaze exercises, and attended a baby shower that some women at the church gave her. The two of us visited relatives that I hadn't seen since I was seven when my family lived in Michigan. And every other day, I called home and talked to the children, who didn't seem to miss me as much as I missed them. My sister Donna and my brother Patrick stopped by often to take them to the park or for ice cream.

But I was still fatigued when I got back to New Jersey. I kept asking my mother and sisters if they thought I would get the chronic form of the disease, and they all kept assuring me that I would get better—indeed, that I already seemed better.

In September 1986, Jana gave birth to a baby girl and my parents drove out to Michigan to stay with her for a week. My father took his video camera to take movies and whenever he got tired of carrying it around, he hung it on a tripod and just let it record. When my parents came home to New Jersey, I borrowed the videotape so I could see what my newest niece looked like.

I lay in bed watching it, missing Jana and feeling inexplicably morose. The camera was trained on her kitchen, and my mother, Jana, and Bonnie (who also was visiting them at the time) were sitting around the table eating breakfast. Then I heard Bonnie ask, "So how's Patricia?"

"Well, I don't know," my mother began, sounding worried and strained. "She doesn't seem to be getting any better. And she's so depressed."

"Do you think she has that chronic form of mono?" asked my sister.

"I don't know what to think," my mother went on, stubbing out her cigarette and sighing. And so the conversation went, back and forth among the three of them, as they discussed my condition, my mental state, the apparently grim prognosis for my recovery.

I started crying. It was so weird sitting there watching them rehash the past six months from their perspective— like being dead and having people talk about you while you listened from some perch. I felt betrayed that they would be so candid with each other but would lie to my face and tell me they thought I was going to get better.

I called my mother at her office and burst into tears. Of course she felt terrible about it. Obviously they hadn't even been aware that the camera was recording. And after that incident, she would not let my father hang his camera on the tripod and let it record without anyone monitoring it.

Those months were tough on Hannah, too. All that spring she seemed depressed. I'd gone back to work in the late spring, and she'd gotten into the habit of calling me there several times a day when she got home from kindergarten. I always welcomed her calls, for although she sounded sad, it was a way of keeping in touch. But I got a lump in my throat when I recalled the phone calls she made to my office as a four-year-old, when she first memorized my number. Back then, every call had to end the same way.

"Bye, Mommy," she'd giggle. "Bye, Hannah," I'd reply. Then: "I love you, Mommy." "I love you too, Hannah." "Bye, Mom." "Bye, Hannah." And we'd hang up at the same time. If I didn't say my part perfectly, she'd call back and we'd go through it again, the right way.

Her kindergarten phone calls were more restrained and subdued. Sometimes they were chilling.

"Will I go to hell if I say I hate life?" she asked me flatly one day when I picked up the phone.

"No, Hannah, of course not, honey," I said, shocked. "But why do you hate life?"

"I don't know," she said wearily. "I know I'm bad."

It seemed strange to have to ask a professional how a

mother should respond to such questions, but it had gotten to the point where I really didn't know how to make Hannah feel better about herself. I would call Susan and ask for advice. In this case, she told me to challenge the notion that anyone is all one way, either all good or all bad.

"Hannah's fundamental feeling of badness is linked to the incidents that happened at Wee Care," Susan told me. "She doesn't necessarily think her *behavior* is bad, but she thinks *she* is evil, she feels a pervasive badness."

Susan said other Wee Care children were feeling badly about themselves, too. One of her Wee Care patients, a five-year-old boy, thought he was very dumb. Whenever he played board games with Susan and made a wrong move, he would slap his forehead with the palm of his hand and say, "I'm so stupid."

Another time, Hannah called me at work to say she had just been playing doctor with Sandra, a kindergarten friend. She'd pretended a pencil was a thermometer, and stuck it in Sandra's vagina, Hannah said.

"Is that okay?" asked my daughter.

"I don't think it's a good idea," I said calmly. "A pencil is very sharp, and that's a delicate area of the body where you're putting it. Whatever gave you the idea to play a game like that?"

"Kelly," Hannah replied without a moment's hesitation.

A few weeks later, she called me at work to say she and Casey MacKenna were sticking crayons up each other's vaginas and did I think that was okay. I reiterated that I thought objects in the vagina weren't a wise idea—from a safety standpoint. I didn't want her to get the idea that exploring her body was wrong or shameful, but at the same time I didn't want her to hurt another child.

Hannah gradually improved toward the end of that summer. She didn't have the frequent outbursts of temper that she'd been prone to for months. Once in awhile, she voluntarily brought up the subject of Kelly. One night on the way home from a visit at my parents' lakefront cottage, she told me sometimes she had "the yucky feeling like I got in my nap at preschool."

I was driving, she was in the seat next to me, and Caroline and Ellen rode in the back. Jim was following in the other car with Robert.

"Taking your nap at school must have been real yucky," I said sympathetically. Maybe talking about it would make her feel better.

"Yeah, it was," Hannah nodded. She seemed lost in the memories. Then she volunteered: "One time, Kelly took off all her clothes and she put forks and spoons down on the floor and lay down on them. And then she made all the kids do it."

Caroline, listening from the back seat, asked incredulously, "Did you do that, too?"

"Yes," Hannah said simply. "Because she made us."

By the end of the summer Hannah seemed more like her old spunky self. I hoped the new school year would get off to an uneventful start. Over the Labor Day weekend we all drove to Boston, where my sister Nina was to be married. One floor of the motel where we stayed was completely occupied by relatives, and my children had a great time charging up and down the corridors and running off to the pool with their cousins.

The ceremony, held in the garden of an arboretum outside of Boston, was followed by an afternoon reception. It was a warm, sunny day, and although the band was set up for dancing in the hall inside, the food and drinks were spread on long tables on the terrace. Children raced up and down the flower-edged walks, and grown-ups occasionally cautioned them to stay off the well-manicured grass.

My three girls were old enough to play on their own, and I didn't feel compelled to keep checking up on them constantly. Every so often I would look over to see what they were up to, and they were usually dancing, eating, or giggling when the bridal couple kissed.

Shana McFee, the little girl who had left Wee Care in the fall of 1984 when her parents divorced, had come to the wedding with her father and his new girl friend. Gerry McFee was an old friend of my sister's, so he had made the trip up from New Jersey. Hannah hadn't seen Shana in months, and the two of them were delighted to be with each other again. They spent the entire day together, occasionally going off into an area of the building that wasn't being used by the wedding party.

In the late afternoon, my niece was overheard telling Hannah and Shana, "You two can't have any cake because you've been bad . . . you were in there pulling down your pants."

I said nothing about this at the time, figuring the less made of it the better. And I didn't think much more about Shana for the next couple of weeks.

But when we got back to New Jersey, Hannah regressed dramatically. She grew weepy again, had violent temper tantrums over the littlest thing, and had terrible nightmares. She began to breathe very heavily, hyperventilating in laboring gasps that were distressing to see. I called the pediatrician and also spoke to Susan about it. They both felt the breathing was caused by stress.

One Sunday evening, Hannah began crying. She sat on my lap and wept so hard and so long that I finally got frightened. She seemed unable to tell me what was wrong, and I was beginning to wonder if a six-year-old could have a nervous breakdown. I called Susan at home, and after the two of them talked on the phone for fifteen minutes, Hannah calmed down somewhat.

Her dreams were disturbing and bizarre. Once she dreamed that Kelly was coming out of a light socket, ghostlike, to get her. Another time she dreamed that Kelly was on the roof. She was going to remove the roof of our house and pull Hannah out of her bed with a giant hook, my daughter said.

I bought Hannah a night-light that sat on her dresser and illuminated the bedroom nearly as much as a regular lamp. Still, she was in and out of my room many times a night. She was a restless nocturnal wanderer, and neither one of us slept much.

Then, a few weeks after the wedding, I got a call from Gerry McFee at work. He had just gotten off the phone with Susan Esquilin, whom he'd called because Shana's behavior had gotten so disruptive he didn't know who else to turn to. Shana's symptoms mirrored Hannah's—and they had all started immediately after my sister's wedding. Gerry's ex-wife, whom Shana lived with during the week, had called him in exasperation and demanded to know what had happened at the wedding to upset Shana so much.

One of the worst aspects for Gerry to accept was her night terrors. I told him about Hannah's night-light, and where he could buy one like it. He seemed to feel better after talking to me, and it occurred to me afterward that he —as a divorced father who only saw his daughter weekends —must feel totally removed from the whole Wee Care mess. Not removed from it in a good sense, but powerless to help his daughter, and lacking the close contact with other Wee Care parents upon which some of us came to depend. At least when I got depressed I could call another Wee Care mother and pour out my worries. Gerry had no one to turn to. I knew by now that it was as hard on the fathers as the mothers. They just expressed it differently.

Jim, for instance, grew increasingly withdrawn from me and disinterested in what I was doing. He spent more and more of his time on the weekends working in the yard. Nights, he sat in front of the television downstairs, while I lay in bed and read. He simply didn't communicate with me.

But with Hannah he was gentle and attentive. When she was having terrible problems sleeping because she was afraid of Kelly, he brought her home a toy robot that he said was so powerful that no one would be able to hurt her. It was a gaudy trinket, about a foot high and made of colorful pieces of metal and plastic that bent in all directions. It looked like a cross between a Gobot and a Transformer.

As the children all exclaimed over it that first night, I kept my skepticism to myself, but I was sure Hannah wouldn't be taken in by such a gimmick. To my amazement, she was comforted by having the toy in her bed.

She and Ellen—and eventually, Robert—began calling the thing Robot, as though this was its name. Only very occasionally would Hannah consent to let one of the others play with it. Robot was special to her, the more so because it was a gift from her father.

Jim had been promising for a long time to make bunk beds for Hannah and Ellen. He finally did build a beautiful set, and installed them in the girls' room. He also bought new clip-on lights for the headboards so they could look at books before going to sleep. Since Hannah, in the top bunk, could no longer reach the night table, he built a special shelf for her and attached it to the wall by her bunk so that she'd have a place to keep her books and the glass of water she always wanted at bedtime.

Both girls were delighted, but the first night I tucked them into their new beds, Hannah cried and couldn't get to sleep because she missed her old bed. I pointed out that she had her same pillow and bedding, and I assured her that if she really wanted her old bed back, then Daddy would move it back into her room.

But she didn't want Jim to know how upset she was, because she thought it would hurt his feelings if she didn't like the new bed. For about two weeks, Hannah vacillated back and forth between missing her old bed and wanting the new one because her father had built it. Through it all, Jim wasn't supposed to know about any of this. Hannah would whisper, "Ask Daddy if it would make him feel bad if I slept in my own bed."

Dutifully I would put the question to Jim, who always said that Hannah could sleep in whichever bed she wanted. Then Hannah would decide to try one more night in her bunk. After a while, she got attached to it and Jim dismantled her old bed and put it in the attic.

Ellen, meanwhile, was so blissfully happy to be sharing a set of bunks with Hannah that she hadn't even asked what had happened to her old bed. And Caroline wisely pointed out to Hannah that she could always use her old mattress when she had a friend stay the night for a "sleep-over."

As the year progressed, Jim and I were not getting along any better. In December 1986, the two of us set off Christmas shopping together at Toys R Us. Halfway there, we got into a fight about—of all things—whether or not Hannah had indeed broken her leg the previous winter. Jim insisted that it had just been a fracture, to which I replied that a fracture *was* a break. He kept insisting that it wasn't, and it escalated until we were shouting at each other like children.

"You just feel guilty because it was your fault," I yelled finally. "If you hadn't had them on that steep hill, it would never have happened in the first place."

At which point Jim braked suddenly, sending our little Toyota bouncing over a concrete curb and careening onto the lawn of a condominium under construction.

"Oh my God, you're going to kill us both," I moaned, and for a crazy instant, I thought he really would. But then he stopped the car and jumped out, slamming the door, and strode off into the darkness. I sat there for a minute, feeling foolish and sheepish but also still angry. I got out and walked around the car, examining the underside and the tires. Miraculously, there wasn't a scratch on it anywhere.

I got behind the driver's seat and pulled back onto the road. When I saw Jim trudging along, I was tempted to just keep on going and I doubt he would have cared much at that point. I stopped, rolled down the window, and said through clenched teeth, "If you want a ride, just *GET* in."

He climbed in wordlessly and we drove along in silence to the store. At Toys R Us, he disappeared and I wandered up and down the crowded aisles alone, unable to remember why I was there. Other shoppers swirled around me, so intent on their purchases that no one even noticed the tears coursing down my face. Merry Christmas, I thought bitterly to myself.

Jim rounded a corner and came toward me, wheeling a full-sized bicycle.

"Do you think Robert would like this?" he asked, as if nothing had happened. I had to smile—the thought of Robert's chubby toddler legs trying to propel such a grown-up bike was comical. Then we both relaxed our guard and finished our shopping as if we were any other set of preholiday harried parents. We never discussed the incident again.

If the Wee Care experience was hard on marriages, it also took its toll on the older siblings of some of the victims. Several felt very guilty that they hadn't been able to prevent the abuse, and were now in therapy themselves. My oldest daughter, Caroline, was only six at the time—too young to feel personally responsible for Hannah's victimization. But she continued to resent all the attention that Hannah got from me, Jim, her grandparents, and the aunts and uncles. Strangely, until Caroline's jealousy became overt, I hadn't even realized how much of my time and attention were devoted to Hannah. I'm sure it was subconscious on my part. Parents of severely ill children must do the same thing without realizing it—coddle and favor an afflicted youngster more than their other children.

I began to make a conscious effort to do more with Caroline and Ellen. Caroline and I went shopping (just the two of us) several times for clothes for her—always a difficult experience for me since she was very particular about her wardrobe. We usually didn't like the same items, but I had learned by then that she wouldn't wear something she didn't like, so I held my tongue and let her do the choosing.

Ellen was at the age where she loved to break eggs and sift flour, so together we baked bread and cookies and pretzels. Several times I brought the ingredients and equipment to make cookies or muffins to her nursery school, and spent a session baking with her class of twelve. She strutted about, so visibly proud to have me there, and always insisted on sitting next to me at "circle time" and accompanying me to the bathroom with each group of children I took, even if she didn't need to go.

It was Robert I felt most guilty about. I'd missed out on so much of his babyhood and could never go back and relive it. My son was five months old when I found out Hannah had been sexually abused, and during the next eight months I was not as attentive and loving to him as I had been with the girls at that age. Then I got mono, and was physically unable to care for him for a long time. He was such a mellow, good-natured child that it was easy to overlook him when a tyrannical older sister demanded more than her share of attention.

Uppermost in my thoughts that awful year were Hannah's self-deprecation and depression, my own seemingly endless illness, and how these were affecting the rest of the family. But the distinct, if distant, possibility of the trial was always gnawing at the back of my mind. I knew we'd have to face it sooner or later, and I dreaded it.

■

As far as Hannah knew, her former nursery-school teacher was still in jail. But Kelly, who had been imprisoned in December 1985, was released two months later. Prior to her release there were several bail hearings. Sara Sencer requested $500,000 cash bail. But Harvey Meltzer, one of Kelly's lawyers, focusing on his client's constitutional right to bail, argued that increasing Kelly's bail would "be nothing more than a punishment before trial, which would be abhorrent to the state of New Jersey."

At the end of January 1986, Judge Harth released Kelly after she posted $25,000 bail. There were certain conditions: she was to remain with her parents in Pittsburgh, and not return to New Jersey unless ordered by the court or required to in order to consult with her lawyers. She had to sign a waiver of extradition, agree to have no contact with children, and keep her secretarial job at an insurance company in the Pittsburgh area. She also was supposed to report once a week to a lawyer in Pittsburgh, who would act as a "quasi-probation officer."

The judge set a May 19, 1986, trial date, but the trial wouldn't actually start for more than a year after that. Kelly's lawyers seemed to be stalling for time. Once the December 1985 indictment was handed down, it took them nine months to decide whether to use an insanity defense. Kelly was examined by half a dozen psychiatrists.

She took the Minnesota Multiphasic Personality Inventory (MMPI), a standardized, well-known test that is used to evaluate a personality. The written, multiple-choice exam has a built-in mechanism to see whether the person taking it is lying or not. Because Kelly scored very high on the lie scale, invalidating the results, she wound up taking the test several more times.

Her psychiatrists agreed that Kelly had major problems with her sexual identity, but they said she wasn't insane. It wasn't until September 1986 that Kelly's lawyers finally decided not to use an insanity defense.

While she awaited the defense's decision, Assistant Essex County prosecutor Sara Sencer McArdle (who, after marrying, used her husband's name) couldn't proceed at full speed with preparations for the trial. An insanity defense might have meant a trial based on the children's initial statements and the grand jury transcripts, and she was reluctant to start lining up witnesses until the issue was decided.

The Wee Care case at that point only accounted for about a fifth of her work time, and Sara used it to get organized. She collected information on which children were seeing which psychologists, and carefully sifted the evidence to develop support for every charge in the indictment. She also began to formulate Wee Care class schedules, compare the children's statements, and devise a teachers' time schedule to see which staffers were in the school on any given day. (By the time the trial began, some of us called Sara the Wee Care computer because she knew every fact there was to know about the case—including all the children's birthdays—and could call them up on a moment's notice.)

Kelly's lawyers then filed several motions attempting to dismiss the indictments. Among them was a motion asking that the indictments be dismissed because of the suggestibility of the young plaintiffs. After Judge Harth listened to all the tapes of the children's interviews with investigators, he ruled that this was an issue for the jury but that he couldn't find anything that would taint the entire case.

Another motion asked for dismissal due to lack of specific dates—understandably, the kids couldn't tell precisely which days they had been abused. Defense attorney Harvey Meltzer argued that without specific dates, he could not properly defend his client. Sara contended there was no way the state could pinpoint the exact days other than negatively through attendance records supplied to the defense showing when Kelly, or any particular child, was absent from school.

At the time, an unrelated south Jersey case was pending before the state supreme court. In that case, known as the *State of New Jersey in the Interest of K.A.W.*, a trial judge threw out an indictment charging a seventeen-year-old boy with sexually assaulting a seven-year-old girl. Defense attorneys for the youth, who was identified only as K.A.W., said the

176

indictment prevented their client from establishing an alibi defense, that is, proving that he was somewhere else when the crimes occurred. The trial judge, who was upheld by the appellate division of superior court, found that the twenty-month period charged in the indictment was too vague to allow the defendant to prepare a meaningful defense.

In the wake of the appellate court's ruling, at least sixteen sexual-abuse indictments throughout New Jersey were dismissed, and defense motions were pending in another sixteen cases.

Judge Harth, presiding over the Wee Care case, denied the defense motion to dismiss the indictment. And in October 1986, the New Jersey Supreme Court overruled the appellate court's ruling. In sending the K.A.W. case back to the trial court for further hearings, New Jersey's highest court ruled that children who have been sexually abused need not remember precisely when the assaults took place before authorities can charge suspected assailants. It was a minor victory for the children.

Meanwhile, earlier that spring, the prosecution filed a motion requesting that the children be allowed to testify via closed-circuit television so they wouldn't have to see Kelly. This meant the children's psychologists, or the parents, had to go into court and testify whether they believed it would be harmful and emotionally distressing for the youngsters to see the defendant face to face in open court. These hearings went on for weeks, and the judge ultimately granted the state's application.

Until the spring of 1986, Sara was the only prosecutor assigned to the Wee Care case. She'd been involved from the beginning, and the parents had come to know and trust her. She was around the same age as many of us—mid-thirties—and she was endlessly patient about explaining the legal proceedings to parents unfamiliar with the law.

Sara was frank and down-to-earth—the kind of person I probably would have sought out for a friend if I had met her under other circumstances. But it wasn't until much later, when I talked to parents around the country who were involved in other sexual-abuse cases, that I realized how lucky we were to have Sara. Some prosecutors purposely distanced themselves from the families of young sex-abuse victims. They didn't return phone calls. Some lacked the easy rapport Sara had with the children. She had a natural talent for making abused youngsters feel comfortable talking to her about an embarrassing subject.

Sara had a lot of experience working with children. She'd been a camp counselor, run Girl Scout troops, and worked in a day-care center one summer during college. She earned a degree in elementary education from Temple University in 1971, and taught elementary school for three years in her home town of Upper Saddle River, New Jersey, and then for two years at an American school in Guadalajara, Mexico.

When Sara returned home from Mexico, she started law school at the University of Toledo, graduating in 1979. She returned to New Jersey, clerked for a Bergen County judge for a year, and in September 1980, joined the Essex County Prosecutor's Office as an assistant prosecutor. She tried various cases in the juvenile section—burglary, robbery, murder, and larceny, for instance—and in September 1984, was asked to head the newly expanded child-abuse unit. Sara had directed that unit for seven months when the Wee Care case broke. And by the time things started gearing up for Kelly's trial, she needed extra help.

Around that time, a young Essex County assistant prosecutor named Glenn Goldberg went to his boss, George Schneider. Since Glenn wasn't working on any major cases that spring, he wanted some additional work to do. Schneider suggested that Glenn cross-examine some of the defense's expert witnesses during the pretrial hearings of the Wee Care case.

Glenn had a reputation for brilliant cross-examination. He had worked for five years as a civil trial attorney for a

Livingston, New Jersey, law firm after receiving his law degree from Rutgers University in 1967. In 1973, he joined the Essex County Prosecutor's Office, where he prosecuted a wide variety of criminal cases.

When Glenn was assigned to help Sara, George Schneider told Sara she couldn't possibly prosecute the Wee Care case and direct the child-abuse unit at the same time. But Sara, who by then felt strongly committed to the case, disagreed. So it was decided that she and Glenn would prosecute the case together.

At first they planned that Glenn would handle the defense witnesses and Sara would mastermind the state's case. But there was so much to do to prepare the state's witnesses that ultimately Glenn began to work with some of the children as well. Soft-spoken and mild-mannered, he was able to develop a quick rapport with them using the amateur magic tricks he had been perfecting since childhood. The youngsters were fascinated when he pulled dice or coins from his pockets and made them disappear or change into other things. It eased the introduction of the always painful topic of Wee Care.

By the end of 1986, the state's case against Kelly Michaels was beginning to shape up. Glenn and Sara began to contact some of the victims' parents to see if they would be willing to let the children recount for a jury what Kelly had done to them.

A year and a half after the abuse had first come to light, many victims continued to exhibit low self-esteem, bedwetting, depression, and night terrors. And the abuse was beginning to show its insidious ripple effect in the children's families. They had shocking stories to tell of how Kelly Michaels had destroyed the fabric of their lives.

C H A P T E R
■ ■ ■ ■ ■ ■ ■ ■ ■ ■

10

Kelly's primary victims were the three- and four-year-olds, whose trust she betrayed and whose innocence she ravaged. They are the ones who for a lifetime will remember what it was like to be young, violated, and defenseless. But the devastating effects of her abhorrent behavior go beyond the youngsters themselves.

In raping them, she robbed our families of their closeness and stability. Her crimes cast a pall over so many lives. She destroyed bonds between parent and child, husband and wife, brother and sister. Grandparents of the Wee Care children and our friends and co-workers suffered, too. Family ties eroded and lives were forever altered in the wake of her repulsive treatment of our children. So much sadness and suffering, so many tears, and all caused by a single young woman.

One of the most poignant examples of this extended victimization was the Bethel family.

Melissa Bethel's family was intact, close and loving before the Wee Care horrors came to light. Sharon and Pete Bethel had their share of disagreements the way any couple does. Many of their arguments centered on Pete's rigorous work schedule. He is a tax attorney who works long hours and often puts in seven days a week. She is a social worker and an active church volunteer. Most of the day-to-day housekeeping and child-care chores fell to Sharon, and the pair would bicker over who had to shop for groceries or clean the bathrooms. But mutual friends and common interests more than compensated for their arguments over domestic affairs, and they were content with their work, their daughters, and each other. Between them they earned a comfortable living.

The Bethels weren't wealthy, but there was always enough money for vacations and new clothes each season for the two little girls. Their house was centrally air conditioned and furnished with lovely rugs and contemporary furniture, and both Laura and Melissa took piano lessons and practiced daily on the new Steinway Pete had bought.

But the Bethels' tranquil life-style was shattered when they found out their daughter had been sexually abused. Melissa, who was already having some behavioral difficulties before her parents found out about Kelly, became fearful and increasingly aggressive in the months after she admitted her victimization. She lost her appetite and grew to look waiflike and vulnerable, her blue eyes huge in her thin face. She had enormous trouble sleeping.

Melissa would discuss some of her Wee Care experiences with her mother, but sometimes a wall would go up in front of her face and she would steadfastly deny having been at school on the days when Kelly was abusing the children. "Mom, there was a good Kelly and a bad Kelly," Melissa explained. "And I didn't go to school when the bad Kelly was there."

Sharon panicked: was her daughter going to develop a split personality? But a psychologist reassured her that this disassociation is typical in abused children. The victim simply pulls inside and allows the abuse to take place, then comes back when it's over.

Sharon spent many hot nights that summer sitting up late with Melissa. When the five-year-old talked about Kelly, she kept coming back to the hitting and the spitting. It really bothered her that Kelly had hurt her classmates to the point where they cried. One night, Melissa described how the youngsters had cleaned up urine and feces from the floor:

"We would build a wall of blocks," she told her mother, stretching her arms high in the air to indicate how tall the wall was. "And then we would make teams. The girls would be on one side and the boys would be on the other side. Kelly would do poo on one side and tinkle on the other. The girls would clean up the pee and the boys would clean up the poo. Then the girls and boys switched places. The girls would clean up the poo and the boys would clean up the tinkle."

She described it as a game, with the teams competing to see which one could finish cleaning up first.

I didn't know Sharon Bethel very well back then. When Wee Care closed, we both enrolled our daughters in the town-sponsored day camp. Sharon worked part-time in the summer, and she offered to drive my girls to the camp. I was grateful because it meant I wouldn't have to be late for work every day for the four weeks of camp. But after just three days, Sharon withdrew her daughters from camp.

She couldn't stand to have Melissa out of her sight for even an hour. She followed her around the house, even into the bathroom, to make sure she was okay. She made several trips each day to the day-camp site to make sure no one was hurting Melissa. She spent a lot of time crying.

"I was devastated not only that a child of mine had been hurt in such a way, but that I lived with her and never put it together," Sharon said. "I, who have worked with children all of my adult life, didn't pick up on it. I never fitted the pieces of the puzzle together. How stupid I was."

One of the hardest things for her to accept was not know- ing exactly what happened to Melissa—how many times

Kelly stuck the knife in her vagina, how many days they played the nude pile-up game, what hurt the most. The not knowing—and the not being able to ask her daughter because this might be construed as tainting the investigation —tormented Sharon. She felt that she could handle everything better if she knew what she was dealing with.

Pete was sympathetic to a point, but he grew tired of the constant talk of Wee Care. Hashing and rehashing every detail, flooding oneself with guilt, seemed pointless to him. And so Sharon began to spend hours on the phone with other mothers because they were the only ones who understood the depth of her grief. Her husband baby-sat with the children on the nights when she was out with the other mothers. He served the girls their dinner when she was tied up on the telephone. But he never asked his wife, "Why are you talking to those people? Why aren't you talking to me?"

When Pete did talk, it never seemed to comfort to Sharon. Once he said to his wife, "It's as if Melissa is damaged goods now. Who's going to want her?"

Sharon was furious. Isn't that a man's way of looking at it, she thought angrily. To think that because his daughter was violated, she was no longer desirable.

"She is not damaged," she said ferociously. "She's going to be all right."

Pete and Sharon drifted apart until they scarcely talked to or knew each other anymore. They were two strangers who handled and reacted to the Wee Care crisis in opposite ways, he refusing to confront his grief, she giving in to it and nurturing it until it became an obsession she couldn't see beyond. The Bethels' twelve-year commitment to each other as a couple came unglued because of the unbalanced way in which they dealt with their sorrow and anger, she turning outward for sustenance from fellow sufferers, he looking inward and trying to hide, and neither finding the solace that can flourish when pain is shared.

That fall, Melissa and Laura were enrolled in grammar

school. Sharon soon felt that Melissa's kindergarten teacher was too strict. She didn't answer the many notes Sharon wrote to her. Sharon started looking at other schools. But no matter how hard she searched, she couldn't find the perfect one for Melissa.

Meanwhile, seven-year-old Laura saw that her mother was paying a lot more attention to Melissa than to her. Feeling jealous and neglected, she got defiant and smart-alecky. She threw tantrums. She fought with her younger sister.

"Why is Melissa always in your bed?" she often asked her mother. "Why can't you sleep with me?"

Sharon, who had no mental energy left to console her older daughter, would wearily explain that Melissa had been hurt and needed her help.

Sharon was barely able to function in her job as a social worker that fall. As with me, when she got into the car in the morning, the tears started. On the road, when she was by herself and no one could see her, Sharon spent most of her time crying. She called in sick frequently, telling her boss she had a headache or a sore throat. That way she could lie alone in bed all day and weep.

It was November when Sharon realized how low she had sunk, and the depth of her depression really scared her. Recognizing that she needed professional help, she began to see a psychologist, who was finally able to convince her that she was a good mother, that she had done the right things for her children. Gradually, she gained control of her emotions again. At least she could get through a day at work without crying.

But she and Pete continued to be like strangers to each other. "Wee Care mentally and emotionally removed me from the marriage," Sharon said. "It took me into another whole set of relationships and problems, and I just ignored what was happening between me and my husband. We really didn't focus on each other. Our energies were not spent on ourselves or each other or our marriage. I just blocked Pete out. He became the extra person in my life."

As she turned away from Pete, she became increasingly involved with the Wee Care case and with a group that works to prevent child sexual abuse. In the summer of 1986, Sharon and Traci McKenna heard about Believe the Children, a California-based organization dedicated to the prevention of child sexual abuse. The two women flew to California that June to attend a conference sponsored by the nonprofit group. When Sharon told Pete she wanted to go, he said it sounded like a good idea. He agreed to stay home with Laura and Melissa.

When Sharon and Traci returned to New Jersey, they were instrumental in forming a New Jersey chapter of the group. They held a garage sale to raise money, and they sold Believe the Children T-shirts and sweatshirts. Getting involved made Sharon feel as if she was doing something useful.

As soon as the pretrial hearings on the Wee Care case began, Sharon started attending them. She discussed this first with her boss, who told her she could go to the hearings whenever she wanted as long as she could verify for him that she had been in court.

A few other mothers also became regular spectators early on. Often they all went down to the cafeteria in the courthouse basement and had lunch together. They discussed the day's proceedings, going over every detail, trading opinions of the various witnesses and their testimony.

Sharon wanted to know everything there was to know about the case. She spent hours sitting on a bench in Judge Harth's eighth-floor courtroom, listening and absorbing. She was intrigued by the legal process, by what happens before a case comes to trial, by all the different issues Kelly's lawyers kept raising. But she knew that she was also in court for Melissa's sake.

"While Kelly was doing this to my kid, I didn't know it," she said. "I wasn't there for my kid. And if Melissa ever

185

were to come to me at eighteen or twenty-one and say, you know, when that happened to me you weren't even there, you didn't do anything—I have no defense. I wasn't. I didn't recognize what was happening. But I wanted to be able to say to her that once I found out, I did everything I possibly could to see that justice was done, that this woman paid for what she did."

CHAPTER
■ ■ ■ ■ ■ ■ ■ ■ ■ ■
11

It is one thing to want to see justice done. It's quite another to allow your child to testify at a criminal trial. But we knew that if Kelly Michaels was going to be punished for what she did, her victims had to become involved in the legal process.

The children were the only eyewitnesses to Kelly's crimes. Their testimony had to be the backbone of the state's case. Parents, pediatricians, and therapists could talk about the children's emotional and physical state. Former Wee Care teachers could discuss the lack of supervision at the school that year, and Kelly's odd behavior. But in the end, it would be up to the children to tell the truth, to convince a jury that their teacher had committed the crimes with which she was charged.

The decision about whether to testify ultimately rested with the children, of course. Six- and seven-year-olds can't be forced to answer questions against their will. But we parents had a choice, too. We could either encourage them to tell their story in court, or we could dissuade them from doing so.

Asking our children to talk about horrendous incidents that had happened to them two years ago—half a lifetime or more for most of them—was like reopening old wounds just beginning to heal. Dredging up unpleasant memories that were starting to fade seemed unnecessarily cruel. When they had already endured so much, why put them through even more?

On the other hand, if they didn't testify and Kelly Michaels walked, how would it feel?

I vacillated between being the responsible citizen and the protective mother. Sending the woman who had molested my child to prison meant a lot. But I had mixed emotions. I had already unwittingly allowed my daughter to be hurt by Kelly. I wanted to shield Hannah from anything that would cause her more pain. I could relate to a ferocious mother bear looking out for her cub—I felt as if I would physically attack anyone who tried to harm my child.

Hannah was still in weekly therapy, but we seemed to be in the midst of a serene period when I could almost convince myself that Wee Care had never happened. (In fact, I was to learn that sexually abused children's symptoms abate and recur over the years.)

There were little reminders here and there, of course. In January 1987, after her first-grade class saw a show about the prevention of sexual abuse, Hannah told me that one part of the play reminded her of a time at Wee Care when she had been the last child left with Kelly at the end of the school day. That she had been by herself with Kelly didn't really surprise me. On nights when rotten weather played havoc with rush-hour traffic, I sometimes arrived close to the 6 P.M. closing time to pick up Hannah. "What happened the day you were by yourself with Kelly?" I asked Hannah now.

"We were up on the stage in the gym," she said. "I kept walking back and forth across the stage, and Kelly kept following me, back and forth, back and forth. And—" She stopped suddenly, and I could see from her expression that she didn't want to talk about it anymore. I couldn't resist pressing her.

"Did anything else happen?" I hoped my casual tone was encouraging. I wanted so badly to know if Hannah had been molested because I was late to pick her up.

"Other things happened," she said flatly. "But I don't remember."

And we dropped the subject.

Kelly's name didn't come up in our house very often, though, and Hannah mostly seemed at peace with herself. She brought home excellent report cards, sang with the first-grade chorus, and tirelessly practiced the tap-dancing routines she and Caroline learned in their Saturday morning tap-and-ballet class.

Unlike Caroline, who dreads having to speak in front of a group, Hannah loved performing for an audience. Their school had "joke assemblies" at which youngsters could get up on stage to tell a joke for the entire student body. (The principal listened to the jokes in advance in his office, and he was on hand at the microphone to help sudden victims of stage fright stumble through their lines.) But Hannah always demonstrated remarkable aplomb up on the stage before an audience of three hundred, timing the punch line perfectly and then laughing harder than anyone else.

She enjoyed performing in skits and plays. In a first-grade presentation of Mother Goose rhymes that winter, she played both the blackbird in "Sing a Song of Sixpence" and the spider in "Little Miss Muffet." Wearing her black stretch pants, sweatshirt, and socks, she gleefully leaped into Miss Muffet's porridge bowl and then snipped off the nose of the royal maid.

Proud as the mother of a Broadway child star, I shot half a roll of pictures, knowing perfectly well that my daughter would only show up as a tiny black dot on the cavernous stage. But that didn't matter in the least to Hannah, who proudly pasted the snapshots into her scrapbook.

Hannah, once she got used to her new bunk bed, slept in the top bunk for a couple of months with almost no nightmares. It amazed me that anyone could sleep at all in a bed crowded with enough stuffed animals to fill a toy store. But Hannah insisted on having her entire collection lined up along one half of the bed. She usually fell asleep clutching her favorites—a battered teddy bear named Joshua, a well-used Cabbage Patch doll called Corinne Amaryllis, and a musical lamb that wagged its beribboned head back and forth in time to "Mary Had a Little Lamb."

At bedtime, the four children and I would sit on the lower bunk and say prayers together. After we asked God to bless the various members of the family and recited the Our Father and Hail Mary, each child prayed aloud individually. Usually these prayers took the form of requests for things the kids wanted and ended with a hurried thank you for something they had received—money to go to the roller rink, for instance.

Sometimes Hannah ended her prayer by saying, "Thank you for the world, God. And thank you for letting *most* of the people in the world be nice." I always wondered if she was thinking of Kelly.

That winter I began to talk to her about the upcoming trial, in terms I thought she would understand. I explained what a jury was, and how important it was to tell only the truth in court. I told her that Kelly had lawyers, and that Sara and Glenn were our lawyers.

I also told her if she testified, she would not have to see Kelly. Absent that safeguard, I myself would have been completely opposed to Hannah's testifying. Knowing how Kelly had terrified her, I didn't want her to have to see that face ever again. Sara Sencer McArdle had asked Judge Harth to allow our children to testify via closed-circuit television. In her motion, the prosecutor relied on a recent state statute that permitted closed-circuit testimony by child witnesses if appearing in front of the defendant, the jury, or courtroom spectators would cause them severe emotional distress.

Judge Harth presided over closed hearings on the prosecutor's application at which some of the parents—along with psychologists who were treating the children—testified. They spoke about the potential harm of forcing Kelly's victims to appear in court in her presence.

Susan Esquilin testified about Hannah and six other victims she was treating. She told the court that having Kelly in the same courtroom would intimidate the youngsters and impair their ability to testify candidly.

"In my mind, there's no question that these children are frightened of her," she was quoted in one New Jersey newspaper shortly before testifying. "Seeing her again would clearly revive memories that are upsetting. They [the children] would have great difficulty testifying."

The hearings lasted for weeks before Judge Harth handed down his decision. Fortunately, it was favorable to the children: the Wee Care victims would be permitted to testify via closed-circuit television from the judge's chambers.

Although we didn't know until the spring what the judge would decide, I had already discussed it with Hannah. I explained that she would not have to see Kelly at the trial because she would tell the judge what happened while she was in a separate room from Kelly. I told her that testifying was a very brave but hard thing to do, and that she was being a good citizen by going to court to tell her story. I said it was important that she and the other children testify so Kelly would be in jail for a long time and thus would not be able to hurt other children.

Hannah listened attentively whenever I broached the subject, and I could see that she was torn about what to do. She wanted Kelly to stay in jail (she thought Kelly was still there) and she wanted to help protect other children. But she didn't want to testify because she was embarrassed,

191

afraid of Kelly, and worried that Kelly's lawyers might yell at her.

But Sara very much wanted my daughter to testify. Hannah had gone before a grand jury two years earlier and said Kelly had inserted a knife, fork, and spoon into her rectum and her vagina. Sara felt that Hannah would be one of her best witnesses. The two drove down to Newark one night so Hannah could see the courtroom and the judge's chambers, but Hannah was unenthusiastic about seeing Sara again. Clearly, the connection to Wee Care was painful.

Soon after talk of the trial began, Hannah's temper tantrums, irritability, and nightmares recurred. Several times she dreamed Kelly was going to come into her room and take her away. I would go in and comfort her, and she was usually able to fall back to sleep. Then late one night, Hannah said to me, "Let's talk about nursery school."

I tried not to look surprised. For nearly two years, she had been reluctant to discuss Wee Care with me. Was this the breakthrough I had been hoping for? Would she finally tell me everything that had happened?

"Ask me questions," she said, almost playfully.

"Well, what kind of questions should I ask?" I said tentatively, but she said she didn't know. So I asked if anything had ever happened in the gym that she didn't like.

"Yes," Hannah replied matter-of-factly. "But most of the bad stuff happened in the piano room."

"What happened in the piano room?" I prodded, sensing correctly that she was unwilling to go further. In the next sentence, she changed the subject.

"Let's talk about my dream some more," Hannah said anxiously. "Kelly was so big in my dream. Will she ever get out of jail?"

She wanted me to say no, but at the same time she wanted me to tell her the truth. I said I hoped a jury would believe the children, but that even if Kelly were to get out of prison, she would not be able to hurt the kids again.

"But if she gets out of jail, won't she be able to find me?"

192

Hannah looked so vulnerable that I felt the old rage at Kelly boiling up in me again. "Couldn't she break into our house even if the doors were locked?"

I hugged her. "No, she can't get in," I said, "and I'll always be here to protect you." And so it went for several nights running, Hannah tense and worried, listening to my reassurances but, I think, not really believing them.

In therapy, Susan Esquilin and Hannah discussed the upcoming trial and the children's role in it. Hannah told Susan she was afraid and embarrassed to talk about what happened at Wee Care in front of people she didn't know. My daughter said she was worried that someone might yell at her, and stressed that she didn't ever want to see Kelly again. But she also expressed that she would not want Kelly to be able to hurt other children.

Later, the psychologist told me she felt Hannah could handle testifying if she were allowed to do so out of the presence of the defendant. She warned me, though, that some of Hannah's symptoms would probably recur.

There was another person who Sara McArdle wanted to evaluate Hannah—New York psychologist Eileen Treacy. Realizing how difficult it was going to be to reinterview all the Wee Care children, the prosecutors had hired Eileen to help them. A specialist in child abuse, Eileen had worked extensively with youthful victims of sex crimes and had testified at the trials of several day-care-center workers accused of molesting their charges.

At Sara's request, some Wee Care parents were having their children evaluated by Eileen to see if she thought it would be emotionally damaging for them to testify. Later, at the trial, Eileen would become an "expert witness" for the state.

Still feeling fatigued much of the time and not up to a long drive on slippery winter roads to Eileen's Bronx office, I asked if the new psychologist could come to Susan's office in Montclair. She agreed. In mid-January, Hannah met with Eileen, who called me later with her assessment. Basically, she told me what Susan already had: that the experience probably would not hurt Hannah so long as she did not have to see Kelly.

"Testifying can even be positive," Eileen told me. "It can be the children's one opportunity to regain the power balance with the abuser. It does a lot to reduce their fears and to enhance the idea of justice."

I talked it over with Jim, who wasn't enthusiastic about having Hannah testify. Quite simply, my husband was tired of having Wee Care dominate my life and so, by extension, his life. And I think there was a part of him that occasionally wished someone in prison would just finish Kelly off so none of us would have to go through this.

The trial became a common subject for my husband and me to bicker about, and we were often on the verge of a full-fledged fight at the end of a discussion on the pros and cons of letting Hannah testify. Jim felt it would be very hard for her to accept if Kelly was not convicted. I agreed, and yet something (a need to avenge Hannah's tormentor? a sense of social responsibility?) kept gnawing at me when I would almost make up my mind to wash my hands of the whole mess and let someone else's kids be the responsible citizens instead.

In the end, Jim and I decided to leave it up to Hannah. I didn't think it likely that she would willingly testify unless we pushed her into it, and I reluctantly acknowledged that our family would not be a part of the trial. We stopped talking about it around the house.

And then one day in March, Hannah asked me if Sara could show her the courthouse again. They drove down to Newark together, and Sara took Hannah into Judge Harth's courtroom, where the trial would be held. Sara pointed out the judge's bench, the two rows of jurors' chairs, the tables where the defense attorneys and the prosecutors sat, the witness stand. Hannah climbed into the witness stand.

"Let's just see if I remember anything," she said to Sara. "You ask me questions, and see if I can answer them."

Sara wasn't surprised when Hannah's answers to her questions about what Kelly had done to her were as firm and concise as they had been nearly two years earlier. My daughter described the nude pile-up game, and she said that Kelly had inserted a knife, a fork, and a spoon into her rectum and vagina.

When Sara brought Hannah home later that night, they both were in good spirits. And when they told me that Hannah had made up her mind to testify, I was mostly glad, too. It just felt as if we were doing the right thing. And yet a part of me was scared—that Hannah might not be a good witness, that we might lose the case. Mostly afraid—for all I'd argued to the contrary with Jim—that testifying might hurt Hannah more than it helped her.

Many other parents were riding the same emotional roller coaster that winter. Some had begun to attend the pretrial hearings. Because our family needed the income from my job, I had to keep going to work and could not be in court. So I didn't feel as mentally caught up in the court case as some parents did.

My sister Kathleen, however, attended nearly all the pretrial hearings. She worked in a small office with a sympathetic boss who let her take off as much time as she needed. Even if he hadn't, I think she would still have been in court.

Of all my sisters, Kathleen was the one I knew the least before the Wee Care tragedy catapulted us together and provided us with common bonds of grief and guilt.

The first five children in my family were born less than a year apart and I'm the oldest. So although my brother Mark and my two sisters Mary and Jana come between Kathleen and me in the lineup, Kathleen is just four years younger than I. Still, though we are relatively close in age, Kathleen and I were never close in the way I am with Mary or Jana. It wasn't that we didn't get along, it was that everything about us was different. I went to a Catholic high school; she talked my parents into letting her attend the public junior high school and high school. We had different friends, different interests, different life-styles.

As a child, Kathleen was placid and easygoing while I was compulsive and competitive. As a teen-ager, I was mildly jealous of her. She had a great shape and always looked terrific in her clothes. My aunt Ruth always said Kathleen had the best legs of any girl in the family, and her long brown hair was thick and straight while mine was thin and just curly enough to be unmanageable. Kathleen made friends effortlessly, got more phone calls from boys than I did, and was generally considered by the other kids in my family to be more hip than I was.

I went away to college in upstate New York, got married, and moved to Manhattan. She stayed in South Orange, met and married Wayne, and had Emily. Even when I moved back to South Orange we didn't socialize often. She was divorced within two years of her marriage. I sometimes invited her and Emily to come over for a pizza dinner, but there were none of the long, late-night telephone conversations between us the way there were with some of my other sisters. Kathleen and I didn't share problems and secrets, didn't confide in each other.

Then we found out that both our daughters had been sexually abused, and our relationship changed. Suddenly, I was drawn to Kathleen in a way I hadn't been before. When I felt as if I was going crazy, when I needed to pick up the phone and talk to someone about Hannah, it was Kathleen's number I dialed instead of my mother's or one of my other sisters'. She kept me informed about what was going on with the trial. She called and told me about parents' meetings, court dates, bits of gossip she had picked up just by being down at the courthouse so much. Kathleen urged me to go out with her and the other Wee Care mothers. She knew my anguish in a way the rest of our family couldn't.

Gradually, I came to know Kathleen and to appreciate what she endured as a divorced mother. The Wee Care ordeal was especially hard on her because she was a single parent and because Emily was her only child. It had nearly driven my sister wild two summers earlier when Emily told her that Kelly had hit her, penetrated her with tableware, made her play with feces. Unlike the rest of us, Kathleen didn't have another adult around to help her make decisions about Emily's care or to help in the day-to-day comforting of the traumatized little girl.

Emily had plenty of nightmares that first terrible summer, and when she and her mother sat up late at night talking, Kathleen felt a tremendous hatred toward Kelly growing within her.

One night, Emily told Kathleen that she still loved her, "even though someone told me not to love my mom."

"Who told you that?" asked Kathleen.

"Kelly," said Emily. "She told us not to love our moms. But I closed my eyes real tight [here Emily screwed up her face] and I still loved you, Mommy."

Emily feared that Kelly could get out of jail. One hot summer night, Emily slammed shut the front door of the house, saying she was worried about herself and Kathleen. Then she told my sister, "Kelly can change into other things." A few minutes later she said, "Kids don't go to jail, right, Mom?"

"No, Emily, kids don't go to jail."

"Kelly said she would push me in front of a car," Emily said. "Upstairs in that chair room [she meant the choir room, with its long benches] Kelly played with no clothes on. I was laughing and she came and picked me up and threw me. I hurt my back. It hurt real bad. I went downstairs by myself and got an ice pack."

Another night, giggling, she said to my sister, "Eat shit. . . . It's slimy, Mommy."

"What do you mean?" asked Kathleen.

"Kelly made a cake out of poops with a candle, and we all had to eat some."

Kathleen despised Kelly Michaels, and she wanted to be in on every step of the process by which the defendant would be tried and judged. She very much hoped five-and-a-half-year-old Emily would testify, but like her cousin Hannah, Emily was ashamed, embarrassed, and afraid. She had been one of the youngest victims, barely out of diapers and talking when she met Kelly Michaels. It would be hard for her to talk about something that had happened such a long time ago.

Still, Emily was keen to see the jail again. Like many of the other children, she wanted to make sure that it was strong enough that Kelly couldn't break out. So my sister and Sara showed her the holding cell in the prosecutor's office. The lock on the cell happened to be broken, and Sara was in the middle of explaining to Emily that someone was coming to fix it when an employee standing nearby shrugged and said, "It doesn't matter anyway. They break out of jail all the time."

Sara tried to signal him to be silent but he kept right on talking about how insecure jails are today. So finally Kathleen walked away with Emily, whose dark eyes were big and solemn.

"What that man said, is it the truth or is it a lie?" Kathleen asked her daughter.

"It's a lie," Emily said fiercely. "Jails are strong."

Emily vacillated about whether or not to testify. One day she told her mother she wanted to tell the judge what Kelly had done, but then the next day she changed her mind and said she couldn't.

"Honey, it's okay if you don't want to," Kathleen assured her. "Other kids are going to go to court. And if you don't feel able to, then that's fine."

Emily started sucking her finger a lot, and her sleeping problems worsened. Sara came to visit a couple of times. One night when she was leaving, Emily asked Sara to come back and see her again. Sara said she would.

"Bring the dolls the next time," Emily said, referring to the anatomically correct dolls. Sara assured Emily that she would. "And don't forget the fork and knife," Emily added.

Kathleen believed that Emily was willing to demonstrate for Sara what Kelly had done to her, but that she didn't want to use anything in her own house to show her. She was relieved that Emily was growing more at ease with Sara. It was beginning to look as though her daughter might have her day in court after all.

Sara spent many hours that fall and winter getting reacquainted with the Wee Care children. Among the youngsters she talked to was Eddie Fernandez, who had told his mother he wanted to go to court and tell the judge what Kelly had done to him. At first Ana thought he was saying he would do it just to please her. But after he reiterated to Susan Esquilin his desire to be a witness, she realized that he really wanted to testify.

But he was depressed in the weeks before the trial. He told his mother, "I wish I was dead. I don't want to live." As the trial drew near, he told her, "I wish a car would kill me."

Ana was in shock. She didn't know what to say. She hugged him and told him, "I love you so much and if that happened to you I would be very sad."

He cried a lot. He told Ana, "Mommy, I wish that never happened to me. Why did that have to happen to me?"

He started having frequent nightmares and couldn't fall asleep unless the lights were on in his bedroom. If Ana turned them off before she went to bed, he would wake up in the middle of the night and call to her from his bed to come turn them back on. When Eddie needed to use the bathroom in the middle of the night, he was afraid to go by himself.

Melissa Bethel's symptoms also recurred when her parents and Sara began to talk of Wee Care and Kelly that fall. Over the previous summer she had begun to seem more like herself, less fearful of Kelly. She even had slept in her own bed in the rented house the family stayed in on vacation.

But once talk of the trial began in the Bethel household, "Things just disintegrated," Sharon recalls. Melissa started sleeping with her mother every night, the aggressive behavior began again, and she made no pretense at all of eating with tableware. She didn't want to talk about Wee Care anymore, and she told her mother so in no uncertain terms. Sharon, meanwhile, continued to follow the legal proceedings carefully.

"I wanted to be a part of it, I felt better being a part of it," Sharon said. "I wanted to know what was happening and how it was progressing, and if I could have any input, I wanted that, too."

She wanted Melissa to testify because she felt the only way Kelly was going to be convicted was if as many children as possible had their say. Still, she worried that her little girl might get into the courtroom only to have absolutely nothing to say.

Sharon knew Melissa would not talk about Wee Care in front of her, but she suggested Melissa might find it easier if her therapist could be in the room when she testified. But even this didn't make Melissa any less reluctant. So Sharon decided to let it ride for a while. The prosecutors didn't have to know for sure whether her daughter would testify until immediately before the trial began. Sharon thought it best simply to stop talking about it for a while.

Sara also spoke that fall to Jodie Minetti, who had done well in kindergarten the year before. She wasn't having as many seizures as she had been two years earlier, and her stuttering had improved. But soon after Jodie entered the first grade when Sara came to visit, Julie Minetti watched in amazement as the talk of Kelly coincided with a recurrence of her daughter's symptoms.

The little girl, who had refused to eat peanut butter at Wee Care but had happily eaten it throughout kindergarten, again developed an aversion to her favorite food. One morning shortly after a visit from Sara, Julie stood at the kitchen counter making Jodie's standard lunch: a peanut-butter-and-jelly sandwich.

When Jodie noticed what her mother was making, she began whining that she didn't want peanut butter. The whining slowly escalated into low-grade crying by the time Julie had finished wrapping the lunch.

"What is it, Jodie?" she asked, feeling irritated with her daughter.

"I want a butter sandwich," insisted Jodie, and Julie experienced a sudden flashback to Jodie's last year at Wee Care. That's ridiculous, Julie thought to herself. This has nothing to do with Kelly. Jodie's just being difficult.

But by the time they got to school, Jodie was crying hysterically. Julie led her weeping daughter into her first-grade classroom and went directly to Jodie's teacher, whom she liked immensely. Julie had even confided in the teacher what had happened to Jodie at Wee Care. Now, out of earshot of Jodie, she explained to the puzzled woman what she herself was only just starting to realize: all the recent talk of Wee Care and Kelly had made Jodie hate peanut butter again.

The teacher comforted Jodie while Julie went home, made a plain butter sandwich, and drove back to school. When she got to the classroom, she learned that Jodie had told her teacher about Kelly. It was the first time Jodie had mentioned Kelly's name in her new school.

The little girl looked relieved to see the butter sandwich, and from then on, Julie made them every day for Jodie's lunch. Neither raised the peanut butter issue again.

But Julie knew her daughter was having a rough time. She began to sleep in her parents' bed again. She started having seizures that the doctor said were stress-induced. Sometimes, as Jodie sat watching television or playing, Julie would see her daughter's face take on an almost trance-like look. It wasn't the look she got right before she had a seizure; it was a remote stare, as though she were twenty million miles away.

"Jodie," Julie would say. "What is it?"

And Jodie would moan, "Kelly's in my head." Sometimes this happened eight or nine times a day. It was upsetting for Julie to see how painful her daughter's memories were.

The child had been interviewed by Eileen Treacy and the two developed a warm rapport over the course of several visits. After Julie told Eileen how Jodie couldn't get Kelly out of her mind, Eileen taught her relaxation and mental imagery that she could use whenever Kelly dominated her thoughts. She asked Jodie what she would like to see happen to Kelly. Jodie visualized Missy, the family's Great Dane, chasing Kelly and biting her on the rear end. Picturing this always seemed to make her feel better when Kelly invaded her consciousness.

Julie Minetti felt an almost physical need to be in court because for her it was a way to gain back control over what she had lost. But she also went for her daughter. Like Sharon Bethel, she doesn't want Jodie coming to her as an adult and asking why her mother hadn't been a part of the legal proceedings. Still, the long days in court caused undeniable friction between Julie and Bob.

"It was a constant sore spot with us," she said. "We're very close—he'd been my boyfriend since I was thirteen and we can read each other's minds. But for the first time, I really didn't understand where he was coming from with Wee Care."

She didn't understand his attitude, although it seemed to her that he wished he could just erase what had happened. Some days she would think he just didn't care. On days when she felt kinder, she knew he was so traumatized by the whole thing that he just refused to deal with it at all.

Julie wanted her husband to be involved. When there was an article in the morning newspaper about Wee Care, she would bring it to him and point it out. She was eager for him to talk to her about the case. She wanted him to share her feelings. But Bob felt that going to court, reading about it in the papers, was pointless. It wasn't going to change what had happened to his daughter. One day she tossed the newspaper down on the bed beside him and headed for the bathroom. She glanced back just in time to see him throw the paper on the floor as hard as he could.

█

Arguments over whether or not their child would testify also plagued the Goldsteins in the months before the trial. By that point, David had moved out and Soma continued to live in their Maplewood house with Rachel and Ted.

But David continued to be very involved with his children. He came on Tuesday and Thursday nights to take them out to dinner and help put them to bed. He also took them every other weekend.

David disliked discussing Wee Care with Soma, but he followed the case in the papers and felt that Rachel should not be part of the trial.

"He wasn't thrilled about her testifying, but a lot of times when he's not sure about something he defers to me," Soma said. "That was one of the things that upset the whole marriage. It was like, if you can't make a decision then let someone else make it for you. Then you don't have to take responsibility for it."

Soma was strongly in favor of having Rachel testify. "I thought it would be good for her," Soma said. "And I wanted to be able to testify, to have my day in court. I felt that we had testimony that would be damaging to the defendant."

The previous year had been particularly difficult for Soma. She hadn't told any of her co-workers about her separation from David, and very few knew her daughter had been sexually abused. She couldn't turn to her colleagues for comfort. And her parents, although well-meaning, didn't really understand the depth of her grief. The couple, who live in Brooklyn, were accustomed to Soma taking charge and carrying on even in a crisis. They didn't realize how much she hurt inside until one day she broke down and cried in front of her father. He was surprised.

"He said, 'Gee, I didn't realize that you took this thing so bad,' " Soma recalled. "They just thought I was very competent. I had never missed work because of Wee Care. Other women look it when they are going through a bad time. But with me, it seemed to them like I was keeping up with everything. They didn't know how bad I felt."

She befriended other Wee Care mothers. Once in awhile, she and Julie Minetti, Traci MacKenna, Sharon Bethel, Marge Farrell, and my sister Kathleen would go to a local restaurant for a drink. Though none of them had been acquainted before, they were at ease with one another and always felt better after an evening out together.

As the trial approached, it became clear that many children were unwilling or unable to testify. The case against Kelly Michaels originally consisted of 235 counts of sexual abuse and terroristic threats against thirty-one children. But by the time the trial began, eleven children had been dropped from the case and the original indictments had been pared by the prosecutors from 235 to 163 counts.

Sara McArdle, with Eileen Treacy's help, had eliminated some children because they both felt the experience of testifying would be harmful, or because the youngsters simply were too immature. In other cases, the children themselves refused to testify, and their parents experienced a whole gamut of emotions that ranged from frustration to anger to a sense of futility.

Having their children refuse to testify was especially hard for parents who were very involved with the case themselves. And since the only parents who would be allowed to take the stand were those whose children were going to be witnesses, it was doubly disappointing. They would have to be passive spectators, watching from the sidelines. They felt they could do nothing to increase the chances that the woman who had molested their children would go to prison.

Peter and Claudia Schwartz, for instance, were deeply committed to seeing the case through to its end. They told their daughter how important it was for her and the other children to testify. Four-year-old Michele had testified before the grand jury in the summer of 1985. She was in group therapy with some other children that first summer, and the Schwartzes had participated in the parents' discussion group held at Susan Esquilin's office that fall.

Michele's behavior over the next year and a half provided the Schwartzes with enough jarring reminders of her victimization that they couldn't put the Wee Care case out of their lives until it was resolved.

But when Eileen Treacy interviewed their daughter, she told the Schwartzes she didn't think the child's testimony would be helpful. She simply wasn't mature enough. Sara let her go down to see the courtroom once, but Michele said she was afraid to testify, that she was afraid of the judge. And so they let the matter drop.

"I felt angry with Michele," Claudia admits. "Sometimes I felt like she wasn't doing the responsible thing, wasn't helping the case. Other parents and other children were doing what had to be done. I felt as though she was acting immature. And then I felt guilty for feeling that way."

Even once they knew Michele would not be a witness, the Schwartzes chose to get involved. They followed the case closely in the papers and went down to court several times to hear testimony. "I wanted to see what was happening," Claudia says. "Emotionally, I felt that I had just as much of an investment in it as the parents whose children did testify. I didn't go through as much as they did, but I felt a part of it all."

Billy Farrell never opened up to the investigators at all or testified before the grand jury. Susan Esquilin was able to establish in one visit that the child had been sexually abused and terrorized, and he spent the next two years in therapy. Billy continued to display symptoms; even two years after the Wee Care case broke, he would try to climb on top of his older sister Linda and lick her. He was still extremely angry at his parents for not protecting him. Marge felt that their household was under a constant state of siege.

Although he would discuss with his mother some of what had gone on at Wee Care, he steadfastly refused to speak with the prosecutors. He kicked and spit when he was asked questions, or crawled under a chair and refused to come out. There was little question but that he would not be a witness at his tormentor's trial.

But his mother, Marge Farrell, was involved with the case from the beginning. When her son attended Wee Care, she did not know any other Wee Care mothers. But in the months after learning about Billy, she grew close to half a dozen of them. In the summer of 1986, Marge also attended a Believe the Children conference in California and served as one of its officers in the New Jersey chapter. She was touched when her father, who was uncomfortable discussing the case with her but who faithfully clipped out all the newspaper articles for her to save, gave her a donation for Believe the Children.

She was luckier than some of the mothers in that her husband, William, played a more active role than other fathers. He often went to parents' meetings, and his was a familiar face in the courtroom. Both Farrells kept hoping Billy would change his mind and testify. "I thought it would really have helped him a lot if he felt he could be a part of it," Marge says. "So it was very frustrating for me not to be able to participate."

Fran Newton felt the same frustration. Although she no longer lived in the same community as most of the other Wee Care parents, she kept in touch and attended as many pretrial hearings as her schedule would allow. But her new husband couldn't understand her need to be there.

"I couldn't not go," Fran said. "I had to be there, to know

what was going on. And there was a sharing there that I liked. I enjoyed getting to know the other parents."

Fran hoped Tiffany would be a witness. Sara McArdle also was anxious for her to testify to rebut the defense attorneys' posture that the children's original interviews with the Division of Youth and Family Services had been tainted. Tiffany had never spoken to DYFS, yet her story of what had happened at Wee Care was the same as the other children's.

But Tiffany was going to a new school now. She had new friends. She occasionally saw Kelly Michaels on television, and she knew from her mother that the children were going to testify on a TV. Tiffany thought that meant she would be on TV, too. Then all her new friends would find out about Wee Care. She had another reason for not going to court: she just didn't want to go through it all again.

"I told it once to the grand jury," Tiffany said stubbornly. "I'm not telling it anymore."

■

By the late spring, it looked as though nineteen or twenty children were going to testify against their former teacher. It was now just a matter of waiting—which I've never been good at—for the trial to begin. If anyone had told me when I first learned Hannah had been molested that more than two years would elapse before the case went to trial, I wouldn't have believed it. And yet, here we were, celebrating Hannah's seventh birthday with a family party and a friends' party.

Now she was taller, lankier, missing her two front teeth— and still unable to leave anyone out when it came to writing the invitations to her party. And so I ended up with twenty guests taking turns sitting at my dining-room table, decorating white T-shirts with vibrantly colored paint that puffed up after it dried. In Hannah's circle, puffy-paint shirts were the hippest thing you could wear to the beach or the pool that summer. Really awesome—or "ausum!" as she wrote in a letter to her aunt.

All Hannah wanted for her birthday that year were pierced ears and a stuffed dog called a Pound Puppy. I took her to the mall to get her ears pierced, then spent two weeks dabbing her earlobes with alcohol and submersing them in hydrogen peroxide when they became infected.

By her birthday, the ears had improved enough for her to wear the new pearl earrings I had bought for her, and my sisters gave her enough earrings to fill her brand-new earring tree.

I'd also bought her a Pound Puppy and a Pound Puppy newborn. When she received two more newborns from her friends, Hannah was ecstatic—now she had a cuddly litter to sleep with every night.

Three weeks later, newspaper articles would describe how Hannah, as the fifth child and first girl to testify against Kelly Michaels, was clutching one of her beloved Pound Puppies as she described to the court how her former teacher had penetrated her with tableware and forced her to engage in the nude pile-up game.

C H A P T E R

■ ■ ■ ■ ■ ■ ■ ■ ■ ■

12

At seven o'clock on a Monday morning, the muggy, pollution-clogged air over the George Washington Bridge foretold another uncomfortable June day. Already the traffic on the Manhattan-bound side of the bridge was sluggish. Impatient motorists—no doubt as frustrated as I that even rising at dawn is no guarantee of a smooth commute into the city—seemed more obnoxious than usual as they zigzagged from lane to lane in order to beat out neighboring vehicles by a single car length.

I am at my very worst in stalled traffic. Jim can calmly read the newspaper or organize the contents of his briefcase, but I quickly disintegrate into a near-frantic state. The immobility is what drives me into a frenzy; I just *have* to know what's causing the delay and how long the wait will be. I've been known to drive in the bus lanes, on the shoulder, even over a concrete curb just to escape a traffic standstill.

On this particular Monday, I'd gotten up early for my annual checkup with the gynecologist/obstetrician who delivered all four of my children. His office is on the Upper

East Side of Manhattan, and I had requested his first appointment so I could drive in early and beat the traffic.

Now my Toyota Corolla was inching along at five miles an hour, sandwiched between two smoke-belching trucks in near-darkness on the lower bridge span. I was trying to keep calm by punching and repunching all the buttons on the AM/FM radio. The news was the same on every station: the trial of twenty-four-year-old accused child molester Kelly Michaels would begin that day in superior court in Newark.

I'd known today was the day, of course. I hadn't slept well in weeks, and my stomach was acting up again to the point where I bought the economy-sized jars of Rolaids and Tums. But in the predawn haze of getting up earlier than usual and rushing out of the house that morning, I'd actually forgotten for a couple of hours that the trial was finally about to start. So when I heard it on the news, it was almost as though I was any other commuter, listening but not really reacting, just wanting to get off the bridge once and for all.

But by the time I was fully awake and cruising down the Henry Hudson Parkway beside the river, it had penetrated. Just as there is no escaping a car-choked highway, so there was no escaping the trial. It would dominate our lives for almost a year. Predictions were for a three- to six-month trial. No one dreamed it would actually last for more than ten months, making it the longest criminal trial ever in Essex County.

That morning I surprised myself. For once, I wasn't crying. I was saddened that we all had to go through such an ordeal, and nervous about our part in it. But I was also resigned. We had taken it this far and we would follow it through to the end.

Back in the office hours later, I kept thinking about the trial, wondering how the opening statements were going. One of the benefits of working on a newspaper is having a VDT screen at your desk on which you can call up any of the hundreds of stories filed by the wire services. Both the Associated Press and United Press International file their stories early and keep updating them throughout the day. By early afternoon, I could read the first Wee Care articles.

The nearest television to my desk is in the sports department. When I heard Kelly's name on the five o'clock news, I practically ran over to the TV. She looked so different from the last time I'd seen her. She had exchanged her hardened, casual boyishness for a softer, more feminine look. The formerly close-cropped hair was longer and styled in a soft perm, she wore makeup, and her summery white dress had a matching white jacket.

She could have been an office worker but for the look of defiance on her features as she strode into the courthouse. Flanked by her family and uniformed guards, she kept her eyes straight ahead. My chest tightened, and I was so glad Hannah and the other children would not have to see her in court. If it was this difficult for me to watch her on TV, how would it have felt for the children to see her in person?

Sara and Glenn had decided to put the children and their parents on the stand first, figuring all the youngsters would be finished by the fall in time for school. But before the children, there were opening statements from the defense attorneys and prosecutors. This was their time to acquaint the jury—six men and nine women, including the three alternates—with the case. Sara outlined the chronology of events leading up to the indictments—how Joshua Peterson had been taken to the doctor by his mother for a rash, how when the nurse took the child's temperature rectally, he said, "That's what my teacher does to me. Her takes my temperature."

Joshua subsequently told his mother that he and two other boys had been "touched by Kelly," Sara told the jury. She then carefully explained the precautions taken by investigators to avoid contaminating the accounts given her by the children.

Glenn Goldberg advised the jurors: "Listen to the children. You will not want to believe what happened to these children. But the end result, unfortunately, is that it happened." He talked about how the former drama student had "created a nightmare" in which she was both producer and director, telling the children "what to do, when to do it, and how to do it." "She choreographed these weird activities," Glenn said. "She was also the star of her own production. And of course she had a captive audience."

Defense attorney Harvey Meltzer said the charges against Kelly arose out of a "witch-hunt type mentality" fueled by hysterical parents and overzealous prosecutors. The entire case, he suggested, rested on a statement made two years earlier by one child to a pediatrician's nurse. Meltzer insisted that the charges were literally "incredible." "And they're too incredible to have happened," he said. "The children were told what happened to them." "Their accounts are not calculated lies," Meltzer went on, but false notions planted by their parents, "like the tooth fairy or Santa Claus."

Anna Peterson, Joshua's mother, was the first parent to testify, and I wondered if she felt as apprehensive as I did about being on the witness stand. I've always dreaded having to speak in front of a group of people, preferring instead the solitude writing offers as a way to communicate. And the idea of describing for a packed courtroom the nightmare we had lived for the past two years terrified me. I wanted the jury to believe me and yet I wondered if they would find it all just too "incredible," as the defense had said.

I still didn't really believe I was actually going to be a witness. When my first daughter was still an infant, I used to look at mothers whose children were older and feel almost envious that they had so many experiences that I didn't. Much as I loved wheeling my baby in her carriage to the park and watching her lie on her back and study the shifting patterns of sunlight that filtered through the leaves on the trees overhead, I couldn't wait until she could climb up the slide, ride a tricycle, play hopscotch.

Swimming lessons, birthday parties, school, trips to buy shoes, haircuts—there were so many experiences I longed for. But in all the time I dreamed and planned for the future, I never once imagined that I would one day testify at the trial of the woman accused of molesting my second child. It was completely out of the realm of my imagination that anything as bizarre and terrible as this could ever happen.

I'm sure it was the same for Anna Peterson. But she got up there and told her story with conviction. Something peculiar had happened in April 1985, the jury learned. Joshua was being tested one day for kindergarten readiness at a local school. All was going well until he was asked to draw the body parts—arms, legs, elbows, that sort of thing. Suddenly, he went wild. He scribbled viciously on the pad, applying so much pressure to his crayons he practically ripped the paper. Then he refused to continue the test. At the time, Anna had no idea what was wrong.

The very next day, the child disclosed to his pediatrician's nurse that Kelly had taken his temperature rectally. Anna testified that her son told her that Kelly "sticks something sharp like the prong of a fork or a sharp fingernail down my penis."

"I said, 'That must hurt,' " Anna said. "And he said, 'Hurt? I was screaming.' "

Anna also said Joshua told her that Kelly had inserted Legos, a plastic building toy, into the rectums of two of his classmates. She told the jury that her son told her, "Her [Kelly] tries to eat my penis." And he told his mother that Kelly once had locked him in a closet.

"I was unnerved," Anna told the jury. "It was unnerving but I knew that it was my job to just listen and to be a quiet listener."

Little blonde-haired Joshua Peterson, looking very grown-up in a suit, became the first Wee Care child to testify against his former teacher. His father, also in a suit and looking sober, sat beside his son in Judge Harth's chambers. Presumably to put the child more at ease, Meltzer had exchanged his business suit for jeans and a plaid shirt.

At first, Joshua appeared cheerful and confident as he colored with crayons and answered Glenn's questions about truth, God, and baseball. But the first time Wee Care was mentioned, he grew sullen. He put his head on the table, looked away, and asked to go to the bathroom. Questioned by Glenn about the nap period at Wee Care, Joshua told him, "One time Kelly took my temperature."

"How did she take your temperature?" Glenn asked.

"She pulled down the pants," Joshua answered.

"Where did she put the thermometer?"

"Bum!" he shouted, later standing and pointing to his behind. Joshua also said he saw two other children have their temperatures taken by Kelly in the same manner.

But as the questioning proceeded, Joshua grew agitated and jittery, hiding under the table and insisting that the camera be shut off. At one point he threw a crayon at Meltzer. And when questioned by the defense attorney, the child said that Kelly was "a nerd . . . 'cause she's not nice."

He gamely resisted the defense attorney's repeated attempts to suggest that he had been coached on what to say.

"Uh-uh, you can't trick me," Joshua said at one point. "My mom said you were going to try to trick me."

During his testimony Joshua wasn't especially graphic, although he said exactly what Sara and Glenn had expected him to—that Kelly had taken his temperature in the rectum. But Eddie Fernandez and Brian DeLuca, who were older than Joshua and so better able to verbalize what had happened at Wee Care, provided such gripping, chilling testimony that some jurors cried. As the spectators, press, and jurors sat in stunned silence watching the color television monitors, Brian DeLuca said Kelly had made the children take off their clothes in the music room and pile on top of each other. He drew a picture of a bloody tampon, and showed how Kelly had held it—between thumb and forefinger.

When Harvey Meltzer asked him to draw the tampon, Brian carefully began outlining a little oval on his pad. Then Meltzer asked the child if that was the right size, or if it had been bigger. When Brian told him it had been bigger, Meltzer asked him to draw it the size it had been. So Brian drew the actual size of a tampon.

"Was it full of blood or just a little blood?" Meltzer asked.

"Full of blood," Brian said, and carefully finished coloring a bloody tampon, string and all.

He demonstrated with dolls how his teacher had inserted wooden spoons and other kitchen utensils into his rectum, and he shocked the courtroom when he described how Kelly had forced him to have oral sex with her.

"I kissed her vagina," he reported, his soft voice tinged with shame.

Asked how that felt, Brian paused for a minute. The camera came in close on his face, and it was obvious to all watching that he was trying to think how best to describe the feeling. Finally he said, simply, "Weird."

"Why?"

"Because I never did it before." The words came out slowly, and it sounded almost like a question, as though he was unsure what made it feel weird. Brian also said Kelly had sucked his penis, but when asked how that felt, it was as if the memory was so terrible he couldn't put it into words.

"I don't know," he sighed wearily.

Eddie Fernandez corroborated what Brian had said. He had been forced to withdraw and then reinsert a tampon in Kelly's vagina. He said Kelly had gone to the bathroom in front of him, and that he had been forced to perform sex acts on other children.

Glenn asked Eddie why he hadn't ever told his mother.

"Kelly told us not to talk about it," the child replied. "She said if you told your mom, she would punch you." As he spoke, he made a fist with one hand and slapped it against his other hand.

Our part in the trial was coming up soon. Like the other parents who testified, I had combed through my notes and my memory to prepare a behavior chart showing my daughter's predisclosure and post-disclosure symptoms: the aversion to naptime. The refusal to eat peanut butter. The acting out. The depression. The aggressive behavior. Each symptom would be noted on a month-by-month chart for the jury.

Sara came over to our house several times, always late in the evening so that my kids would be asleep and we could talk without interruption. Even by 11 P.M. the air was still close and sticky in our un-air-conditioned house, and we drank gallons of iced tea. Sometimes we just sat around talking after we finished discussing the trial. Sara was easy to be with, and never seemed too busy to spend time with a parent who needed reassurance or encouragement. She never talked down to us, and I liked her genuine concern for our children. Her inexhaustible energy supply amazed me—she devoted twelve or fifteen hours a day to the case without complaining.

On evenings when Sara was at our house, Jim disappeared upstairs to read. He was silent on the subject of Hannah's testifying, but I sensed that he disapproved. He never read the articles about Wee Care in the newspaper, never watched any broadcasts about it. And if I broached the subject to him, he smoothly moved on to another topic.

He was not interested in attending any parents' meetings, nor did he want to go down to court with me. After a while, I stopped asking him to. I didn't want to make him angrier at me than he already was, and was grateful that he didn't openly criticize me for my interest in the case.

Sara had said she didn't need Jim to be a witness, but then changed her mind. It was Jim who had showed our daughter the class picture after her interview two years earlier with Lou Fonolleras when Hannah had pointed to every child in the photograph.

Since I wasn't there for this conversation, I couldn't testify to it. Sara felt it was important for the jury to know about it, and she promised Jim that if he testified he wouldn't be on the stand very long, perhaps ten minutes. To my surprise, he agreed to testify.

And so Sara told us the schedule for our family: Hannah would testify first, followed by Jim, then me. My daughter's testimony was only expected to take about an hour; the defense attorneys did not cross-examine the children much longer. Then I would go on the stand for my "direct," which is when the prosecutors question one of their witnesses. Probably I would need to return a second day for my "cross," when Meltzer and Clark would question me.

Hannah was scheduled to testify on Tuesday, July 14, so Glenn and Sara came over the night before for a visit. Hannah had never met Glenn before, and it was important that she feel comfortable with him. He had brought along his magic tricks, which delighted all four of the children for a while. Then Glenn and Sara wanted to talk to Hannah alone.

Caroline went upstairs to read, and I took Ellen and Robert outside. It was a sweltering, unbearably humid night, and I sat on the front lawn watching the two little ones chase fireflies. Pretty soon it was so dark I couldn't see them at all, but could only hear their delighted shrieks whenever they clapped the lid of an empty mayonnaise jar over one of the doomed insects.

The only lights came from the gas street lamps and the beams of the headlights on the few cars that passed in front of our house. It felt good to stretch my legs out in the cool grass and listen to the sounds of children and crickets. I wondered what they were talking about inside. Glenn and Sara appeared so confident that Hannah would be a good witness. I hoped she wouldn't disappoint them. It was odd, to be hoping for this the way you hope your child does well at a sport, or in school.

For Hannah's sake, I just wanted it to be over. She'd known for months the trial was coming, and she seemed small and sad to me that summer. It didn't seem fair that she should have to unearth so many gruesome memories just when it seemed like they were starting to fade. I only hoped that the experience of testifying wouldn't be frightening for her. I couldn't remember having to do anything scarier than go to the dentist when I was seven years old.

One of the worst parts about it was that I wouldn't be in the room with Hannah while she testified. At least if I could sit with her, hold her hand, and offer encouragement, I would feel as if I was doing something to decrease her anxiety. But all of us knew that Hannah hated talking to me about her Wee Care experiences. It was unlikely that she would have been a good witness with me in the room. Also, as a witness myself, I was sequestered (for the protection of the defendant) until after I had testified. So I would have to wait for Hannah outside, not knowing what she was saying or thinking. I felt as if I was deserting my child, whom I had promised to protect.

As Sara and Glenn were leaving that night, I asked Sara what Hannah should wear the next day.

"A dress," Sara advised. "She's going to court, and it's an important day."

So the next morning, Hannah put on her favorite dress— a short-sleeved, pastel-striped knit—and I swept her long, light brown hair up into a high ponytail. She insisted on wearing her gold heart-shaped locket, too, and packing a bagful of stuffed animals and coloring books. Jim helped her load everything into the car and Maria came down to say good-bye.

Although she didn't discuss it with Hannah, Maria followed the Wee Care case closely in the papers and on TV, and her broad Jamaican face, normally so serene, grew dark whenever she and I talked about it. Lips tight and eyes flashing, Maria would always begin muttering about what happened to child molesters in Jamaica. I couldn't understand everything she described in her heavy accent, but it was clear that in her country they were dealt with swiftly, severely, and unhampered by any court of law.

Now Maria was too overcome to speak. She broke down, sank on to one of the stairs, and began sobbing in earnest. The only other time I had seen her cry openly was the day a year earlier when I left to visit Jana in Michigan for two weeks.

She feels this is somehow her fault, I thought in amazement, just as she blamed herself for my not getting better from mono last summer. I sat down awkwardly beside her and hugged her. It's going to be okay, I told her. Hannah will do just fine. She finally wiped her face and went back to Robert and his Cheerios.

Riding down to Newark that steamy July morning, I felt apprehensive, as though I was about to take a tough examination in school or undergo some painful medical procedure. Sara had instructed us to meet her in the courthouse basement, not to come through the lobby where we might run into Kelly and the hordes of reporters and TV camera crews that gathered there each morning.

She and George McGrath, a detective in the prosecutor's office, met us in the basement. We were quiet in the crowded elevator, and when we got there, George and Sara took Hannah to Judge Harth's chambers.

Jim and I waited in the judge's library during Hannah's testimony. Susan Esquilin sat by her side as she testified. I paced back and forth, too nervous to edit the article I'd tucked into my briefcase. Sara and Glenn asked Hannah questions for about half an hour and then there was a lunch break.

My friend Kate had taken the day off from *Newsweek* to come to court, and she joined us in Sara's crowded office for sandwiches. Hannah ate part of a bagel with cream cheese, but she was worked up and hyper, and spent the hour running around. After lunch, Meltzer questioned her for about forty-five minutes.

My sister Kathleen and the other parents weren't there because as witnesses they were sequestered until after they testified. But my sister Nina and my sister-in-law Bernadette (Mark's wife) were in the courtroom to hear Hannah's testimony. Both told me later that they, and many other people who watched my daughter on the TV monitors, were crying.

I watched the videotape of Hannah's testimony four months later, sitting in Sara's office one morning. Spellbound, I couldn't take my eyes off the TV screen long enough to take notes in my steno pad. And I had never been so proud of my daughter.

She was a spunky little witness who won the spectators' hearts with her wide-eyed innocence, her candid demeanor, her childlike vulnerability. She clutched her Pound Puppy newborn, whom she told the judge she had named Trixie. When Glenn asked Hannah whether she knew what Meltzer's job was, she said frankly, "To make the jury think that Kelly didn't do anything." When he asked her what knives were for, she said to cut with. Forks? To eat with, she told him. Asked what she used spoons for, she thought for a minute and then giggled, "To slurp."

Meltzer asked Hannah if Glenn and Sara had come to our house the night before, and then wanted to know what they talked about. He probably hoped she'd tell him that the prosecutors told her what to say. But Hannah answered simply, "We talked about lies and the truth."

At one point, she described how Kelly had made her poke her cousin Emily.

"Did you poke her?" Meltzer asked.

"Yes," Hannah answered.

"Did you hit her hard or hit her soft?"

"I poked her, not hit."

"Oh, what did you poke her with, your finger or something else?"

220

"My finger," said Hannah.

When asked where she poked Emily, Hannah said she didn't remember. Meltzer asked her if it had been on the nose, and she said no.

"Is it that you don't remember, or are you bashful about telling us?"

"I don't remember," Hannah said. It was an answer she often gave when she didn't want to say what really had happened.

My daughter discussed the pile-up game, and demonstrated with dolls how the children had piled on top of each other. She said Kelly had stuck a knife, a fork, a spoon and her finger into her "private spot."

"How did it feel?" she was asked.

"Yucky," Hannah replied. Asked to show where Kelly had stuck her fingers, Hannah climbed on a chair and indicated her rectum and vagina. It was clearly embarrassing for her.

When Meltzer began to question her about getting poked in the vagina with a knife, her eyes had that flat look again. She looked so young and yet the look of intractable sadness on her small face made her appear older than seven.

"Okay, when Kelly put the knife into your vagina, did it hurt?" the defense attorney asked her.

"Yes."

"A lot?"

"Yes."

"Did you scream?"

"No."

"How come?"

"I don't know."

"Did you jump?"

"No."

"Did you say ouch?"

"I don't know."

Meltzer was not abusive with my daughter, but I lost any

221

respect I had had for him when he next tried to trick her. It was a sleazy thing to do, and ultimately didn't help the defense's case, because Hannah didn't fall for it.

Meltzer had a copy of the pretrial report that Eileen Treacy had prepared on Hannah. The report detailed a conversation between Hannah and Eileen about our family's pets—finches named Tweetie and Sweetie, and fish.

That day in court, Meltzer began to question Hannah about these pets as if they had discussed them before.

"You used to have two fishes called Sweetie and Tweetie, didn't you?" he asked her.

"No, birds," Hannah said.

"Birds? You're kidding," Meltzer said. "I figured that was a funny name. What about . . . you have fish, though, don't you?"

"Yes," Hannah said.

"Do you remember telling me about the black mollies and catfish and zebra fish?" Meltzer asked.

"Yeah, and the catfish."

"Yeah. Yes. Did you ever speak to me?"

"Yes."

"Besides today? Remember about a year ago we spoke?"

But to this Hannah answered no quite firmly. It was obvious that she would not let herself be led by him.

At the recess, Sara was angry at the impression left with the jury by this last exchange between Meltzer and Hannah: that she had forgotten an event Meltzer clearly implied had occurred just a year earlier. How then, was his implication, could Hannah really remember what happened at Wee Care more than two years earlier?

Meltzer had never met Hannah before and was pretending he had. He knew from Eileen Treacy's report that she had an aquarium of fish at home. Meltzer hoped to "lead" Hannah, to show that she was suggestible by having her agree with him that they had met before. But my daughter didn't fall for his lead.

222

When court recessed, Sara took the matter up with Judge Harth. She felt the questions were objectionable and unfair, and asked that the jury be told that Hannah had never seen Harvey Meltzer.

When court reconvened, Harth had the clerk read back the conversation about the birds and fish to the jury. He then instructed the jury that Hannah had never met Meltzer before, that there had been no conversation between them a year earlier.

I was furious when I learned what Meltzer had tried to do, but proud of Hannah for not letting herself be led by him. I hugged my daughter and told her how proud of her I was and how brave she had been.

And then it was Jim's turn to speak publicly for the first time about what had happened to his daughter. In his tie and sports jacket, he looked composed and sober that day. Only I noticed that morning that his face, normally so deeply tanned from sailboarding and hours of yard work, was strangely pale.

He'd been my boyfriend for three years before we got married fifteen years ago, so I've known him almost half my life. I know his habits better than anyone, right down to which sections of the Sunday *New York Times* he reads and how he likes his eggs. But I would never have predicted that, after avoiding the subject of Wee Care for two years, he would be overcome with emotion and break down twice on the witness stand.

Glenn Goldberg began asking Jim about his conversation with Hannah on June 10, 1985, in which she had pointed out all the children in her class picture as Kelly's victims.

"And where were you when you talked to Hannah about that?" Glenn asked.

"In the living room of our home," replied Jim.

"What was your conversation with Hannah?"

"We had just finished dinner," my husband said. "And I asked her if—I had a few minutes alone, inadvertently, although I must say I tried to arrange that I would have a few minutes with her—I asked her if she had been involved."

Jim stopped talking, took off his glasses, and wiped tears from his eyes.

"Why don't you just take a deep breath?" Judge Harth said gently.

"It is very difficult to talk about," Jim replied, and then he recovered and was able to answer questions. But several minutes later, his emotions got the better of him again when Glenn showed him Hannah's Wee Care picture and asked him to explain what he and Hannah had talked about that night.

"I asked her if there were others involved in some of the games that her teacher, Kelly, had played that some of the other children had discussed with their parents," Jim said.

"And what was the response?" Glenn asked.

But Jim was so choked up he couldn't speak, and the judge told the jury to take a break. Then, the normally stern judge said to my husband, "Mr. Crowley, I certainly understand the situation, the stress and things like that. I don't know what might best help you, but sometimes I have observed, in difficult situations, witnesses taking very deep breaths. That might help."

Harth also offered to send a court officer for a soda or a glass of water. But Jim seemed fine by the time the jury returned to their seats. When Glenn asked what Hannah had said to him about her classmates' involvement, Jim told the court that Hannah had said that all the children were involved.

"So my question was, then, point to the ones who were involved," Jim said. "And she pointed one by one to all the children in the photograph."

Jim was only on the stand for a short time, and when court recessed, he took Hannah home because she was growing restless. I didn't have to tell him to stop on the way home and get her a treat of some kind; no doubt he would buy her an ice cream as well as a small trinket. The two of them were very close, even though they didn't gab for hours the way Hannah and I did.

I recalled that at one time Hannah had been bothered that they didn't converse more. She worried because she didn't talk to Jim as much as she did to me, and asked anxiously if I thought his feelings were hurt. I assured my daughter that her dad didn't mind and that he knew she loved him, and I knew that this was true. Jim isn't as gregarious as I am, and yet he and all our children have a stable, close relationship.

I knew just how Hannah felt, though. For me, conversations with my mother are effortless. Talk just flows between us naturally, and there's never a lack of things to say. It's been like this for as long as I can remember. With my father, whom I love as fiercely as my mother, I have to work a little harder.

When bad things happen to me, I tend to unload them on my mother rather than my father. More than once, he has picked up the phone when I've called and asked me how things are. "Fine," I say brightly, and I don't burst into a torrent of tears until he hands the phone over to my mother. Hannah is the same way: if she can't fall asleep at night, she comes in and finds an excuse to lure me out of our bedroom and into the hall so she can tearfully tell me what's bothering her. She wants to put up a brave front to her dad.

Now, as I watched the two of them walking away hand in hand down the dingy corridor, Jim carrying Hannah's bags of toys in one hand, I felt flooded with love for them both and remorse for being so angry and short-tempered toward Jim lately.

It seemed that, in those months, I was always angry with him when we were together, and yet, when we were apart, I felt tender toward him. In his absence, I would remember all the nice things he was constantly doing: shopping for me because he knows how slow sales clerks and long lines drive me to a frenzy . . . washing my car . . . fixing things—he knows that everything I touch has a tendency to break or disintegrate on contact, and he patiently, uncomplainingly, repairs them. Why, then, was I always so mean to him? Why didn't I try to understand and cope with his grief? For it was clear to me that he was as deeply affected and hurt by the whole mess as I was. He just showed it differently.

I wanted to tell him I was sorry for being so critical of him, but it was time for me to take the witness stand. And so I didn't say anything to him about it, then or later at home. I wasn't even able to deal with my own grief yet, and was not generous enough to reach out to my husband.

In court, looking out at a sea of faces, I concentrated on answering Sara's questions as completely as I could. I always talk too fast, in a rush of words, probably because when we were growing up there were so many of us we had to speak quickly just to get a word in edgewise. Now I tried to tell my story slowly, so the jury would understand everything, and I found it easier than I thought. From the looks on their faces, I felt as if they believed me. Every time I felt tearful I looked at Kelly, and the hatred and anger that welled up inside made it hard to cry.

When court was dismissed for the day at four o'clock, I walked out into the crowded corridor feeling completely exhausted. Nina and Kate were waiting, and Nina's eyes filled with tears as she hugged me. Someone told us to take the elevator to the basement to avoid the TV camera crews. When my sister lit up a cigarette outside, I felt like smoking for the first time since I had quit ten years earlier.

Outside, the sun had disappeared and the sky was an angry dark gray. Huge drops of rain pelted us suddenly as we ran across the parking lot to Nina's car, and by the time we drove home, the streets were flooded and the gutters swirled with dirty water.

I had never felt so exhausted in my life. When we got home I suggested we go out to dinner and leave Robert home with Maria. I told Hannah she could invite a friend to come with us to a Mexican restaurant. She jumped up and down and promptly said she wanted it to be Melissa Bethel. My daughter was very worked up, and ran about the house acting raucous and uncivilized. I decided to ignore it. After her day, she had a right to be rambunctious.

Later, I learned that the papers and television news broadcasts had described Hannah as "a wide-eyed seven-year-old" and her testimony as "dramatic" and "graphic." TV viewers were warned beforehand that the testimony might be disturbing for their children to hear.

A TV reporter said of Jim's testimony, "At one point, the father was so overwhelmed the jury was led from the room as he regained his composure. His breakdown made the defendant cry, too."

The next morning I kissed the kids good-bye as usual and headed down to Newark, alone this time, for another day of court. In his cross-examination of me, Meltzer seemed to be trying to pin Hannah's behavioral changes during the period of abuse on having a new baby at home. He also tried to portray me as a very busy working mother who was so wrapped up in her career she didn't have time for her children.

The only time I started to cry was when he asked why I had initiated therapy for Hannah in the fall of 1985.

"Just seeing her that depressed," I said. "You know, just having her call me up at work and feeling so helpless. Not being able to do anything for her—" I felt so choked up suddenly that I couldn't continue, so the jury was told to take its midmorning break. By the time court reconvened, I was back in control.

Later, Meltzer asked me if my daughter was one of the plaintiffs in the civil action against Kelly and the day-care center.

It occurred to me that he was probably trying to portray me as a money-hungry opportunist, but I told him precisely why we had decided to sue the school, and when we had made our decision. "It wasn't right away," I told him. "I guess it was probably that fall after I had done some reading. And I had talked to my mother a few times and realized from my conversations with Susan that Hannah as a teenager would likely have some problems.

"That she might, you know—it could go one of two ways. She could be promiscuous. She could be frigid. We just won't know till she reaches adolescence. I looked up in my own child-care books and I saw that—I read that children who are sexually abused bear the scars for life. And, at first, you know, I just didn't want to get into it [a lawsuit], but then I thought if she is really fifteen or sixteen and is going to have big medical bills, I would like to have a way to cover it."

I told the court that my husband and I had spoken to a lawyer, and that we had filed a civil suit against Kelly and against Wee Care. And that pretty much wrapped up my cross-examination.

On what is called "redirect," Sara asked me how much time I spent with my children. She obviously didn't want the jury to leave with the impression that I was so busy I never saw my kids. I said I felt lucky to have a housekeeper who did the laundry and cleaning, because it gave me more time with my children than many mothers have. And I explained that although I work full-time, I spend all my evenings and weekends with my kids. My husband and I have very little social life outside the family, I said, and any socializing we do is usually with friends who don't mind if we bring the children along. It's always been this way for us, and I wouldn't have it any other way. I hoped the jury understood this. It was so hard to know what they were thinking.

◼

Soon after my testimony was finished, we took our vacation at the Jersey shore at a rented condominium that was near the ocean and had a pool as well. The weather cooperated, and we had hot, sunny weather every day. Hannah and her sisters spent hours floating on inner tubes in the condo's pool and perfecting their belly flops. We walked along the boardwalk, went on the rides, saw *Snow White,* and ate lobster at an outdoor restaurant. Hannah looked tanned and less strained, and the sun left golden streaks in her long hair.

Jim relaxed, too, and often took the girls to the beach or looking for shells in the afternoon while Robert napped and I read in the air-conditioned comfort of the condominium. It felt so good to get away from the trial, if only for a week. And other parents still faced the ordeal we had just been through.

My niece Emily testified a couple of weeks after Hannah. She had asked if her grandma could be with her. My mother had already testified about the behavioral changes she had seen in Hannah. But since she would not be testifying about Emily, the court allowed her to sit in the judge's chambers while Emily testified.

Emily was asked the same kinds of questions as the other young witnesses, to make sure that she was qualified to testify—if she knew the difference between the truth and a lie, if she would tell a lie to make her mother or Sara or her friends happy, if she knew that she was in court to tell the truth.

Emily seemed terribly shy, and she kept looking down as she spoke. Her soft voice could hardly be heard at times, and often she shook her head or nodded instead of saying yes or no. But she basically corroborated what others before her had said.

"Would you like to have Kelly for a teacher again?" Sara asked her at one point, and Emily said no. Why not? "Because she hurts kids."

"What did she hurt kids with?"

"Knives. Spoons. Forks."

Later she demonstrated on a doll how Kelly had penetrated her vagina with a knife, and she pointed to her backside when asked where Kelly had hurt her with a fork. After she talked about how Kelly once made her cousin Hannah pinch her, Sara observed that Emily had a scratch on her face and asked if Kelly had put it there.

"No," Emily said.

"Yes, she did," said Sara.

"No, she didn't."

"Yes, she did."

"No, she didn't." Then Meltzer objected, saying, "I believe that this prosecutor is attempting to place before the tribunal something that is not a true statement."

But Judge Harth allowed it. "What she is doing . . . is seeing if the child is led by her suggestibility," he said. "Accordingly, I find it perfectly proper."

Like the other children, Emily pretty much repeated what she had told investigators and the grand jury two years earlier. There were times when some of the young witnesses contradicted themselves or said they couldn't remember. But it was amazing how much the children did remember, and how articulate they were. The long delay in the start of the trial had not worked to Kelly's advantage after all. In fact, her victims made much better witnesses at age six or seven than at age four or five because they were more verbal, more mature. And they had not forgotten what she did to them.

They were a brave group, and sometimes they did such surprising things in court they even caught the prosecutors off guard.

When Oliver Madison's testimony began, he was doodling on a pad of paper and waving at the camera that was broadcasting his testimony into the courtroom. The boy described himself as one of Kelly's "very special helpers," and said one of his duties was to clean urine and feces off the floor. "And when the kids ran away, we had to bring the kids back to Kelly," he said. He used dolls to demonstrate how Kelly had touched him and the other children and how he had touched her. Asked why he touched his teacher sexually, Oliver said, "Because she wanted us to."

He told the court his classmates would "tiptoe" between

the music room and the gymnasium because "Kelly didn't want the other teachers to know where we were going." And he said that Kelly warned him, "Don't tell your mother or I'll hurt your mother and your grandparents."

When Glenn asked him how Kelly sounded when she said this, the child said, "She sounded mad, angry, frustrated."

"How did you feel when she said it?"

"Scared," Oliver said.

He grew restless, frequently squirming in his chair or walking around a table. Once he threw a small football to the judge. Then, when the attorneys for the opposing sides were embroiled in a legal argument, he wrote a note and handed it to a startled Judge Harth. Written in block letters, the note read, "I'm going to get Kelly for hurting my friends. Kelly is a bad person."

Defense attorney Bob Clark later asked Oliver who had made him write the note.

"Nobody," Oliver said. "She hurt my friends. I'm going to get her for that."

Oliver was on the stand for a day and a half, longer than most of the children, and Clark seemed bent on antagonizing the little boy. Once, Clark said to him, "Why don't you look at me when I ask you a question."

Oliver looked at him and said, "Why should I have to?"

After court, Oliver seemed to need to let off steam. "After he finished testifying was when he went totally off," said his mother. "I mean, it was like he exploded. He just ran and ran. It took three court attendants to grab him and hold him. And then he ran down from the eighth floor to the basement. He and Sara and Glenn, they all ran. He felt good."

His mother took him for a drive before they went home so he could calm down, and she asked him, "Are you okay now?"

"I feel good," Oliver told her. "I said everything."

Although some youngsters seemed to feel vindicated after they went to court, others became depressed and fearful. Jodie Minetti, sitting on her first-grade teacher's lap, testified that Kelly had molested her with tableware. At one point she stood on a chair and demonstrated how she had been prodded and poked. Asked where she slept at night, Jodie said she slept with her mommy.

"When do you think you'll be able to go back to your own bed?"

"Tonight, because I won't have to think about Kelly anymore," said Jodie, a big smile on her face.

But three days after she testified, the little girl was in medical trouble.

"Jodie's blood level [it was related to the medication she took for seizures, which in turn were related to stress] shot up and we took her to the emergency room," Julie said. "She almost died. She had twenty seizures that July after testifying. She has a great fear of Kelly, that Kelly is going to come and get her."

Melissa Bethel became depressed again soon after her testimony in court. Her mother Sharon told Melissa's therapist about her daughter's intense separation anxiety, and the doctor kept giving her the same advice. "It was the typical psychologist's thing to say," recalls Sharon. "The doctor would say, you must explain to her beforehand that you need to go out and then firmly leave her with her father and turn around and walk out the door because she is reading your fear of leaving her."

The therapist stopped this advice the day Melissa decided she didn't want to stay at her office without her mother. For twenty minutes she screamed and cried, grabbed onto her mother's knees, and sobbed to the point where the therapist couldn't talk to Sharon or Melissa.

"After that experience," Sharon said, "the therapist didn't give me quite as many of those psychological platitudes about what you're supposed to be doing with your child."

Like Jodie and Melissa, Eddie Fernandez seemed depressed after testifying. Initially, he'd been very happy. "He felt great, so proud afterward," recalls his mother, Ana. "And he told me, 'Mommy, one of the things Kelly used to say to us was that when we grow up, she wanted us to do this to other children. But I know that is wrong and I never want to hurt any child.' "

But in the following weeks, Eddie became increasingly depressed, expressing a desire to die. "I wish a car would kill me," he said over and over. "I wish I was dead. I wish it never happened to me." He said to his mother: "I'm a bad boy. I'm so bad."

"No, you're not bad, you are a child," his mother told him.

One day she found him in the bathroom examining the contents of a box of tampons.

"I'm just curious," Eddie said. "I know this is what Kelly had, that she took it out with blood on it."

Unlike some of the children, who wanted nothing to do with the trial once their part in it was over, Eddie liked to follow it on television, and he asked Ana to let him know when it came on the news.

It seemed to be on the news nearly every night that summer and into the fall. Although nothing that followed could be as dramatic or as disturbing as the children's stories, many other witnesses were nearly as compelling. The case against Kelly Michaels was slowly building. And some of the testimony most damaging to the defendant came from two prison guards and from an inmate who had befriended Kelly while she was incarcerated.

C H A P T E R

■ ■ ■ ■ ■ ■ ■ ■ ■

13

By the end of the summer, the jury had heard from the children as well as their parents, psychologists, pediatricians, and teachers. Several grandparents, including my mother, also took the stand.

I was very worried about my mother. As a partner in a major law firm, she has a terribly demanding, high-pressure job anyway, and the trial placed even more stress on her. My mother is a beautiful woman, tall, dark-haired, and slim. She dresses elegantly in suits softened by silk blouses, brooches, and thin strands of pearls. She carries a monogrammed leather briefcase and wears tiny eyeglasses on a gold chain. Both were gifts from my father, who loves to shop and spoils her terribly with expensive jewelry and clothes.

Yet when she comes to our house from the office, she gets right down on the floor to play with my kids and doesn't seem to mind getting rumpled or smeared with baby food. She is equally comfortable being the master of ceremonies at a Bar Association dinner or having snowball fights with her grandchildren. My parents have been married for nearly forty years and are still so much in love. Daddy affectionately calls her the O.L. (for old lady)—and has done it for so long that when we call and he answers their phone, we often ask, "Is the O.L. there?"

Once, after Jim and I had been arguing, I asked my mother how it was that she and my father hardly ever seemed to fight. She smiled at me and said sweetly, "I guess it's because I make all the little decisions and he makes all the big decisions. And so far, we haven't come to any big decisions."

I couldn't tell if she was joking or not.

Next to each other, my parents love their children more than anyone and they are very close to each one of us. I'm sure no only child ever felt more cherished than my brothers and sisters and I. My parents have always been there for us, and different as they are, we love them equally.

My mother is the voice of reason and the first person we turn to in times of trouble. She is a terribly strong, incredibly smart woman who has weathered unbelievable crises and sadness in her lifetime. Her grandchildren bring her great joy, and it hurt me to see her involved in something no grandmother should be—a trial concerning sexual abuse of her granddaughters.

My mother was very concerned that Kelly would somehow escape conviction, and the stress was visible in the way she clenched and unclenched her fists, bit her lips, was short of breath. She seemed to be taking it harder than I was, and I found myself chiding her, telling her she had to calm down. Since the start of the trial, she'd been smoking a lot more. She looked drawn and tired, and was as obsessed as I was. We discussed it constantly on the phone late at night, after Jim and my father had gone to bed.

It hurt to see my father feeling so badly about it, too. He is a writer and an artist, a wonderfully gentle man who never loses his temper, would do anything for my mother or one of his children, and has a fabulously dry sense of humor. My father didn't discuss the trial with me very often. I think it was just too painful for him. But he kept abreast of it through the newspapers and was always helping us during those stressful months in ways he knew how —bringing over dinner, running errands, taking the kids for a ride.

All my brothers and sisters were interested in the trial, and though we had to be careful not to discuss it in front of any of the children, it was often a main topic of conversation at my parents' lakefront home that summer and fall. By the end of the trial, nearly all of my siblings had come to court. They were there for Hannah and Emily as much as for Kathleen and me, because they were unusually close to their nieces and still couldn't believe this had happened. It saddened me that they had to see this ugly side of child-rearing before they even had kids of their own.

◼

Sara and Glenn called a parents' meeting midsummer to update us on the trial. The mood was so different from what it had been at meetings during that first awful summer. Two years earlier, parents could barely hold back tears, and their anguish and anger were almost palpable. But at Traci MacKenna's house that hot July night in 1987, everyone seemed calmer.

Parents chatted among themselves, a couple of mothers had brought homemade cookies and brownies, and after the business was over and some people had left, the rest of us sat around and watched a videotape of the TV news coverage of the trial.

I saw the coverage of our testimony, with artists' sketches of Jim, Hannah, and our pediatrician. He had testified that Hannah's hymen had been open when he examined her in the summer of 1985. Seeing the broadcasts about Jim and Hannah brought a wave of fresh pain. I hated how the correspondents prefaced their coverage of Wee Care with that warning to parents. If it was that upsetting for other people's children to hear about, what had it been like for my own four-year-old to experience?

Still, sitting around and watching the news on tape that night wasn't all grim. By the end, we were actually giggling. We teased the prosecutors about how they looked on TV. Sara complained she was too fat. She jokingly told Glenn that since she appeared so much shorter, from now on he would have to kneel when they were interviewed together. We discussed Meltzer's creeping baldness. We talked about Kelly's two obese sisters, who often came to court with her and whom we had nicknamed Big and Brutal. Someone mentioned that Meltzer had named his pet dog after Kelly. Someone else said Kelly was planning to write a book about her ordeal, then wisecracked that she should name it Peanut Butter and Kelly. By the time the meeting broke up, I was practically in tears from laughing.

Maybe it was gallows humor, but it felt good to be sitting around with the people I had shared so much with, and to be laughing with them instead of crying. For that one night, letting down our hair with each other relieved some of the excruciating tension that had been building for weeks, even years.

None of the Wee Care parents had attended the trial up till then. As sequestered witnesses, we were not permitted to attend the trial until after we had testified, so that our testimony would not be "tainted" by hearing other witnesses. But there was another reason for staying away. There was a lot of soul-baring going on in that courtroom, and more than a few tears were shed. It was a private time, and we stayed away out of mutual respect for one another. By the fall, though, when the parents and children had finished testifying, many parents started going down to court.

The prosecution was still presenting its case. The defense would then have its turn, and we knew they were planning to trot out several expert witnesses—psychiatrists and psychologists who would say that Kelly couldn't have

237

done what she did because she didn't fit the profile of a child molester.

And then there was the million-dollar question: would Kelly herself take the stand? There was lots of speculation, but her lawyers didn't have to say yes or no until the last minute.

■

One brilliantly sunny morning in August, the jurors were bused to the sixty-one-year-old St. George's Church, where the Wee Care preschool had been housed. The prosecutors had requested the tour, and the defense did not oppose the motion. The school's layout was considered important because a key issue in the trial was whether or not Kelly had the opportunity to perform hundreds of acts of abuse unobserved.

The jurors, the judge, attorneys, reporters, and Kelly and her family spent about two hours touring classrooms, lavatories, offices, the choir room, and a gymnasium on several floors of the church building. One by one, they filed into a small, dark, musty furnace room in which some children said they had been locked. A plastic partition separating the block room from the art room was closed and the lights were turned out so the jury could observe "naptime" conditions.

Afterward, Sara told reporters the tour showed how many nooks and crannies there were for Kelly to abuse the children without being seen. Meltzer contended that noises could be heard by other teachers and that much of the school was too open and central for observers not to have seen what was going on. In court later that day, Judge Harth described the building as "somewhere between a complex, a maze, and a labyrinth."

News photographers weren't allowed into the building and the tour was closed to the public, too. By now the rooms formerly occupied by Wee Care had been vacant for nearly two years. We'd heard that church officials had even had the place exorcised. One television reporter told me that when she and her camera crew signed out each morning on their way to the courthouse, they no longer wrote "Kelly Michaels trial" in the log book. They wrote "Demon Seed" instead.

I had purposely avoided driving past St. George's because it would upset me to see the Gothic-looking place where my child had been tortured. But one summer evening, driving home from somewhere by myself, I made an impulsive detour and pulled into the church's parking lot. It was dusk, and I stood in the outdoor play area looking at the tire swings and climbing equipment. It seemed like half a lifetime ago that children used to shout and play here, and ride tricycles on the asphalt that was cordoned off from the rest of the parking lot.

It was spooky to stand there in the silence. The door to the school was locked, but I walked over and peered in the windows of the gymnasium. If I'd done this two years earlier, I wondered, would I have noticed anything unusual? For the hundredth time, I told myself that I had to put it behind me.

But that fall, I started attending the trial whenever I could. I liked to get to the office very early and work at top speed, not going out to lunch or letting myself be drawn into any of the informal gossip sessions always going on around the newsroom. Then I'd drive like a maniac to the courthouse, often getting there after the lunch break.

Among the prosecution witnesses to take the stand during those days were psychologist Susan Esquilin and Anne Felsten, a psychology student.

Susan told the jury she initially thought that the Wee Care parents were "exaggerating" in their descriptions of the children and the behavioral changes they exhibited in the winter and spring of 1985. But after meeting with thirteen of the victims, she changed her mind. She said: "When I saw the children, I saw the absolute terror of separating from their parents. I saw the high levels of anxiety. . . . I saw the panic at playing ordinary children's games. . . . I saw them as very unstable at that point . . . they were an extremely traumatized group."

Susan displayed some of the artwork that had been done by her Wee Care patients in the previous two years. The drawings, vivid and unsettling, corroborated much of what the children had said in their testimony.

In one of the group-therapy sessions, Susan had instructed the youngsters to draw a picture of "someone who does bad things." Half of them drew Kelly. One little girl used felt-tip markers to draw a distorted representation of her former teacher. In her picture, Kelly has no hands, a symbolic effort by the child to strip her tormentor of power over her, according to Susan. Another child had drawn Kelly with an appendage between her legs. The little boy who drew it told Susan, "Kelly touches my penis." Susan testified that a third child said of her drawing of Kelly, "Kelly gives us doody, she gives us sissy and peanut butter and jelly. Yuck!"

The psychologist showed the jury a picture by Eddie Fernandez. It was a rough rendering of Kelly, done in red crayon. Susan quoted Eddie as saying, "This is Kelly in the bathroom. She's happy. She's hurting children. But I don't like it." In still another picture, a little girl had drawn herself and another child with Kelly in the Wee Care gym. At Kelly's feet are feces and a yellow puddle of urine. The pictures said so much more than the children were able to verbalize.

Anne Felsten, the psychology student, testified next, and her testimony was also disturbing. She said that three-and-a-half-year-old Keith Parsons had attempted to assault her sexually in June 1985 when she'd sat in on an interview between him, a social worker, and a DYFS investigator. Miss Felsten, then a Rutgers University undergraduate, had been enlisted as an observer for the session. At one point, she told the jury, the other interviewers left the room and she was alone with the little boy.

"He was drawing pictures and looking over at me," Miss Felsten told the court. "He came at me suddenly. He put his hand down the front of my shirt very quickly."

Shocked, she asked Keith who else he touched "like that." With a knowing smile he told her, "You know who." Miss Felsten then played a guessing game with the child, running through a list of names, all of which he responded to negatively. But when she asked him if it was Kelly, he replied "Yes."

Repeatedly, she said, the boy told her, "Take your clothes off." When she told him that she couldn't, he tried to remove her belt and pull off her pants. Miss Felsten attempted to get the child to act out his aggression on a pair of anatomically correct dolls.

"He literally ripped their clothes off," she recalled in court. She demonstrated how he had held the female doll's legs apart. She said as he looked at the genital area, he said, "It's wet." The child licked the doll's genital area and also licked Miss Felsten through her clothing, she said. And when she again used a guessing game to learn from the child whether he had ever licked anyone else's genitals, he responded with a "yes" when Kelly's name was mentioned.

Under cross-examination, Miss Felsten said, "You have to realize that when this was going on, I felt like I was being raped by a three-and-a-half-year-old."

A couple of weeks after Anne Felsten testified, three women—none with any special interest in the case—took the stand to talk about Kelly's candid jailhouse musings. They included two prison guards and an inmate serving time for aggravated manslaughter. They provided stunning testimony that some courtroom observers called the "smoking gun" in the Kelly Michaels trial. It was certainly a turning point for doubting Thomases who until then still wondered if she could really have done such things to children.

The evidence these three women provided against Kelly was damning, and obviously upset the defendant very much. At times as they testified, Kelly shook her head from side to side and clasped her hands together tightly. She looked as if she was fighting back tears.

First, Essex County correctional officer Betty Sheffield told a rapt jury about a conversation she had witnessed among a group of inmates. It had taken place when Kelly was incarcerated in the Essex County Jail Annex in Caldwell two years earlier.

Ms. Sheffield said she heard Kelly telling the inmates that she had undressed in front of the Wee Care youngsters and that she didn't believe she had done anything wrong. Ms. Sheffield had asked Kelly what she meant. Mimicking Kelly, Ms. Sheffield put her hand on her hip and replied in an impudent tone, "I really feel that a person's sexual preferences are her own business." (Though it never came up in court, Kelly made no secret of the fact that she was gay. Ms. Sheffield didn't go into this.)

Ms. Sheffield explained that another guard had called her over to eavesdrop on Kelly, who was alone inside her locked cell and speaking with some prisoners standing just outside it. (Kelly was segregated from the other inmates to avoid harassment.)

Later, the other guard, Wanda Dean, testified she had overheard Kelly discussing the way "show-and-tell" was conducted in her class: "I heard her talking about, these are my eyes, these are for this. And the nose . . . the mouth. It sounded pretty normal. Then she mentioned breasts. That struck me as off guard to be telling a child," Ms. Dean said.

Outside the courtroom, Ms. Sheffield told reporters she heard Kelly say she told the children that breasts "are for feeling."

Ms. Dean testified that she told the other inmates to move away from Kelly's cell, and then warned the defendant it was unwise for her to discuss her case with them. "She said to me she didn't think what she did was wrong, and that she didn't hurt them [the children] the way they said that she did," Ms. Dean testified.

242

A couple of weeks later, at the beginning of December, the jury heard from Charlene Munn, a twenty-three-year-old inmate who said she had befriended Kelly when the two were incarcerated at the county jail. During a conversation they had about the nude pile-up games, Ms. Munn said she asked Kelly, "Did you really harm those kids the way they said you did?"

And Kelly said, "Not all of them," according to Ms. Munn. Ms. Munn also testified that Kelly had admitted spanking the children.

Charlene Munn's testimony devastated Kelly, who broke down and cried. Normally she appeared so cool and arrogant, sitting with her two lawyers beside her and her family directly behind her. She was constantly writing, filling up notebook after notebook with God-knows-what. But that chilly fall day, she lost her composure. And I'm sure the sight of a weeping client made Meltzer feel more waspish than usual. On the way out of the courtroom that day, as he passed the sizable crush of parents clustered around the door, he looked Kathleen right in the eye and said nastily, "Just wait'll it's over, sweetheart. Then you'll see."

Kathleen was furious. Glenn and Sara heard what had happened and the next court day, Glenn put the entire incident on the record before Judge Harth. Glenn didn't identify my sister by name but just said Meltzer had made the comment to one of the parents. When the judge asked Meltzer to explain, the defense attorney got up and said one of the parents had made "a gesture" toward his client. Then Meltzer told Harth the parents must have "overheard a conversation" he was having with his client on the way out of the courtroom.

But the upshot of it all was that the prosecution witnesses were assigned a room for their own use at the courthouse. Until then, the Michaels family enjoyed the use of a little room off the main corridor of the eighth floor, where they gathered daily for breaks and lunch. It constantly amused me to see the boxes of candy bars and soft drinks that they carted in there each day along with their big blue lunchbox. Kelly's father was a chain smoker, and he would barely be out of the courtroom before lighting up.

The victims' parents, though, had to make do with the hallway or the drab, cheerless cafeteria for the lunch hour and the frequent, often lengthy recesses. A couple of parents had asked Sara about getting a parents' room. So far, she had done nothing about it because she didn't want it to seem as though we parents had special privileges. After the incident between Meltzer and my sister, I think Sara probably figured the less the defense attorney and the parents saw of each other, the better.

The bureaucratic wheels were set in motion, and within a couple of days, the Michaels family was politely asked to vacate their room. It was given over to us, and it came to be known, simply, as the parents' room, although reporters and friends came in, too. Some parents chipped in and bought a dorm-sized refrigerator that was always stocked with orange juice and yogurt, and someone else brought in an electric coffeepot. On one wall, someone had hung a Pin-the-Tail-on-the-Donkey poster from a children's birthday kit. Taped to another wall were the latest newspaper clippings about the trial.

It was a bare, harshly lit room with folding chairs and two rickety tables, but it was a wonderful sanctuary to retreat to when the courtroom scenario and the sight of the Michaels family became too much. Every morning, the table would be loaded with bagels, doughnuts, and fruit that parents took turns bringing in. Everybody complained they were gaining weight, but the daily volume of carbohydrates never diminished, and I never heard any protests about that. Worrying keeps me thin, but I did eat more bagels that year than ever before or since. I think if I hadn't munched on bagels I would have started to smoke again.

By the beginning of December the prosecution wrapped up its case, which had taken five and a half months to present. The last of the state's ninety-six witnesses was psychologist Eileen Treacy. Her chief role was to explain the patterns of behavior exhibited by victims of child sexual abuse, and to use that model, known as "child sexual abuse syndrome," to assess each of the twenty youngsters in the case. This is a process called "validation," Eileen testified, a task she has performed hundreds of times as a witness in other sex-abuse cases. Eileen stressed to the jury that she never says outright that abuse occurred—she only testifies whether the children's statements and behavior are "consistent with a child who has been sexually abused."

She outlined five phases through which child sexual abuse generally proceeds. There is engagement, in which the abuser woos the child and wins his or her trust, often through bribes and games that the child likes. Next comes sexual interaction, in which explicit acts, including sexual assaults, occur. The secrecy phase overlaps with the previous phase and entails threats made to the child to ensure silence. Then there is disclosure, sometimes deliberate but more often accidental. In the suppression phase, the child often avoids or denies the subject. Eileen uses a checklist of behavioral symptoms to assess whether a child has passed through those phases and she requires evidence of at least four of the five phases.

Eileen testified that she also analyzes other stresses that might have caused the child's behavioral changes. The list of symptoms ranges from changes in a child's eating and sleeping patterns to bed-wetting and thumb-sucking. The list also includes sexual symptoms, and Eileen told the jury she pays particular attention to these because they are less likely to be precipitated by other stresses in the family. The replication of sexual acts, advanced sexual knowledge, excessive masturbation, and sexual play with toys are among the symptoms on her list.

Under cross-examination by Meltzer, Eileen explained that experts have not been able to agree on broad guidelines for a diagnosis of child sexual abuse. This is because youngsters who have been molested react differently, depending on their age and personalities.

At one point, Meltzer asked Eileen if four-year-olds lie.

"Children lie. Adults lie. People tell lies," Eileen answered. "It should be noted that children lie to get out of trouble, not into it."

After Eileen's six days on the stand, the state was done. Now it was the defense's turn to present its witnesses.

Meltzer and Clark called their first witness on December 15, 1987—the Rev. R. Craig Burlington, the rector of St. George's Episcopal Church. The gist of his testimony was that church personnel were in and out of the building often enough that Kelly would not have had time to sexually assault her young charges. Two church secretaries testified that they had never noticed anything out of the ordinary in the building.

Several expert witnesses came next. The first was Ralph Underwager, a psychologist who was the director of the Institute of Psychological Therapy in Minneapolis and who had previously testified in dozens of cases in which child sexual abuse had been charged. Underwager presents himself as a specialist in the field of suggestibility, and Kelly's lawyers hoped he could convince the jury that leading questions from adults induced the Wee Care children's allegations.

Underwager acknowledged that for a long time he was a spokesman for an organization called VOCAL—Victims of Child Abuse Laws. He said he had left the group, which was composed of individuals who claimed they were falsely accused of sex abuse, just two weeks earlier because of infighting among the members.

In his testimony at the Wee Care trial, Underwager criticized the techniques used by the investigators. He said that the use of anatomically correct dolls teaches explicit sexual activity. Underwager, a huge man whose appearance reminded me of Orson Welles, talked about a study he had done on the use of these anatomically correct dolls. Underwager said he compared the reactions of abused and nonabused children, and found that more than half of the total group "played with the dolls in ways that showed overt sexual behavior."

In what he called his Time and Motion Study, Underwager also assessed how long it would take for one of the acts of abuse to have occurred. For instance, he said it would take anywhere from thirty-five minutes to two hours and forty minutes for the nude pile-up game, because it involved gathering the children, bringing them to the off-limits room, and arranging them in various configurations. The prosecutors brought out in cross-examination that Underwager had never been to St. George's Church or had any idea of its size.

After Underwager, the defense called David Brodzinsky, a psychology professor at Rutgers University. He contested the validity of the checklist that Eileen Treacy presents to parents when she suspects child sexual abuse. He told the court that some of the behaviors on the list, such as bed-wetting, soiling clothes, and night terrors, are normal for preschoolers.

Brodzinsky explained to the jury that to test Eileen's checklist, he had asked the parents of ninety-six children enrolled in a Rutgers day-care center to fill it out. Half the parents completed the forms, rating the intensity of the behaviors on a scale of one to four. The parents also were asked to complete a corresponding questionnaire of life experiences that would indicate whether the children were under stress, such as from an illness within the family, or a divorce or separation.

Brodzinsky said that twenty-seven of the Rutgers children exhibited five or more of the behaviors their parents ranked in the intense range. And, he noted, there was "little relationship" between the behaviors and any stresses that might have been mentioned in the corresponding life-experience questionnaire.

It emerged in Brodzinsky's cross-examination that the

Rutgers parents were never told that the results were being used to assist the defense in Kelly's trial. Also, Brodzinsky had sent out the letter to them as the head of the Rutgers psychology department—as if he were doing the research for the university and not in preparation for being a defense witness in a sex-abuse trial. He sent the parents the forms on university stationery, and said "we" are conducting a study of children's daily activity. Glenn Goldberg argued in court that Brodzinsky's results could not be compared to Eileen's checklist because Brodzinsky told the parents to check off "behaviors." Eileen, on the other hand, focused on "behavior changes."

A third defense psychiatrist, Dr. Elissa Benedek of Ann Arbor, Michigan, testified that the Wee Care children did not act like abused children. (She had never met any of the children, and she had only watched a couple of the videotapes of their testimony.)

Dr. Benedek, a clinical professor at the University of Michigan who specializes in child psychiatry, told the court that one child whose videotape she had viewed was "basically flat and disinterested," while another boy "seemed to be annoyed at having to do this one more time." Neither child, she maintained, showed "the emotion of a child reliving any trauma." She said if the Wee Care children had been abused, they would be "severely disturbed." And she explained away behavior changes such as bed-wetting by saying they could be caused by parental discord, the birth of a baby, or sickness within a family.

Dr. Benedek watched the videotape of Dennis Hammer's testimony in the courtroom. The child had been feverish the day before, and at one point on the tape his mother, Jane, reached over to touch his forehead. At this, Dr. Benedek laughed aloud. Glenn turned off the tape and asked what she found so amusing. "Well," Dr. Benedek sniffed. "I really question *that* maternal gesture after what this parent has put her child through."

Infuriating as it was to have someone like Elissa Benedek

stand up and profess to tell us our kids were not abused, I don't think her testimony really hurt us. Glenn Goldberg's cross-examination of her was wonderful. He brought out that she had very limited experience with preschool children, for one thing. She conceded to Glenn that she spends just three to five percent of her time treating child sex-abuse victims, and that preschoolers comprise just a portion of that percentage.

Glenn showed Dr. Benedek a self-portrait done by one of the Wee Care children. In the picture, the child had scribbled with a red crayon in the area between his legs. He had told his mother that this was blood, and insisted that she hang the drawing in the kitchen. Glenn asked Dr. Benedek why she thought the child would make such a drawing. And Dr. Benedek replied that it didn't surprise her because the children had been asked repeatedly about blood by the investigators.

"Dr. Benedek," Glenn said in his characteristically low, pleasant voice, his bespectacled face as bland as a mask, "what if I were to tell you that drawing was done three months before the Wee Care investigation began?"

"Well," Dr. Benedek replied, looking huffy, "I'd like to know how, when, and why it was saved!"

Judge Harth looked annoyed. He told the psychiatrist that why it was saved was unimportant and asked her to say why she thought the drawing was done.

"I frankly don't know," she said.

"Any idea?" asked Harth.

"No," conceded the witness.

Her testimony was so weak that I doubted the jury believed her. Still, I was far from sanguine about the ultimate outcome of the trial. Sometimes in court I studied the jury for some reaction, but their faces were maddeningly inscrutable. I lived each day with the reality of a sexually abused child. But the jury had to listen to and weigh an exhaustive body of evidence presented by both sides. Would they find in our favor? If they didn't, how could I possibly tell Hannah that they hadn't believed her and that her tormentor was going to walk away from it all scot-free?

And if Kelly took the stand in her own defense, would that help or hurt us? None of us knew whether she would testify or not. Out of courtesy, Meltzer was supposed to give Glenn and Sara a day's notice before putting his client on the stand, but he wasn't absolutely required to.

He certainly gave no hint that he planned to call Kelly as a witness on Monday, February 22.

The previous week, he'd told Judge Harth that on that particular Monday, he planned to call as his next witness the woman who had presented a puppet show at Wee Care back in January 1985. Presumably, she would get on the stand and say that she had talked to the children about abuse and that if these kids had been molested, they would have told someone. It didn't promise to be an exciting morning at the trial, which is probably why the courtroom was nearly empty at 9 A.M. that Monday.

The only parent there was my sister Kathleen. Most days, she didn't get down there until around 10 A.M., because she took Emily to school and went home to change and have another cup of coffee first. But for no particular reason, she drove straight down to Newark from Emily's school that day and was in the courtroom by 9 A.M. sharp.

Inside, she sat on the left, on what had come to be known as "our side" of the courtroom. The Michaels family and any spectators there for the defense, such as Meltzer's wife or Bob Clark's girl friend, always sat on the right. It reminded me of the way guests at a wedding sit on opposite sides of the church, depending on whether they know the bride or the groom.

On this morning, except for Kelly's family and perhaps one reporter, Kathleen was the only spectator in the courtroom. To Kathleen's surprise, Meltzer stood up and said, "The defense calls Margaret Kelly Michaels to the stand."

Perhaps, anticipating the crowd of parents and reporters who would converge on the courtroom if they knew Kelly was going to take the stand, he figured it would be less nerve-wracking for his client if she could testify in a nearly empty courtroom. Perhaps he thought he was pulling a fast one on the prosecutors by not telling them ahead of time.

At any rate, Glenn and Sara were furious. They jumped up and approached the bench, where Harth listened to arguments from the attorneys for both sides. While they wrangled, Kathleen ran out to the pay telephone. She had just enough change for one call, so she called my sister Beth at work. Beth contacted other parents, and those parents made calls, too. By the time Kelly began to testify an hour and a half later, the courtroom was filled and people were being turned away.

When I got the message, I ran to tell my co-worker Jack, who was covering the story, so he could report on Kelly's testimony. There was no way I could go to court that day because it was so hectic at work, but I juggled my schedule so I could be there for her second day on the stand.

When I arrived on Tuesday, I was shocked at the chaos, the tight security, the crowds lined up waiting to get into the Kelly Michaels trial. Two poker-faced guards were stationed at the door to the courtroom, and spectators had to go through a metal detector. Another guard pawed through purses and briefcases in search of hidden weapons, and everyone had to sign in.

By nine o'clock in the morning, the courtroom was overflowing and Wee Care parents were being turned away. Some who had attended a lot of the trial were standing out in the hall while first-time spectators had front-row seats. It didn't seem fair. People were getting angry, and the mood was tense.

Then Judge Harth stepped in. Everybody in the courtroom was told to write down their names and their interest in the case. Then the judge announced that seating for the rest of the trial would be on a priority basis. Wee Care parents would be seated first, followed by members of the press and relatives of the Wee Care children. If there were any seats left over, they would be allotted on a first-come, first-serve basis. He said everyone would get their seats back after the lunch hour, during which the courtroom was emptied and locked. That meant we wouldn't all have to stand in line again. I could have hugged him.

I had waited so long to hear Kelly's version of what had happened at Wee Care. I didn't really expect to hear the truth from her, although a part of me hoped that she would finally break down under tough cross-examination.

In the end, Kelly's testimony was undramatic, at times tedious, almost anti-climactic. Meltzer led her through a description of her daily schedule at Wee Care and her duties there. His questions covered virtually every allegation raised by the state's witnesses, and she explained away or denied every one. She said she had never played a licking game or a piling-on game with her charges. Instead, she said, they played the games the children knew, such as Tag and Duck Duck Goose. Kelly said she had not had the time or the opportunity to molest the children. She went through a list of the children named in the indictments, reviewing the days and hours they had attended the school.

Meltzer read off the names of the twenty children listed in the indictment, asking Kelly if she had ever touched them sexually or abused them. Kelly answered him twenty times with a "no" that was both emphatic and defiant.

On the witness stand, she was dramatic, using her hands expressively and appearing at times almost to be acting. Her demeanor never changed, and she maintained a puzzled, quizzical look. (Glenn later suggested to the jury that her animated gestures, pauses, and use of her hands while testifying all were for dramatic effect. He suggested that Kelly, a former drama student, was showcasing her acting talents for the jury.)

Frequently in her testimony, Kelly echoed questions before responding. At times, she reversed herself after answering and changed her mind, giving a different response. She was caught outright in a couple of lies. Glenn brought out the fact that she had lied on a résumé three years earlier, something she acknowledged doing "for completeness' sake." When questioned about her conversations with the prison guards, she denied having talked to them at all except to ask to go the bathroom or take a shower.

Kelly was cool and self-assured, never losing her composure even under cross-examination. Perhaps the closest she came to it was the day Glenn surprised everyone by pulling an electronic piano out of a box and challenging Kelly to play "Jingle Bells" on it—"like you did for the children." The request visibly unnerved her, and defense attorneys objected and accused Glenn of "grandstanding."

But Harth ordered the witness to perform, and Kelly struggled through an abbreviated version of the song, first using one finger and then two. Glenn called attention to the fact that she had not played any chord. He asked why she had listed piano playing under the heading of "special talents" on a résumé for Wee Care. On that résumé, Kelly indicated that she had twelve years of experience with the piano.

"I never said I had world-class experience," she replied smoothly.

Her cross-examination was important mainly because it established that Kelly had indeed had time alone with the children, and thus opportunities to abuse them. Sara was able to show that on many days, Wee Care was so short-staffed Kelly had no aide in her class, and no supervision from her superiors. And when she did have an aide, that helper was often called away to do other tasks, such as cut up fruit-snacks for all fifty children. Kelly was unable to remember much about her months at Wee Care. She said she couldn't recall which children were in her class, or her own schedule, or which children were there on certain days.

Watching and listening to Kelly evoked mixed feelings in me. It was a relief that her story seemed thin. Yet her frequent "I don't remember" and "I can't recall" responses angered me. Meltzer had insinuated that our children were making everything up when their memories failed them. He expected our youngsters to recall how many children had been in the room at a particular time, what their names were, and whether certain incidents had happened in the morning or the afternoon, before Christmas or after. If an adult couldn't remember even who was in her class, how could five- and six-year-olds be expected to recall such details?

Kelly, the last of the defense's twenty-two witnesses, finished testifying at the end of March. Now all that remained before jury deliberations were the attorneys' summations.

The weather had turned suddenly warm and springlike, and the courtroom was so warm I felt sleepy. Some days we took our sandwiches outside to sit in the sun. The summations lasted for eight days. Glenn and Sara finished by showing pictures of the twenty children as they recapped for the jury the charges against each one.

The still pictures, freeze-frames of the children during their testimony, only stayed on the TV screen for about twenty seconds. But it was an effective ending—images of those small, vulnerable faces, some missing their front teeth, others framed by pigtails or baseball caps—stayed with the viewer long after the photograph had faded from the screen.

Then it was Judge Harth's turn to give the charge on the law to the jury.

"Use your common sense," he told the seven women and five men. "No one can ask more of you. You cannot ask more of yourselves."

Kelly was charged with 131 counts—some charges had been dropped months earlier when a trial court ruling permitting hearsay testimony in child sexual-abuse cases was reversed by a higher court. In light of this ruling, some of the earlier hearsay testimony had to be stricken, with the result that particular counts had to be dismissed. (Hearsay testimony is that offered by someone who was not present

254

and therefore has no personal knowledge of the events he or she is describing. In our case, if a parent testified that her child had told her Kelly spread peanut butter on his genitals, this would have been hearsay testimony because the parent wasn't present when it happened.)

If convicted on all counts, Kelly faced up to eight hundred years imprisonment and fines ranging up to $100,000 per count. Harth reiterated to the jury that they all had to be in agreement on each count, and that each charge would be considered separately. He named college student Mark Burnett as jury foreman.

The jury began to deliberate on March 29, 1988 at 1:20 P.M. Three hours later, they asked to see and hear "all available material" on each child named as a victim in the indictments. They specifically wanted the audiotapes of the interviews conducted by the investigators for Glenn and Sara, plus all the videotapes of the children's testimony during the trial. Interestingly, the jurors did not request any evidence from the twenty-two witnesses from the defense's case. Nor did they ask to have read the testimony from any of the expert witnesses from either side. Once the jury had requested all the children's videotapes, we knew deliberations were likely to continue for a long time.

Several parents took up a vigil in the empty courtroom, reading or writing to pass the days. They could watch the videotapes of their children's testimony with the jury. For most, it was their first chance to see their youngsters in court.

It looked as if deliberations were going to last a long time. The waiting was agonizing. I went to work every day but operated on automatic pilot. In the middle of the night I'd wake with a start and be unable to fall back to sleep. I'd gotten into the habit of checking on the children to make sure they were not just covered but still breathing. Obviously, I was losing my mind.

I always lingered at Hannah's bunk, where she slept in the luminous glow cast by the Mother Goose night-light.

With her arms around Joshua (the teddy bear she'd slept with since age one) and her thumb in her mouth—she was embarrassed to suck it in front of her friends but still resorted to it in bed—she looked so small and vulnerable.

I knew some of the Wee Care parents were planning to tell their children Kelly had been convicted even if she wasn't. I couldn't do that because I could never lie to a child of mine. Upsetting as it might be, Hannah would learn the verdict when I did.

Courts and trials and jails belong in an adult world, not a child's. And yet Hannah was introduced to this world the first time Kelly Michaels laid a hand on her. For my daughter to put it behind her, the ordeal had to come full circle and reach a conclusion, from the committing of the crime to the bringing of justice.

But what if this ending were not about justice? What if the jury believed Kelly, not Hannah?

Sometimes I wondered why I had ever involved my family in the trial in the first place. Maybe it would have been better simply to sweep the whole Wee Care mess under the rug. If Hannah said she couldn't remember, if she didn't want to talk about it, then fine . . . just let it go. No therapy, no grand jury, no trial. Ignore it and go on with life. It certainly seemed like a simpler road.

What happens when this route is chosen? Do sexually abused children suffer any less? Do they really forget what happened to them? Does it make more sense to not talk about it and to act as though it never happened? Some Wee Care parents did that. And so, many years ago, did my own parents.

CHAPTER

■ ■ ■ ■ ■ ■ ■ ■ ■ ■ ■

14

Many people marvel that the Wee Care children endured being molested for so long without telling. But as a victim of child sexual abuse, I understand perfectly. My parents, when they learned of my Uncle Barney's deviant behavior, chose not to discuss it with my sisters and me. Perhaps they felt that keeping quiet would ensure that we would one day forget it had ever happened.

But that's not the way it works. Like other childhood experiences, the episodes unquestionably influenced my growing up, helping to shape the kind of teen-ager, and then adult, that I became.

Perhaps what has been affected the most is my own sex life. I wouldn't say I'm frigid. But I don't think I've ever been uninhibited and really giving of myself in bed either. I can never seem to erase the image of Barney's flaccid, limp penis completely from my mind. And thirty years later, thinking of his hand sliding under my panties makes me recoil in disgust. "Yucky"—Hannah's word for how she feels about what Kelly did to her—is perfect.

Being sexually abused as a child has had a lifelong effect

on my sisters, too. One has never been able to enjoy oral sex because it reminds her of how Barney used to kiss her vagina. Another has a very low self-esteem, despite the fact that she is beautiful, brilliant, and successful in everything she does.

Would therapy, or even just talking about it, have helped us? Who knows for sure whether dealing with it when it happens can ease the pain and hurt later on. I like to think that having Hannah in therapy is doing some good, that perhaps she won't suffer as much as an adult because as a child she had someone she could talk to about her shame and feelings of guilt.

Knowing she can talk to me or to Jim about it seems to make her feel secure, too. My sisters and I, close as we are to my parents, never felt we could discuss Barney with them. They never told us not to, but we didn't want to hurt them and, besides, we were ashamed of what we had done. On the positive side, having been molested myself made it a lot easier to believe my own daughter when it happened to her.

I know how hard it can be to hurt those you love (your parents) by telling them you were molested. And I know how difficult it is to "tattle" on the molester. Almost always, the child abuser is known and loved by the victim. It's a teacher, a baby-sitter, an uncle. It's terribly confusing and painful for a child to separate her love toward her tormenter from her knowledge that what that person is doing is wrong, and then to act on her instinct, do what's right, tell.

The child fears losing the tormenter's love, risking the parent's anger and tears. In my case, I could deal with Hannah calmly. I didn't get hysterical (never in front of her or my other children, anyway!), and I showed her my love and support. Maybe the reason I could do this was because my mother was so calm with us, and believed us right away.

What I never understood until recently is how many grown-ups walking around out there were sexually abused as children. Gradually, as friends and acquaintances found out about Hannah, many came to me with their personal stories of how they had been molested in childhood. A couple were Wee Care parents who relived their own victimization when they found out about their children.

Wee Care parent Ginny Williams was herself molested as a teen-ager by a friend's older brother. Although she didn't talk about it with anyone at the time, she remembers it as if it were yesterday.

Ginny had a girl friend in the neighborhood who often invited her to stay overnight. Ginny liked those sleep-overs, but her friend's brother, two years older than she was, often came in to fondle her and touch her sexually after her friend had fallen asleep. Ginny was too ashamed to tell anyone, and so she kept silent. She continued to see her friend but didn't know how to tell her about her brother.

Learning about the abuse at Wee Care brought memories of Ginny's own childhood secret to the surface again. They are all the more painful because she doesn't even know for sure if her daughter was abused by Kelly, and Miriam won't talk to her about it. Every day, Ginny looks at her child and wonders.

Plump, dark-eyed Miriam Williams was in Hannah's class at Wee Care, and since she went to school three days a week, she actually was there more hours than my daughter. Unlike Hannah, Miriam has never admitted to anyone that Kelly molested her. But her behavior—both during the period of abuse and since—is disturbingly like Hannah's and that of the other children who admitted they had been abused.

When Ginny and her husband first learned about the charges of sexual abuse at Wee Care, they didn't believe Miriam could be involved because she was such a strong-willed child. It seemed doubtful she would let anyone do anything to her. Miriam was interviewed by Lou Fonolleras, but denied any personal involvement although she admitted having seen Kelly touch other children "in a bad way" at naptime. She repeatedly denied that Kelly had done anything improper to her.

Still, Ginny wondered. So much of her daughter's behavior in the past six months just didn't sit right. For months, Miriam had been reluctant to go to school in the morning, whining and crying and clinging to her mother. There was also the reluctance to nap there, and that winter Miriam wet her pants frequently, although she had been completely toilet-trained from the age of two. It seemed to Ginny that Miriam was always bringing wet underwear home, but when her mother asked her about it, the child would say she couldn't hold it, or that the teachers wouldn't let her go to the bathroom.

In the previous six months, there also had been nightmares from which Miriam woke up moaning or screaming. But the daughter of a friend of Ginny's was having nightmares around the same time, and Ginny just figured that they were something children went through.

Once Ginny found out about Kelly, all these behavior patterns took on new significance. She urgently needed to know if Miriam was involved. At bedtime, Al went up and sat with his younger daughter, gently asking her about Kelly. And Sara McArdle interviewed Miriam. But if the child had been sexually abused by Kelly, she was keeping it to herself.

Ginny tried to let it go. Periodically she got calls about the parents' meetings, but she never attended any of them. She thought about putting Miriam in therapy, but couldn't see the point of it since the child refused to acknowledge that anything had happened to her. Occasionally, Ginny brought up Kelly's name, mentioned seeing articles in the newspaper about her. But Miriam acted as if she didn't even remember who Kelly was.

The Williamses live near a family whose two children had both been at Wee Care with Miriam. Paul and Annabelle D'Amico, who had been five and four years old at the time, had both testified at grand jury and were planning to testify at the trial. Miriam still played occasionally with Annabelle even though they were no longer in school together.

Ginny wasn't encouraging this friendship, though. She had walked in on the two girls several times when they had their pants down and were touching each other sexually. When they were at her house, Ginny no longer let the two children play upstairs alone. She kept them downstairs where she could monitor their games. She felt as if she didn't know Annabelle's mother well enough to tell her what was going on, but whenever her daughter played at the D'Amicos' house, she called over there to ask her daughter where and what they were playing. And she didn't know whether she should worry or not.

"I played doctor, too, as a kid," Ginny said. "And so you wonder, is this normal or is it not normal? I didn't know. I drove myself crazy. Things still happen that make me wonder, and then I think, is it my imagination? If she comes to touch and hug me and hits my breasts, I wonder if that's normal."

Miriam began having nightmares again when she was in the first grade. By second grade, they were happening at least twice a week. She would cry and talk in her sleep, but Ginny couldn't make out what she was saying.

When the Williamses' noticed a correlation between the nightmares and Miriam's play dates with Annabelle, they decided to have their daughter see a therapist. She began going to a South Orange psychologist on a weekly basis. Miriam and the therapist played games together and talked, but never about Wee Care. Ginny says the therapist told her that her daughter was disturbed, that she had a lot of anger and aggression. But Ginny, frustrated because her daughter was not discussing Kelly Michaels, pulled the child out of therapy. She felt that it wasn't helping.

What she wants most is to know whether or not Miriam was abused, and then for her to talk about it. "It's important for me to know what happened so that I can deal with it and help her deal with it," Ginny says. "If she was touched, is it going to affect her? Is she ever going to talk about it? I've been told just to wait till she's ready to talk. If she is able to talk about it and deal with it, then fine. But what is she going to be like otherwise? I worry about what she might be like in fifteen years."

Ginny has never been in therapy to help her deal with her own feelings as a victim of child sexual abuse. But Dana Ernst, another Wee Care parent, whose child did not testify, sought professional counseling as an adult to help her come to terms with having been molested as a child.

When the allegations against Kelly Michaels first surfaced, Dana experienced the tremendous guilt, disbelief and denial that all of us did. Her depression was magnified because she herself had been abused as a schoolgirl.

Over the course of one summer, a group of older boys in the neighborhood had touched Dana in places she knew they shouldn't and had forced her to touch them. It had started innocuously enough, with kids playing doctor together to relieve the vacation boredom. But then the boys had selected her to go to a special place and play the game in a different way. Some of the things they did to Dana hurt. At first, she felt important. Later on, she felt tarnished and ashamed.

Somehow—Dana doesn't remember how—her parents found out. They questioned her, then talked to the boys' parents. The abuse was stopped, and Dana's parents never referred to it again. They severed their social ties with the boys' families, and Dana was not allowed to play with those children anymore. "It was very disturbing because I felt responsible for what had happened," Dana says. "I felt I had done something wrong. I felt like I was the only one it had ever happened to, like a freak."

Dana buried the whole experience as best she could. Until the summer that the Wee Care case surfaced. Eventually she began to see a therapist and, gradually, to deal with her own molestation. She has found therapy useful for helping her come to terms with the terrible secret she had lived alone with for so long. "It helped to talk about it," Dana said. "We can all get over sexual abuse, but to do so in a positive way, you need to talk about it."

Two years after Hannah was molested, I wrote an article about it for *Family Circle* magazine, using the pseudonym Cathy Smith. After it was published, reader mail poured in. Some of the letters chided me for not having stayed home with my child instead of going out to work, implying that by doing so I could have prevented the abuse. But the most touching letters came from women who had been molested as children. Most said they had never told anyone before, and they requested anonymity if the magazine published their letters.

One woman wrote that she found my article "heartbreaking" because it brought back so many "ugly, hideous memories" for her. Now in her late forties, she was only seven years old when the neighborhood grocer began to molest her. Scared, convinced that it was all her fault, she never told anyone. Then, when she was in the third grade, three high-school boys molested her. This woman described herself as a "happily married mother of two college-aged sons, a past president of the PTA, and a successful career woman." She is active in her church and various civic organizations. But inside, she still carried a lot of anger: "I've survived three serious suicide attempts, a nervous breakdown, and reoccuring violent mood changes," she wrote. "Inside, I believe the anger remains, buried under layers and layers. I wish I could make it go away. . . . Why does that grubby old man still have me convinced that somehow it's my fault?"

Another woman wrote that she was a victim of sexual abuse from age five to seven. The man who molested her was a neighbor and her best friend's father. The two mothers shopped and played cards together. He was respected in the community. He threatened to hurt her if she told. When her parents finally found out, they tried to ignore the situation. She was frightened and wanted to discuss her

263

fears with them. But all they could say was, "Let's not ever talk about this again." The woman wrote: "They thought if they ignored it, it would go away. How I longed for someone I could talk to, someone to explain to me what had happened to me. I was really very confused."

Another letter came from a thirty-seven-year-old nurse and the mother of two children. She prefaced her note by saying she had never before told anyone what had happened to her, though the horror is still "vivid" in her mind. She was four years old the first time her stepfather told her mother that she needed a nap and that he would lie down with her. In the bedroom, when he played with her genitals, she had a dreadful feeling that it was wrong. "I still have a hard time relaxing," she wrote. "I still have some guilt about sex. . . . But I am enjoying it more and beginning to learn to trust my husband. I realize now that [the abuse] was not my fault. But the child in me is still there and the pain is still there and the stigma of talking about it is still there."

Still another letter came from a doctor in her mid-thirties who is engaged to be married. She wrote that she had been brought up in a nice, middle-class suburban family. Her parents often left her with maids and baby-sitters, one of whom had a boyfriend who used to "do that which I can still, after years of therapy, only refer to as 'bad things to me.'" The "bad things" went on for two years before the baby-sitter moved away. Although she told her parents, they didn't believe her. "To this day I still wake up screaming and sweaty. Fifteen years of good therapy have made it possible for me to function normally most of the time, but I still wake up screaming." Despite therapy, she still finds it hard to trust anyone and always is a little on guard. "After years, the anger subsides," she wrote. "For me, it took years of drug abuse and promiscuity, but I finally turned out okay."

Common themes run through these handwritten letters —powerlessness, self-blame, and a sense of despair. The authors all experienced a sense of futility, feeling it was hopeless to tell because they wouldn't be believed anyway. They were guilty, afraid, ashamed. No matter how many years elapsed, they never forgot what happened to them.

It's impossible to forget being victimized as a child. I never talked about it, and neither have most of the women who told me their stories. Perhaps Hannah's generation is luckier than mine in that these days, sexual-abuse victims are encouraged to seek treatment, to vent their feelings about what happened.

Hannah's psychologist feels it's important for young sexual-abuse victims to be evaluated at least. Their parents should consult a therapist and determine—based on the nature of the experience and the child's reaction to it—whether or not treatment is needed. In some cases, say, where the abuse was a single event, no treatment may be indicated.

If a child who needs therapy doesn't get it, Susan says, the concern is that the child doesn't deal with it. He or she doesn't forget the experience, but may split it off from his or her awareness and not allow himself or herself to be in touch with the feelings that are connected with the event. These feelings, which can range from anxiety and guilt to intense rage and vulnerability, are painful and often conflicting. "You worry that the experience is going to come back in a way that the child isn't fully in touch with or doesn't have the ability to manage and control," Susan says. "It might affect the child's life in the future."

For instance, when sexuality becomes important during the teen-age years, the victim may engage in promiscuous behavior or may avoid sexuality. As adults, they may engage in abusive acts against children. Because those painful childhood memories have come back to haunt him, a sexual-abuse victim might act out on them impulsively, without allowing himself to feel responsible. He might rationalize molesting a child himself by saying the youngster seduced him, or that the child enjoyed it. Susan stresses that this is not the typical outcome, but says that it may occur. "While a large percentage of people who molest were molested as children, many people who were sexually abused as children do not go on to molest children," she said.

However, those who were molested as children are at risk for a number of problems in adulthood. The most common long-range effects of being abused as a child include problems in terms of self-esteem and sexual adjustment, and a difficulty in forming trusting, intimate relationships. Sexual-abuse victims may constantly get themselves into abusive relationships when they grow up, or they may not be able to form healthy, strong relationships. Hopefully, Susan says, abused children who have been in therapy are less likely to have such problems when they grow up. We just won't know until this generation of sexual-abuse victims are adults.

Today there's an openness, a frankness that didn't exist back when Barney was molesting his five great-nieces. In those days, parents didn't press charges against molesters. They even tried to shield the abusers. My parents, devastated as they were, still wanted to protect Barney and not ruin his life. As far as treating us, the wisdom of the day seemed to be the less said about it, the better.

Years later, after my sister Jana moved to Michigan, she occasionally visited Barney and Anna. Jana was a married woman by then, and Barney was aging and feeble. She visited them mostly out of a sense of duty. Jana noticed that Barney had built himself a small lean-to that was attached to the garage. It had a peephole in it, looking out onto the backyard. Jana is convinced that this was his hideaway, where he could molest little girls in the neighborhood without detection. The peephole allowed him to keep watch in case anyone—Anna, or a neighbor—should unexpectedly head in his direction.

The children's mothers probably let them visit Barney because they trusted him and his loving wife, who made the best cookies on the block. No doubt they thought of him as a kindly old retiree who loved playing croquet in his backyard with the neighborhood children. I'm sure Barney's victims never led their parents to believe anything different. And even if they had, it's unlikely he would ever have been prosecuted.

My sisters and I are the lucky ones, lucky because my mother believed us, lucky because we have each other. Of course, had my uncle been tried and convicted, other little girls might have been spared what we endured. But even today, prosecuting child molesters is a tricky business. It's expensive, time-consuming—and frustrating.

Some legal experts hold that children just don't make good witnesses. Young children are unsure of themselves, can't remember details, sometimes recant their testimony. Many sex-abuse cases must rely on the testimony of witnesses barely able to write their names and remember the days of the week, such as our own Wee Care children. Juries are asked to believe the unthinkable, often of people who don't look as if they would hurt a flea. Kelly, for instance, looked like a fresh-faced college co-ed, just the kind of baby-sitter parents consider a real gem.

Would the jury believe what she had done to our children?

C H A P T E R

■　■　■　■　■　■　■　■　■　■

15

"Not guilty," said Mark Burnett, and time stood still. Just moments before, the judge had instructed the jury foreman to respond individually to each of the 131 counts with which Kelly was charged. The court clerk was to read off the charges. Then Burnett would answer either "guilty" or "not guilty." Kelly had just been acquitted of first-degree sexual assault by anal penetration of Joshua Peterson.

I was sitting in the front row of the courtroom. On one side of me were Joshua's parents, Anna and Dan. Their faces were impassive. My mother sat on my other side, and we held hands tightly. When Burnett said "not guilty," she squeezed my hand so hard I winced. Then she leaned over and whispered, "I don't think I can take this." I scanned the faces of the jurors, but they were as inscrutable as ever. I didn't think I could take much more either.

■

The tension that had been building since the jury began to deliberate two weeks earlier had reached an unbearable level by Friday, April 15, 1988. The day was ominous and gray, and it was drizzling off and on. I had been writing at home, but I couldn't seem to sit at the computer for more than five minutes. I wandered from room to room, straightening shelves, rummaging through closets. Every time the phone rang, I jumped.

The jury had finished listening to the last child's videotaped testimony the day before. Some people said that meant a verdict was imminent. At ten o'clock that morning, my friend Jack called me from the courthouse. He thought I should drive down to Newark immediately.

A few minutes later, my sister Beth called. "You better get down here," she told me. "Otherwise you're not even going to get in."

I was shivering and queasy by the time I arrived at the courthouse half an hour later. News photographers milled through the main lobby. They weren't allowed to take pictures in the courtroom so they stayed on the first floor to capture for that night's TV viewers the sight of Kelly's family entering and leaving the building. As usual, Kelly had arrived in protective formation, flanked by her parents, brother, sisters, and lawyers, and led by sheriff's officers.

Upstairs, in the corridor outside Judge Harth's courtroom, the mood was expectant. Everyone else was as nervous as I was. One of the reporters told me she had caught a glimpse of the jury room as the jurors filed out of it for their midmorning break. The reporter could see that the children's behavior charts had been removed from the wall, where they had hung since the start of deliberations. And Mark Burnett, the young black jury foreman with a serious face, had turned up in court that day wearing a suit. The reporter said she bet the verdict would come after lunch.

Someone suggested getting a sandwich, so a group of us went down to the cafeteria. Eating was impossible. My stomach—a reliable tension barometer—was even more jittery than usual. Back upstairs, the guards had unlocked the courtroom and were scanning everyone with a metal detector and checking handbags and briefcases. For the first time, the Michaels family was being searched for weapons. After all the weeks of putting up with this indignity myself, it was mildly satisfying to see Kelly's huge father being searched, too. Did the judge really think that if Kelly was convicted, her family might turn on us parents with an arsenal of guns?

Inside, we sat and waited, still unsure if there would be a verdict today. Sara, looking pale and worried, was wearing a black dress and a burgundy blazer. I smiled. Jack had once remarked to me that Sara always wore black on important days. Glenn stood at the prosecutor's table, looking more serious than I had ever seen him. I thought how stressful this must be for them, too. They'd poured their all into this case for months, and now it was over. There was nothing else they could do.

Defense attorney Bob Clark ambled past and Glenn smiled and said to him quietly, "Well, Bob."

"Good fight," Clark replied amiably. Glenn smiled that bland smile and said, "That about sums it up." They shook hands then, two fighters ending the match on good terms.

It took a long time for everyone to be seated because there were not enough spots. Parents and press were let in first, but it was still mass confusion and the hall was packed with would-be spectators by the time the courtroom doors were closed.

After warning the spectators against any emotional outbursts, Judge Harth instructed the court clerk to begin reading off the charges. When Burnett responded with that first "not guilty," there was a moment of shocked silence. Was Kelly actually going to be acquitted?

And then, as the clerk continued to drone off the charges, I began hearing Burnett intone the word "guilty" over and over again. It was the sweetest word I had ever heard. And the jury foreman said it over one hundred times in half an hour.

Vaginal penetration with forks, spoons, and knives—

guilty. Anal penetration—guilty. Oral sex with the children —guilty. Urinating on them—guilty.

In all, Kelly was convicted on 115 of the 131 counts with which she was charged. The convictions included 34 counts of first-degree aggravated sexual assault—each carrying a maximum twenty-year sentence—and two counts of threatening the children to keep them silent. Interestingly, she was not found guilty of first-degree aggravated sexual assault (by anal penetration) on Joshua Peterson, although the jury did find her guilty of second-degree aggravated sexual assault (by anal touching) in that instance.

When Mark Burnett had finished reading off the verdict, defense attorney Meltzer asked that the jury be polled on all the charges.

"Is this your unanimous verdict?" Harth asked each juror about the first four counts in the indictment. Several jurors answered yes. But juror Essie Belle Brown shook her head and said no. Harth looked as if he hadn't heard her correctly. When he asked her to repeat herself, and it was clear that she had indeed meant no, the judge ordered the jury back to their room to deliberate until they could reach unanimity.

It seemed like they were out forever. And while they were gone, the courtroom buzzed with speculation. Some spectators looked puzzled, others worried. A few parents cried. I was in shock. We had come so close to a conviction. Now it seemed that one juror had been holding out and didn't really believe Kelly was guilty after all.

Ten minutes later, the jury returned and moved through the rest of the polling without a hitch. They were in agreement that Kelly was guilty as charged. (A few days later, Essie Brown clarified in a newspaper interview that she felt very strongly that Kelly *was* guilty, and that her "no" answer had been misperceived. There was speculation that on the charge she disagreed with, Ms. Brown had wanted Kelly to be convicted of first-degree sexual assault instead of the less serious second-degree charge.)

After the verdict was finally in, there was a lull while Judge Harth and his clerk tallied up how many convictions there were. I let myself relax a little. Parents hugged each other, and tears of relief streamed down their faces.

Members of Kelly's family alternately cried, shook their heads, and stared straight ahead. John Michaels, her father, had rolled his eyes at some of the guilty verdicts. Now he appeared to be trying to restrain Kelly's mother, who looked ashen. As she strode out of the courthouse a few minutes later, Marilyn Michaels remarked to television reporters in that high voice that seemed so out of place in such a big body, "We have only begun to fight."

Kelly had listened with tears in her eyes as the verdict was read, vigorously shaking her head from side to side occasionally. At the very end, when it seemed as if the verdict had finally sunk in, she began to tremble and to cry uncontrollably. "I can't believe it. I can't believe it," she said over and over.

All four lawyers got up and began to argue before Judge Harth. Meltzer wanted Kelly's $25,000 bail to be continued pending appeal. Sara stated quietly that Kelly was a danger to society and should be held without bail. In the end, Harth revoked Kelly's bail and ordered her remanded to the Essex County Jail Annex in Caldwell. He scheduled sentencing for May 26.

The sheriff's officers snapped handcuffs on Kelly's wrists and prepared to lead her away. Meltzer asked if his client could have a few minutes with her family, and Sara started to say she had no problem with that. But Harth would not permit it, and Kelly was led away. She turned back once and said to her family, "It's okay. It's okay."

I watched her walk out of the courtroom through a wall of tears. Sharon Bethel, sitting on an aisle seat in the second row, had a perfect view.

"The sound of those handcuffs being snapped on her made my stomach turn because there's still a part of me that feels sorry for this sick girl," Sharon said. "The other thing that turned my stomach is how when they took her away, they wouldn't even let her take her purse. She had a red purse and they grabbed it and handed it to her mother. And I thought to myself, this is what prison is. You don't even carry your own purse with you. She walked out of that room with just the clothes she had on her back. That to me was just devastating."

When it was all over, we sat in the courtroom, unsure of what to do next. Judge Harth made a little speech to the jurors, thanking them for giving what had amounted to practically a year of their lives to the Wee Care trial. He ended by saying that he would be very grateful if, after they collected their things from the jury room, the jurors would come back to his chambers and allow him to shake their hands. I thought that was a really nice gesture on his part. I felt like personally hugging each one.

As they rose to leave, I heard one juror wisecrack, "They're going to have to get a new chair to replace this one. I've worn it out."

As the jury filed from the courtroom for the last time, all the parents stood up. It was our silent expression of respect and appreciation for the verdict. Then we all spilled out into the hallway, hugging and kissing, laughing and crying. The mood was buoyant and giddy, and the reporters looked almost as happy as the victims' relatives.

During the trial, parents had kept silent, but now some of them were giving interviews to the press, their faces in silhouette so they could not be identified. But all I wanted to do was go home and tell Hannah that the jury had believed her.

My mother and I took the elevator to the basement so that we could avoid the crowd of photographers on the first floor. She had walked up to the courthouse from her office —we'd called her on such short notice that she hadn't even had time to get her car out of the underground garage near her building. I would drive her back to work.

A brilliant late afternoon sun had burst out of the clouds,

and it was warm and springlike as we crossed the parking lot. I could feel some of the pent-up tension drain away. Already the news of the conviction was on the radio. I still was having trouble believing it myself.

At a busy intersection in downtown Newark, my mother climbed out of my little Toyota. She looked the picture of dignity, every bit the proper attorney in her high-heeled pumps, linen suit, and tiny eyeglasses on a gold chain. With some of the tension gone from her face, she looked so much younger than sixty. Her eyes sparkled as she turned briefly to look back at me. "Wheee!" she laughed, and as she walked away from me she was practically skipping.

I'd arranged for Casey MacKenna to come home from school with Hannah that afternoon because her mother didn't think she'd be home from court in time. I ran up the stairs and found the two girls playing in Hannah's room. When I told them the news, their faces lit up. They jumped up and down with excitement, hugging me and each other. All of our faces were wet from crying. Maria shrieked with joy, and Jim sounded quietly pleased when I called him at his office.

Caroline, nearly ten, and Ellen, nearly six, both joined in the festive mood around our house that afternoon. Though they had been too young when Wee Care first happened to understand its implications on all of our lives, over the years they had seen it bring much upheaval and tension to our household. I think they were as glad about Kelly's conviction for their own sakes (now life would return to normal!) as they were that she was going to jail.

That night, there was a huge victory party at Bunny's, a nearby pizza joint. The owners were as jubilant as the Wee Care parents who were there, and they poured free champagne for everyone until after midnight. Sara McArdle attended, and Detective George McGrath, and even a couple of the sheriff's officers. The next night, there was another party at Bunny's to which Glenn Goldberg and Eileen

Treacy came. Lou Fonolleras arrived late with his wife, and he looked shy and surprised when everyone applauded.

But though we all acted as though it was a happy time, it was also very sad. A young woman had been convicted of heinous crimes, and would be going to prison for a long time. And her conviction didn't erase what she had done to our children. Nor did it recapture for them their stolen innocence.

Sara, interviewed by one TV network, expressed it perfectly when she said: "I feel good and I feel sad. It is not a happy day when someone is convicted of something like this. It wasn't happy for the state to prosecute and it wasn't happy for the parents and it wasn't happy for the children to have to undergo."

Still, the jury had believed them, and this was important not just to our children but to youngsters everywhere. It meant that kids can and do make credible witnesses and that these kinds of cases can be won.

The Wee Care children each reacted differently to the news. When Ana Fernandez told Eddie the verdict, he was initially jubilant. "Mommy, we made it. We made it!" he said happily. But later he grew quiet and pensive. He told his mother, "I'm happy because Kelly is in jail and can't do this to other children. But I feel sad in a way, because I think she is sick. Who else would do this unless they were sick?"

Eddie told Ana once again how Kelly said she wanted the Wee Care children to do to other youngsters what she had done to them. "But I know that is wrong and I don't want to hurt any child," Eddie assured his mother. "I love children. I will never hurt kids."

Melissa Bethel didn't want to hear what her parents had to tell her.

When Sharon got home from court that day, she said to her daughter, "I have something to tell you."

"I don't want to hear it," Melissa shouted, and she ran upstairs. As she often did when she was upset, she kept hurting herself. First she closed her hand in a door, pinching her fingers. Then she ran into the bathroom, climbed into the cabinet beneath the sink, and bumped herself. She kept crying, running around, acting frantic. She didn't want to talk about Kelly's conviction.

"That was a hard day for Melissa," Sharon said. "But once she understood that it meant that this was truly the end for her, that Kelly was in jail and that the jury had believed her and the other kids, then she settled down."

We all settled down. After months of feeling stressed out, of going to court, reading about and thinking about the trial constantly, life was finally going to return to normal.

But the sense of relief was short-lived.

Three days after the verdict, defense attorneys Meltzer and Clark convinced the appellate court to set Kelly's bail at $1 million, pending sentencing. They argued that Kelly's freedom would not jeopardize anyone, and stressed that she had been free since January 1986 without doing anything improper.

The three-judge panel said it would accept $100,000 in cash or a property bond of the same value. This meant Kelly's family could put up their Pittsburgh home as security, and that Kelly would be free pending sentencing.

Wee Care parents reacted with outrage and anguish. At first, I didn't even believe it. What, I wondered, was the sense of having a trial if she was going to go free anyway? What does a guilty verdict mean in this country? Kelly Michaels was a monster who just wouldn't go away, one of those werewolves that appear to be dead but just keep bouncing back up over and over.

While Kelly waited in jail, Glenn, Sara, and two other attorneys in the county prosecutor's office, Virginia Lincoln and John Redden, went to the New Jersey Supreme Court. Arguing that it would be "difficult to imagine a case in which a defendant's dangerousness has been better illustrated," they urged the court to withhold bail from Kelly. A thirty-four-page legal brief by Glenn, Sara, and Deputy

First Assistant Prosecutor John Redden stated: "One might well wonder what more is necessary to demonstrate the defendant's dangerousness. How many children must come forth and undergo the ordeal of testimony and cross-examination before the fact that she is a danger will be accepted? Must yet more children be victimized before this fact will be accepted? The answer to this question must be no."

State Supreme Court Justice Marie Garibaldi stayed the bail order, asserting that the issue should be decided by the full court. Meanwhile, Kelly remained in custody. The prosecutors were given several days to file a brief with the state's highest court. The supreme court said it would consider the bail request at an administrative conference the following Tuesday, April 26.

We spent the weekend calling and writing to congressmen. My sister Donna had contacted a local radio station, and the station's talk-show moderator was anxious to air Wee Care parents' views on the bail issue. I agreed to participate, although I was so nervous beforehand the palms of my hands were dripping. Once I got on the air and began to tell my story, though, I forgot how scared I was. I was still so angry about what had happened that it was easy to talk about it.

The day after the radio show, the supreme court voted 6 to 1 to deny bail for Kelly. At the session, which was not open to the public, the justices overturned the bail order granted the week before by a three-judge appellate panel and reinstated the order of the trial judge.

I was so relieved by the court's decision to keep Kelly in jail that I felt dizzy. It seemed as if the supreme court was saying that convicted child molesters can't just walk away. Kelly would stay in jail where she belonged.

Her sentencing, scheduled for late May, was delayed by a series of psychological examinations that are required by law for convicted sex offenders. She probably would not be sentenced before August. But the Wee Care case continued to be in the news that summer.

In June, in a case called *Coy* v. *Iowa*, the United States Supreme Court handed down a decision severely limiting state efforts to shield young sex-abuse victims when they testify at criminal trials. The justices, voting 6 to 2, overturned the conviction of an Iowa man who had been sentenced to ten years in prison for sexually molesting two thirteen-year-old girls. The highest court in the land said that the defendant's rights to a fair trial had been violated by the use of a one-way screen that was placed in front of him at trial to prevent the children from seeing him.

Justice Antonin Scalia, writing for the Court, said that such one-way screens violate a defendant's rights. "It is difficult to imagine a more obvious or damaging violation of the defendant's right to a face-to-face encounter," he wrote, saying the defendant's rights were not outweighed "by the necessity of protecting victims of sexual abuse."

As I read this, I felt angry. What about Hannah's rights, and the rights of the other three- and four-year-olds whom Kelly Michaels had molested, I thought.

But Coy's lawyers argued that the screen made a guilty verdict practically inevitable by creating a presumption that he was guilty. They also said the screen violated the defendant's constitutional right to confront his accusers, because it prevented Coy from confronting the girls face to face. Coy's lawyers said there was no evidence the girls were in danger of being traumatized.

We were all worried that this Supreme Court decision might be grounds for appeal in the Wee Care case. After all, our children had testified on closed-circuit TV. But there was an important difference between the two cases. In the Wee Care trial, there had been more than just the presumption that seeing Kelly would traumatize our children. In three weeks of pretrial hearings, the youngsters' parents and psychologists had outlined carefully what the potential effects would be if the children testified in front of Kelly.

In the written decision, Justice Scalia had noted ". . . we leave for another day, however, the question as to whether any exceptions exist" to the usual face-to-face confrontation. And Justice Sandra Day O'Connor, in her concurring opinion, insisted that a defendant's right to face physically those who testify against him "is not absolute." She recognized the protection of child witnesses as an important public policy justifying something other than face-to-face confrontation and identified the New Jersey statute, which permits young victims to testify via closed-circuit television after a judicial finding of necessity, as one of several which provide "appropriate" procedures.

Still, it was inevitable that Meltzer would use the Supreme Court decision as grounds for an appeal. He already had asked Judge Harth for a new trial, arguing that the verdict was "inconsistent" and that he and Clark had been kept from "preparing a credible and informed defense."

That summer, Meltzer accused his former co-counsel, Jed-Mathew Philwin, of prejudicing Kelly's case by telling the prosecutors that she was a lesbian and that jail guards had seen her father fondling her. Philwin, who dropped out of the case long before the trial began, had wanted to present to the jury the theory of "diminished capacity," meaning that Kelly was victimized herself and could not be held accountable.

In pretrial hearings, defense psychiatrist Jonas Rapaport had testified that Kelly had told him she had a homosexual affair. But her sexual preferences were never brought out at the trial. Still, Meltzer now argued before Harth that he had a "gut feeling" the jury had learned of the homosexuality and of Kelly's alleged victimization by her father. He said rumors had circulated around the Essex County Courthouse during the trial.

But Judge Harth denied Meltzer's plea for a new trial, saying there was more than enough evidence to convict her. Harth also scheduled a late July hearing to consider a request by the *Village Voice*, a Manhattan weekly newspaper, to open the official court record of the trial.

The request stemmed from an article that freelance writer Debbie Nathan was working on. Ms. Nathan had written a cover story for the *Voice* in September 1987 about an El Paso, Texas, case in which two day-care workers were convicted of sexual abuse. The slant of her article was that the prosecutors there had fashioned a witch hunt, and that the two defendants were innocent. Miss Nathan referred to various day-care center abuse cases around the country as "junior McMartins." "McMartin" is a nationally known sex abuse scandal in California, in which the founder and some staffers at the prestigious preschool were charged with molesting more than a hundred children in their care.

We'd heard that Meltzer had contacted Ms. Nathan and asked her to do a story on Kelly. And she did. The cover headline that August, superimposed over a picture of an angelic-looking Kelly, read simply, CHILD MOLESTER? Inside, the story's headline read, VICTIMIZER OR VICTIM? WAS KELLY MICHAELS UNJUSTLY CONVICTED?

The story was very sympathetic to Kelly and made it sound as if our children had made the entire thing up. Ms. Nathan had written it without talking to parents. She had never attended any of the trial, or any of the pretrial hearings. Nor did she speak with Sara, although Glenn spoke with her off the record.

Though Ms. Nathan had prepared the heavily biased story without the aid of transcripts, she still wanted the official court record, which had been sealed to protect the identities of the children and their families.

But at a hearing a month later, Harth ruled that the transcript would remain sealed. "If this court today will not protect these children, which court should?" he said in denying the *Voice*'s request. Unsealing the transcript would create a risk that the names of the children would be disclosed, causing "substantial harm . . . that could be incalculable," the judge said.

At that hearing, Harth read two letters he had received from victims' parents. One expressed fear that the child might consider suicide when he reached adolescence and realized what had happened to him when he was four years old. The letter said the child "has already suggested he would kill himself if any of his friends found out."

After being denied copies of the transcripts by the trial court, the *Village Voice* filed an appeal. And in January 1989, a state appeals court ruled that the transcripts could be unsealed and made available to the public, provided that the identities of the victims were deleted. It was a unanimous decision of the three-judge panel, which concluded that the need to protect the young victims and their families had to be balanced against the right of the press and public to access criminal proceedings.

Shortly before the day of Kelly's sentencing, Sara McArdle met with Wee Care parents. We learned from her that on the actual day of sentencing, parents whose children had testified would be able to speak before the court. Many parents seemed to want this opportunity. As one mother put it, "I've been through hell and I want to speak."

But Sara cautioned us not to get emotional, or to appear to be gloating that Kelly was going to prison. "We know that in the end we all lost," Sara said, and her face was very serious. "And even though Kelly's going to jail, it would have been five million times better if it hadn't happened at all. So you should make the judge understand this."

The day before Kelly was scheduled for sentencing, Harvey Meltzer made a bid for a new trial. Referring to the recent U.S. Supreme Court decision, he argued that Kelly's Sixth Amendment right to confront her accusers had been violated because the children testified via closed-circuit television.

Sara cited the fact that the Supreme Court had left open-ended whether there were viable exceptions to the right of confrontation. Reiterating Justice O'Connor's reference to the New Jersey statute, and that pretrial hearings had been held to determine if it would be harmful for the Wee Care children to see Kelly, Sara carefully distinguished the Iowa trial from the Wee Care case.

Meltzer responded that the Wee Care children had not been brought to court for the judge to assess their trauma, nor were defense experts permitted to evaluate them. But Sara said a defense expert conducting "a one-hour interview two years after the event" could not have been on an "equal footing" with the psychologists and parents who testified about Kelly's effect on the children.

Harth denied Meltzer's motion for a new trial, saying he thought the New Jersey law "satisfies the confrontation clause, while still respecting the fragility of the children." The judge maintained that in the Supreme Court's decision, "It was the Iowa statute and only the Iowa statute that was found unconstitutional."

On August 2, the day Kelly was to be sentenced, I sat with my family as usual in a packed courtroom. Hannah, happily ensconced with her two sisters in a town-sponsored day camp at the park near our house, didn't know I was going to court. As far as she was concerned, the verdict meant that Kelly was in jail indefinitely.

Kelly looked so different that day from the way she had during the trial. Instead of a figure-revealing pastel dress, she wore a plain red blouse and a black skirt. She was very pale and had lost a lot of weight. Her hair, styled in a trendy perm just months earlier, hung limply to her shoulders.

The defense attorneys and the prosecutors argued before the court. Although we'd heard that Kelly's lawyers planned to trot out a lot of character witnesses, not one appeared. Meltzer argued that Kelly's crimes were part of a "brief period of aberrant behavior" and that she would not be likely to commit similar crimes again. He contended that her punishment could be the maximum consecutive sentences for the two most serious crimes. In Kelly's case, that would be two of the thirty-four first-degree aggravated sexual assaults of which she was convicted.

Meltzer's rationale would have equaled a forty-year sentence, but he argued that Kelly should be given a fifteen-year term since she had no prior criminal record and had shown no "abhorrent sexual compulsivity" prior to her Wee Care crimes.

Then it was Kelly's turn to speak. She sounded defiant as she stood before the judge and maintained her innocence. "I declare today as I declared three years ago my innocence," she said. "I have every confidence that one day the appellate court will vindicate me." Kelly said she had spent a lot of time in prison praying. Alluding to a "deep, abiding faith in God," she said, "I stand before you here today ready to face whatever lies ahead."

It was amazing that she was able to keep up such a tough exterior. There was no remorse in her voice, and I wondered if she ever thought about our children. I hoped she wouldn't get out of jail until Hannah was grown up.

Now it was Sara and Glenn's turn to speak. Sara argued that Kelly's crimes had inflicted lasting damage on the victims. "There's no way to compensate the children," she said. "There's no way to give them back the innocence they lost at three, four, or five years old.

"Every child experienced tremendous impairment of their daily emotional functioning," Sara continued. She talked about how some of the individual children were faring. Brian DeLuca had recently tried to molest another child. Oliver Madison, when he talked about Kelly to his therapist, often called his mother from the doctor's office to make sure she was all right.

At the last minute, the parents had decided that instead of each of us getting up to speak, just one volunteer would speak for us all. Soma Goldstein's statement was brief but moving:

"Our lives have changed dramatically and drastically

over the past three years," she said. "Our lives will never be the same and our children will never be the same."

And then it was Harth's turn. He called the facts in the Wee Care case "sordid, bizarre and demeaning to the children." He talked about the "gravity and seriousness of the harm inflicted on the victims." He called the impact of the assaults "devastating and incalculable" and pointed out that Kelly had abused her position as a teacher.

Referring to the "bizarre behavior, the number of victims, and the continuity of the crimes," he said he felt there was a substantial risk that the defendant would commit another offense if given the opportunity. "If ever a case cried out for deterrence—cried out in anguished cries— this is the case," he said. From the way he was talking, I was sure he was going to throw the book at her. Instead, he sentenced her to forty-seven years in prison, with a parole eligibility of fourteen years.

We were stunned and disappointed at the leniency of the sentence. This meant that Kelly would likely be out of jail by the time she was forty. I didn't want her set free until she was an old woman. Parents wept openly. The prosecutors were disappointed, too.

Chief County Prosecutor Herbert M. Tate, Jr., said: "One of the concerns we have is what kind of message this case sends out. The message for twenty victims is that they are looking at a sentence of less than one year per person."

■

That night my brother Johnny came to our house to celebrate his birthday. He'd brought along his newest girl friend, and I'd also invited my parents. After dinner, we sat around the table and discussed the sentencing. Everyone felt angry and cheated. To be eligible for hundreds of years in prison and then to be able to get out in just fourteen years—it seemed so unfair.

But as we talked, I was able to put the sentence in perspective. True, it was more lenient than we'd hoped for.

But Kelly won't be eligible for parole until Hannah is twenty-two. Her victims will be adults by then, old enough to attend Kelly's parole hearings, to speak up and say what this woman did to them and why she should never be given the opportunity to hurt another generation of children. Even more importantly, since Kelly would at least be in jail until the Wee Care children were grown up, by then they will know that she can't get through the bars of her jail cell to hurt them, that she can't go through walls, that she can't hurt their parents, kill their grandparents, cut their throats with a knife. Instead of perceiving her as an omnipotent, superhuman being with magical powers, they will recognize her for what she truly is—a weak, pathetic woman with a twisted set of sexual mores.

■

There were two Wee Care celebrations that summer, one for the adults, after the sentence was handed down, and one for the children after the trial ended. The parents threw a big party for Glenn and Sara at which there were enough Swedish meatballs, fried chicken, and Chinese stir-fries to feed an army. We talked about our summer vacation plans and where to find the best buys on back-to-school clothes. The Wee Care scandal had been at the foundation of our friendship and it would continue to bind us together as our children matured. But it wasn't the only thing we had in common anymore. Truly, we had become close friends.

The other celebration was much more important, because it was for the children. During the trial we'd talked for months of having a party for them regardless of the verdict. It wasn't to thank them for going to court but to let them all have a good time together. Someone suggested the roller-skating rink. It sounded ideal—a good place for the kids to let off steam. We didn't tell our children that the party was to celebrate a verdict. Instead, we simply called it the Wee Care party.

I reserved the entire roller rink for a Sunday afternoon in

June, and we telephoned as many Wee Care parents as we could reach. Though some parents wanted nothing to do with a party, the turnout was surprisingly good, especially considering that it was a very hot Sunday. I hadn't seen some of the children since Wee Care closed three summers earlier and I couldn't believe how grown-up they looked. Hannah recognized every one of them, though she was shy about going up and saying hello.

She loves to roller skate, and was in high spirits that day as she cruised around the rink holding hands with Melissa Bethel, Casey MacKenna, or her sisters. Even Jim had agreed to go, and he strapped skates on himself and three-year-old Robert. The two of them made their way slowly around the rink while I kept an eye on the three girls and chatted with mothers I hadn't seen in months. Glenn brought his girl friend, Sara and Kevin McArdle were there, and Susan Esquilin came with her twin daughters.

Afterward, we went to Bunny's for dinner. Once again, the entire back room was taken over by Wee Care families. It was noisy and convivial, and although the jukebox drowned out most conversations, everyone seemed to be enjoying themselves.

Looking around the room at the happy, relaxed families, I felt as if we really were going to make it. It was good to be with these people, to be laughing instead of crying.

Carrying Robert to the bathroom, I threaded my way past the table where Hannah was sitting with Caroline, Melissa Bethel, and Casey MacKenna. Oblivious to me, the four of them were toasting each other with Coke-filled beer mugs.

I walked by just in time to see Hannah hoist her heavy mug high above her head, and to hear her say, "Three cheers to the end of Wee Care. Three cheers to the end of Kelly."

C H A P T E R

■ ■ ■ ■ ■ ■ ■ ■ ■

16

But it wasn't the end of Kelly. The verdict didn't make everything right again. We all didn't live happily ever after once she went to prison. Her jail sentence wasn't our victory. There were no winners, and all of us lost something.

Whether Kelly makes parole at age forty or stays in jail for life, she will always haunt the darkest part of our children's memories. She degraded and demoralized her victims, forcing them to see a sordid side of sexuality. She instilled in them a terror that may fade but will not disappear. We're healing, but it's a slow process.

Nine-year-old Eddie Fernandez has been in therapy for more than three years. He still can't sleep at night without all the lights on in his bedroom. If his mother turns them off before going to bed, he invariably wakes up and calls for her to come and switch them back on again. He is still afraid to go to the bathroom by himself, so Ana often is summoned in the middle of the night to escort her nine-year-old son to the toilet.

Eddie won't let his mother take a bath with the door shut. He follows her around from room to room in their house, afraid that Kelly can find him and his mother and hurt them.

Sometimes he puts on the videotape Ana made of the Wee Care news broadcasts. Sitting alone before the television, he becomes completely absorbed in the sight of his former teacher sauntering in and out of the courthouse, day after day and month after month.

Though they no longer attend the same school, Eddie and Brian DeLuca remain close friends. Recently, Eddie told his mother that Brian had tried to touch his penis. When Ana asked Eddie why he had allowed it, Eddie told her that Brian said it was all right. Ana reminded him gently that this was not all right. Now she closely supervises their activities.

After refusing to attend church for a long time, Eddie finally consented to attend Sunday services with his mother and sister. He even made his First Communion. But he perceives himself as a bad person. One Sunday not long ago, when he was talking in church, his mother told him to hush. He turned his serious gaze on her and asked, "I'm a bad boy, aren't I? I'm so bad."

"No, you're not bad. You are a child," his mother said. "But I just want to let you know that in church, we are quiet."

Ana encourages Eddie to talk about Kelly when he feels the need. At his request, she clipped out newspaper articles about the trial, and together they pasted the clippings into an album. Ana wrote about some of his Wee Care–related symptoms in a diary she plans to give him when he's older.

"Eddie said he's happy I'm doing that," Ana said. "You know, there are some parents I know who don't want to talk about Wee Care. It's like they are running away. But how long can they run away from the reality of something that happened to their children? I think it's important to be open to the children because it happened to them and, one way or another, it's going to affect their lives in the future."

288

Melissa Bethel's life is quite different from what it was before Kelly Michaels came into her life. Her parents no longer live together. Pete's truck is only pulled up in the driveway when he comes over to pick up Melissa and Laura. The two girls live with their mother.

After the Wee Care verdict, Pete initially was euphoric on learning of Kelly's conviction. He and Sharon went down to Bunny's together with other parents to celebrate. But a few days later, when it looked as if the appellate court might let Kelly out of jail, Pete grew morose and despondent.

"That the jury had believed his kid and now these judges were going to turn Kelly loose . . . that was just devastating for Pete," Sharon recalled. "The day of the supreme court hearing, he took off from work, which is very unusual, and came with me to the hearing even though it was closed. And even though the decision went our way, he became very depressed. I have never seen him so depressed."

A month went by, and the Bethels planned to spend the Memorial Day weekend in Vermont with friends. The four of them were all going to drive up together on Friday afternoon, so Sharon decided to work that morning. But when she arrived home at noon, she found a note from Pete saying he had left and taken the girls.

Sharon was nonplused—and hurt. That evening she called their friends in Vermont and was told that her husband and daughters had arrived. Sharon, who didn't feel like making a nine-hour drive by herself, spent the weekend at home alone, upset and angry. When Pete brought the girls home Sunday night, he just dropped them off and told Sharon he was going to stay at a motel because he needed time to think. He stayed away for a few weeks, growing increasingly gloomy and introverted. Finally, he began to live in a two-family house that the Bethels owned in another town. Melissa's therapist told Sharon she felt that Wee Care had a lot to do with Pete's depression.

"She said that Pete probably thought, here's the verdict, now everything is going to go back to the way it was before," Sharon said. "And yet, life still isn't rosy. It's still just ordinary life."

Melissa's therapist recommended a marriage counselor, but though the Bethels went a few times, it didn't seem to help. A clergyman in their church recommended a psychiatrist to Pete, who began weekly visits. Still the depression persisted. He occasionally didn't go to work. One day, Sharon and the girls arrived home to a dark house. When she called the utility company, she was told that the electricity and gas had been turned off because the bills hadn't been paid.

Sharon had the locks changed so Pete wouldn't be able to get in and remove the mail. She was afraid he might just throw the bills away. Still devoted to his daughters, he sees them regularly and has begun to contribute some child support. Sharon maintains the house and tries to keep the bills paid. Although the Bethels have not decided whether to divorce, they are trying to sell all the property they own jointly.

Melissa Bethel still struggles with her nocturnal fears of Kelly. She won't sleep anywhere except her mother's bed, and she would never stay overnight at a friend's house. If she is visiting a friend and it starts to get dark before her mother arrives to pick her up, she gets nervous. She starts pacing and calls home to tell her mother to hurry.

Academically, Melissa performs poorly. When she started second grade in the fall of 1987, she really fell behind in her work. Still thinking about the trial and testifying, she was simply unable to focus on her schoolwork. At the end of that year, her mother decided to switch Melissa and her sister from the Catholic school they had been attending into the public school. In the third grade, Melissa still is below grade level. She watches a tremendous amount of television because she says it's a great escape.

"TV makes the time go by," she tells Sharon. "TV takes my mind off things."

Sharon is trying to keep life on an even keel for Laura and Melissa. She has money worries now where she once didn't. She works longer hours, and so her daughters, ages ten and eight, often let themselves into an empty house after school. Sharon devotes a lot of time to her church, and often on Saturday mornings she is busy decorating the parish bulletin boards or cooking for a church function.

When Pete first left, Sharon cried a lot, lost weight, and was depressed. But she is beginning to rally. She got a perm, and she sees her friends often. Now she's not sure whether she would want Pete to move back in with the family, but they haven't filed for divorce.

■

Soma and David Goldstein aren't officially divorced either, although they haven't lived together in more than two years. David sees his children two nights during the week, and they stay with him many weekends. Rachel, who began to wet her bed in the summer of 1985 when she was interviewed by the prosecutor's office, still wets her bed often. She is very shy and doesn't make friends easily.

Soma and David see each other almost every other day when he comes for the children, but they don't kiss each other, and there's no hugging. Soma knows she ought to initiate divorce proceedings, but she still is so exhausted from the Wee Care trial she just hasn't the energy for another legal battle.

Every so often, David talks of getting back together. He looks hurt when she mentions divorce. One day recently, when Soma's parents were visiting her, they started dropping hints for Soma to get back together with David. "Even though they know he hurt me and them, they see that he's a good father, a good earner," Soma said. "So my parents said to me, he's not so bad after all, did you ever think about maybe getting back together, just until the kids grow up? And I said, but my little one is four. That would be for fourteen years. What about my happiness? That really floored my mother. You don't think about happiness. You think about raising the kids, and a family life, and what's good for the kids."

On the weekends, Soma sometimes goes out on a date. She's busy with her work, and the children take up nearly all her spare time. Still, she worries for the future, both for herself and for her daughter. "I'm afraid for Rachel, afraid of the unknown," Soma said. "I don't know what she's going to be like when she reaches puberty. And I feel afraid for myself, because I don't like being alone. I guess I fear being alone for the rest of my life."

※

Although the Wee Care crisis soured some marriages, it strengthened others. Donald and Cathy Baird recently celebrated their twelfth wedding anniversary by renewing their vows at the Catholic church they attend. It was a far cry from their ninth anniversary three years ago, which they spent sharing other parents' grief at a Wee Care meeting.

Cathy has lost the weight she gained after learning her son was molested. She has made friends and is active in both her sons' schools. Benjamin, nine, and George, six, look like the quintessential California children—tall, lean, golden.

A year ago, Cathy felt as if she was having a nervous breakdown. She was so saddened by what had happened to Benjamin that she cried constantly, didn't go out of the house, just wanted to be alone. She went to a psychiatrist. She asked him: why now?

"The doctor told me that I had spent all the time up until then keeping everyone else in the family level," Cathy said. "Once I knew they were going to be okay, my body chose that time to fall apart."

Therapy helped Cathy come to terms with her feelings. "I would look at Benjamin and realize he's just not the same child after Wee Care," she said. "I felt like it was all my fault. But I began to realize that I was just a parent doing what I thought was best."

In second grade, Benjamin's behavior became violent. He began attempting to lie on top of his mother. He tormented his younger brother George the way he had while he himself was being abused.

He started to see his therapist again. After the second visit, Benjamin woke up one night while his parents were out. He sat on the edge of his bed and cried as if his heart would break. "Something terrible's going to happen to my mommy," he told the puzzled baby-sitter. Cathy feels that when Benjamin talks about Wee Care, he thinks there will be repercussions from Kelly.

Benjamin hasn't played with his Wee Care friends in the three years since the Bairds moved to California, but Cathy knows her son still thinks about Kelly. Once when Cathy and Benjamin were in the car together, the child began to talk about the things Kelly had done to him. Cathy stopped the car and listened, and then she told him, "I'm sorry you were alone. And if I could take it all back, I would. But I can't."

Cathy was crying and hugging Benjamin, and he was crying, too.

"She really was nice," he wept.

"I know she was," Cathy said softly. "A lot of the kids really did like her. Some of the stuff she did wasn't bad, it was just inappropriate for four- and five-year-olds."

Benjamin seemed to find that comforting. Cathy soothed him for a long time before she finally started the car and drove home. There was no further talk of Kelly that day.

But another day, after being particularly abusive to his brother, Benjamin burst into tears and told his mother, "Kelly gets into my brain and I can't get her out. I don't want to think about her because she makes me so sad."

"Three thousand miles," marvels Cathy. "We've moved three thousand miles away and it's been more than three years since it happened. And still he can't get Kelly out of his head."

◼

Claudia and Peter Schwartz think about Wee Care a lot, and when they do, they still feel angry. Eight-year-old Michele doesn't talk about Kelly at all. Once in a while she and her mother run into a former Wee Care pupil, but Michele always pretends not to recognize the child.

When Claudia told Michele that Kelly had been found guilty, Michele "acted as though I had just told her there were four cities in Czechoslovakia with populations over twenty thousand," recalls Claudia. "It had absolutely no relevance to her life." They didn't go to the roller-skating party because Michele didn't want to.

Claudia has decided that her career isn't as important as she once thought. She now works part-time instead of full-time so she can spend more time with Michele. "Wee Care made us more conscious of how valuable your family is and how important it is that you take the time to be with your family," Claudia said. "And it made me start feeling more maternal, less interested in what was out there and more interested in what was here at home."

Because they wanted to become "more of a family," she and her husband decided to have another child: two-year-old Ariel is a curly-haired, pudgy replica of Michele.

◼

Eight-year-old Jodie Minetti still has seizures, and as often as not, she sleeps on the floor of her parents' room. She has been in therapy for more than three years. Julie and Bob are still together, and the strain between them during the months when Julie was attending the trial is beginning to ease. Bob even came to the roller-skating party with his wife and daughter.

Julie still finds herself wishing she had listened more

back then, picked up on the subtle changes in her daughter that she wrote off as cute or quirky.

"If a friend called me up and her kid was in day care or went to the baby-sitter, and my friend said, 'It's so funny, my kid really wants to wear her pajamas under her clothes,' or say there's another behavioral change," Julie said, "I would tell her, 'Don't just say it's nothing.' It may be nothing, but there's a reason why kids react the way they do. My advice is, if your kid is having a change, there's a reason and you have to find out what it is. If your child is saying he doesn't want to go to school, then you better find out why."

In my own family, life is undeniably more serene than it was three years ago, when I couldn't make it through a day without crying, and Jim and I were strangers. He is more affectionate, less critical now that I don't drive down to court regularly. We can watch a movie on television together or write out a shopping list without getting into an argument. We quarrel about the same things as other married couples—how the money will be spent, the housework shared, the children disciplined. After steadily drifting apart, we've begun to grow together once again.

Wee Care will always be an unresolved issue for us, but then, what marriage doesn't have its rough spots? We've healed the wounds, accepted the scars, and gone forward. We've accepted that we have different ways of handling tragedy.

More importantly, we've learned that we still do love and respect each other. Kelly Michaels didn't break up our marriage, and maybe it wasn't the worst thing in the world for Jim and I to come to know each other's darker side.

Just as Jim wasn't happy that I chose to involve myself in Kelly Michaels's trial, so was he less than pleased when I decided to write this book. On an emotional level, it was because he wanted to end this unhappy chapter in all of our lives. On a practical level, he knew it would mean more baby-sitting on his part.

"You're always biting off more than you can chew, setting these impossible goals for yourself and then expecting to drag me into it," he told me angrily one day. "You have this idea that you're superwoman, and you don't think of anyone but yourself."

This tirade came on a particularly hectic day, when he was up to his ears in work. I was working full-time while trying to write this book at night and on the weekends, and I told him he simply had to watch the children while I wrote for a couple of hours. We were both stressed out, and we shouted back and forth.

Gradually we got over our anger. We apologized. He took the kids to two movies in one weekend, bought me new covers for the computer and printer, chauffeured the girls to piano and ballet. He moved the computer from the third floor to our second-floor bedroom so I could listen for the children at night while I worked. Though he would never tell me, he knew how much this book meant to me.

Actually it wasn't my idea. Soon after the trial began, my friend Jack suggested that I write a book. I jokingly put him off at first, telling him that it could be a book of Kelly's favorite peanut butter recipes. (He knows how much I love to cook.) But Jack kept at me about it, and he offered to write the book with me since he had been covering the trial right along anyway.

My confidence in my ability to do anything well—writing included—was at an all-time low at that point. (Sometimes it seemed that my own lack of self-esteem mirrored Hannah's.) The more I said that I couldn't write a book, the more Jack kept insisting that I could.

We started working on an outline together, but then Jack's wife, who was four months pregnant, was told she had to stay in bed for the rest of the pregnancy. Between working at the paper and taking care of his wife and two kids, Jack had less and less time for the book. One day, he told me he couldn't do it with me.

I was crushed, just devastated. Already, though I'd just begun to work on a proposal and first chapter, I had begun to feel that the book was a part of me. I wanted so badly for other parents to know what we'd all gone through, and what our children had been like during this time, so that they would be on the alert with their own youngsters. Writing made me feel as if I was doing something useful and worthwhile, something that would help other families.

It also gave me back the control I felt I had lost three years earlier. We were powerless when our children were molested, and we could not have prevented it. That's a scary thing to deal with. But writing about the experience helped me regain control, and maybe some of my lost self-respect, too.

Later that same afternoon that Jack told me he couldn't do the book, I was supposed to meet with Susan Esquilin myself, to discuss Hannah's progress in therapy. Instead, I tearfully told her that Jack had backed out on me, and she spent the hour trying to talk me into writing the book myself. Susan, ever calm and reasonable, had a ready answer for every one of my excuses for why I couldn't (a full-time job, four kids, no previous experience at book writing). And by the end of the session, she had convinced me to try it on my own.

There's a funny twist to this part of the story. After I started to work solo on this project because Jack's wife was pregnant, I found out (surprise!) that I was pregnant, too. I, who had never planned to have any more children, was due just four months before this book was supposed to be handed in.

Samantha has spent countless hours of her infancy sitting on my lap in front of my computer. She's listened to the hum of the printer, drooled on my notebooks, tangled herself up in the telephone cord while I'm on the phone checking facts.

Samantha is the light of my life and a daily source of joy—a placid, happy baby who is nearly always singing and smiling. She looks the most like Hannah, with her fair hair, long aristocratic fingers, and big round eyes. But (another surprise!) instead of the brown eyes all our other children have, Samantha's eyes are blue. And she's plumper than the others—she weighed twenty pounds when she was not quite five months old. My friend Len dubbed her Megababy, and the name has stuck.

When I'm holding Samantha, when I listen to her trill her wordless songs or watch her wave her chubby fists, I find myself hoping fervently that I will always be there to protect her from harm. That she should never go through what Hannah did is something I will strive to ensure.

Of our older children, Hannah is unquestionably the best with Samantha. They all love their baby sister, of course, and play with her endlessly, but Hannah is the quintessential little mother, always ready and willing to take over when I need my hands free. Hannah was thrilled when I told her I was writing a book about Wee Care, and offered to watch Samantha so I could work on it.

Hannah helps me give Samantha a bath every night, even though it means she has to give up fifteen minutes of her before-bed reading time. She coaxes Samantha to stop fussing when no one else can, and she can bounce the baby to sleep on her lap while making this funny noise (it sounds like a ringing telephone) that Samantha loves.

How unlike Hannah's behavior with Robert four years earlier, when she was sullen and occasionally violent around her newborn brother.

Hannah is in the fourth grade now and her teacher tells me what a wonderful writer she is, and so good at editing her classmates' work. She's a Brownie, and this year made the rounds of the neighborhood tirelessly with her Girl Scout cookie order form. She wants to sell two hundred boxes so she can acquire the painter's cap pictured in the Girl Scout catalogue. It's not unlike one you could buy in a store for three dollars. Hannah doesn't care when I say this to her, though. She wants that particular hat.

Birthdays continue to be important: she planned her last party, when she turned nine, months in advance. She couldn't make up her mind whether to have a bowling party (she never had one before, and they're getting popular), a roller-skating party (she loves to skate, but her friends might remember she took them to the rink last year), or a sleep-over party (this was really just wishful thinking, because Hannah knows I won't consent to having fifteen children overnight in my living room.) Ever generous and expansive, she couldn't leave out any friend and so the guest list kept changing, growing longer. In the end, she opted for a barbecue and a make-your-own-sundae bar.

My daughter excels in gymnastics, spends hours playing her keyboard and weaving bracelets out of embroidery thread. She can't decide whether to be an artist, a nurse, or a veterinarian when she grows up.

Because she is so gentle and patient, six-year-old Ellen and four-year-old Robert insist that Hannah tuck them in after I do every night. She gets them settled in their beds in the room they now share, and she lets Robot sleep on a doll blanket on the floor between them. Hannah reads to them endlessly, and is never too busy to play dinosaurs with Robert and Barbie dolls with Ellen. She helps Caroline find her shoes or her violin in the morning when my oldest daughter is running around the house hysterically.

She knows to keep out of Caroline's way when her older sister is moody. But Hannah is always the one Caroline calls when she's in trouble. Hannah still is the consummate peacemaker in the family, always comforting the child who's been punished, or mediating between two who have had a fight.

Not that Hannah is a goody two-shoes. She gets into her share of trouble the way any fourth-grader does. Not long ago, she ran in from school out of breath and all upset and told me that she had gotten detention for two days. (At her

299

school, detention means sitting in the lunch room after eating instead of being allowed out on the playground.)

How did she get detention, I asked. Well, it seemed as if Hannah had gone up to the lunch counter in the middle of her meal to get a straw for her milk, and when she returned to her table, two of her friends had put some peanut butter and jelly on the seat of her chair. So Hannah, in retaliation, scooped up some spaghetti sauce on a spoon and pretended she was going to flick it in her friend's hair. She didn't actually shake the spoon, she said, and yet a little bit of the sauce just went flying off the spoon and landed on the other child's head. All three girls were confined for two days to the lunch room during playground time.

At age nine, Hannah still likes to snuggle down on the couch with the younger children and me for bedtime stories. She sucks her thumb and believes in Santa Claus.

She has been in therapy for nearly four years, and she is terrified of Kelly Michaels. We have our good periods, when Kelly's name rarely comes up and there are only small, jarring reminders like the one I got last spring when I happened to pick up a notebook of Hannah's.

My daughter is always writing stories, so steno pads filled with her prose and artwork are strewn around the house. On that particular day, I noticed a pad she'd left on my dresser and was horrified by the picture inside. It showed a man and a woman coupling, the huge-breasted woman on top. Hannah had drawn a vagina on the woman and a penis on the man. Underneath the picture she had printed, "Sara and Ken loved each other very much. They loved hugging and kissing each other. Before long they were cresting [I'm sure she meant caressing] each other under their clothes."

We never mentioned the drawing to each other. I tucked it away in a drawer and I imagine she's forgotten about it by now. It was upsetting to find such a disturbing drawing so long after Hannah was molested. Looking at it, I felt all the old anger and hatred toward Kelly bubble up inside me again.

Hannah doesn't have the vocabulary or the experience to verbalize many of her dark thoughts and yet she now sometimes wants to talk to Jim and me about Kelly. Quite a difference from three and a half years ago, when she shied away from the subject of Kelly Michaels.

Last September, Hannah suddenly became afraid to sleep alone in her room.

We'd moved Ellen and Robert into a room together so Hannah could have her own bedroom, which she'd wanted for a long time.

Though initially she seemed happy in Robert's old room, soon she became agitated each night at bedtime. She wouldn't say why, just that she was scared. So she started to occupy the floor in Caroline's room until I finally bought a fold-out cot because I couldn't stand the sight of her sleeping on the rug night after night. Eventually, Jim moved Hannah's bed into Caroline's room, and Samantha now occupies Hannah's room. Hannah insisted on having her Mother Goose night-light on as well as the bathroom light and the hall light. Still, she was vague about just what it was that scared her so.

She hadn't been in therapy over the summer, but when I took her back to Susan Esquilin that fall, she burst into tears and told the therapist she was terribly afraid of Kelly. Hannah insisted that Kelly could break out of jail and get her. Susan explained that jails are very secure places, and that Kelly could not get out. But Hannah, having spent a lot of time imagining Kelly's escape route, disagreed. "She could either break through the bars or take a sharp shovel and dig her way out," she told Susan. "Or else she could not eat and get skinny enough to slip through the bars."

Convinced that Kelly could enter our house through the windows even if all the doors were locked, Hannah became afraid even to sleep in Caroline's room. Caroline's closet has a tiny window in it, and Hannah was sure Kelly could get in.

I demonstrated how perfectly the locks on our doors and

windows work. I bought Hannah a powerful flashlight so she could check under the beds and in the closet after dark. On nights when she was still pacing around past midnight, I dragged her fold-out cot into our room. And when thinking about Kelly gave her such bad stomachaches that she vomited, I fixed her the hot water bottle and gave her Pepto-Bismol.

Still, all that fall and winter, the fear of Kelly persisted. When her frequent bad dreams brought her to my bedside in the middle of the night, I listened to her talk until she got sleepy again.

She believed that her schoolmates disliked her. "Nobody in my class will play with me at lunchtime," Hannah sobbed, and big tears rolled down her cheeks and dripped onto her nightgown. "The only one who will talk to me is Ida, but she just wants to sit in the front of the line so she can be the first one in the door after lunch. And I don't want to just sit there. I want to play something but Ida always says she doesn't want to. And whenever I ask someone else to play, they're already playing with their friends and they won't play with me."

Right before Christmas, we were driving home together from somewhere when Hannah burst into tears and told me she felt guilty because she had never told me about Kelly. She was upset that I had had to find out from someone else, and insisted she should have told me herself while the abuse was going on.

"But Hannah, you were just a little girl," I told her. "How could you tell me? None of the kids told their parents. We didn't expect you to, you were much too little. I'm just sorry I didn't find out sooner so that it wouldn't have gone on for so long."

"You feel bad about that?" asked Hannah anxiously. She looked stricken that she might be responsible for making me upset.

"No, no," I said quickly. "Now I don't, but I did for a very long time."

302

"But now you don't feel bad anymore?" asked Hannah.

I stopped the car, and thought for a minute before answering. "I felt just terrible when it all happened." I realized I was crying. "I don't think anything ever hurt me so much before. But as the time goes by, it gets a little easier for me to think about. It hurts, but not as much as it did back when it first happened."

Hannah considered that for a minute, but then started crying again. It was so heartbreaking to watch her struggling so.

"It's all my fault for not telling you," she said. "And besides, I'm the only one of my friends who still goes to a therapist. Melissa doesn't go anymore and neither does Casey. Only I do, because I'm weak."

"You mean they told you they don't go anymore?" I asked, and she nodded.

"Well, maybe they're not going this week or this month, but they will go again," I said firmly. "Maybe right now they don't need it and so they stopped. You didn't go all summer either, remember? And you were fine. You go when you need someone to talk to."

I told Hannah that other Wee Care children were still in therapy. Knowing she wasn't the only child still seeing a psychologist made her brighten some. I reminded her that Melissa had to sleep with her mother every night, and that brought a giggle. She seemed impressed to hear that even some of the grown-ups went to a psychologist to help them deal with Kelly.

But Hannah remained as restless as a cat on winter evenings, following me from room to room. She needed to check the locks, switch on more lights, examine closets with her flashlight.

Each night brought something new to make her feel guilty: she felt bad that she didn't look after her hamster as well as she should. She was convinced that she didn't take good care of her stuffed animals. Once my daughter told me with a perfectly serious face that some night her stuffed animals might come alive because she didn't hold them right. She worried that she didn't talk to her father enough; she thought his feelings might be hurt. She felt bad that Maria had to do the dinner dishes every night, because she might be lonely by herself in the kitchen. When my aunt died after a long bout with cancer, Hannah whispered to me that it was her fault because she hadn't prayed enough for her aunt to live.

One evening, Hannah collapsed weeping on the bed and told me she was sad because she was growing up. I assured her that she would always be my little girl, no matter how old she got. I spent so much time with her that sometimes I wondered if my other kids were jealous, though they didn't show it. Perhaps they sensed that Hannah needed extra love and reassurance. And she was so good to all of them they never resented her.

One night not long ago, Hannah wandered in and sat down at the kitchen table next to me. It was nearly midnight, and everyone else was sleeping. I was peeling apples for applesauce. Watching television makes some people forget, but cooking keeps me from going crazy. Now Hannah sat hunched over on a stool, watching me work, chewing on apple skins, lost in thought. I could see that she was struggling to put her thoughts into words.

"It's just that I can't get her out of my head," she whispered finally, the tears bright in her eyes. "I keep thinking about how it was when she touched me. It felt so yucky."

I looked at her, so filled with pain myself I could scarcely speak. If I could have taken it all away, could have suffered for her, I would have done so gladly. She was crying now, the quiet kind of sobbing I had come to dread more than the loud howls children employ when they are angry or hurt. This was a deep, anguished sound that was far too grown-up to be coming from a child. Impulsively, I decided to share with Hannah something I never thought I'd tell a daughter of mine.

"I know how you feel," I said softly.

"You do?" She sounded surprised, as if she hadn't heard what I'd said. And I told her about Barney, and how her aunts and I had allowed it to go on for years without telling Grandma. We sat and talked that night for a long time about how the pain she was feeling would lessen as she got older, and how she shouldn't feel as if what had happened had been her fault. For the first time, I think, she believed me when I said that no one expected the Wee Care children to have told.

■

I think Hannah will always need more from me than my other children. I only want to provide whatever it takes to make her feel good about herself, to mature into a happy, secure woman.

Sometimes I recall that night four years ago in the restaurant when Jim urged me to look at things in perspective. Hannah hadn't been raped and murdered by an unknown assailant, her body left to rot in a field somewhere. Though I couldn't appreciate what he said at the time, I know now he was right and just trying, in his own way, to comfort me. Hannah is with us still, so we are luckier than parents whose children die. She will survive, and God has given us a second chance to nurture her.

As for me, I'm much more vulnerable than I was before Hannah was molested. I cry more easily than I ever used to. Even life's small pleasures—Ellen's first-grade class reciting a poem for the school assembly, a surprise phone call from Jana in Michigan, the sight of the early-morning mist rising from the lake behind my parents' house—bring tears to my eyes.

I'm much more fearful and less sanguine than I was in the days before Kelly abused my daughter. Disaster has a way of creeping unbidden into my life, and so I'm always waiting for the worst to happen, sure some unseen evil is about to befall my children, my husband, my family. If one of my kids has a fever for more than two days, I'm convinced it's leukemia. If a child goes to the bathroom a lot, I suspect diabetes. Diarrhea? Maybe it's cystic fibrosis.

If Jim is an hour late getting home from work, I picture him in a fatal car accident. If my mother is held up at the office on a night she is due at my house for dinner, I am sure she has been mugged and is lying, unconscious and bleeding, on a Newark street somewhere.

My mother and sisters tease me about my fears, but I don't like myself this way, though I don't know what to do about it. It's as if, burned badly once, I walk around now waiting for the other shoe to drop.

I'm too protective of my children, something else I wish I could overcome. Hannah asked if she could go to sleep-away camp with the Girl Scouts next summer, but I can't let her go. Imagine the countless opportunities those counselors have to molest their charges when they are alone with them every night for a whole week.

Jim and I rarely go out anymore because I hardly trust anyone with my children. No baby-sitter other than a family member or Maria is good enough. I don't miss not going out on Friday or Saturday nights, though. In my twenties, I had my weekend evening plans lined up a month in advance and got depressed if Jim and I didn't have social engagements both nights of every weekend. But now I like to stay home. And when we get invited to a party, my husband often goes by himself.

A day doesn't go by that I don't think about Wee Care and experience the small, accompanying stab of pain. But as with a death, the intensity of the grief has diminished with time.

Of the several stages I passed through after learning about Hannah—disbelief, rage, guilt, depression, and acceptance—the hardest for me to come to terms with was the guilt. As women, we are expected to be perfect mothers who ensure that everything goes well for our children. We working mothers have even higher and more unrealistic self-expectations. And when things don't proceed as they should—the child brings home a C instead of a B—we immediately blame ourselves. If we weren't working, this wouldn't have happened.

When something really traumatic does happen to the child, such as sexual abuse, our entire maternal role is called into question. We doubt our competence and motivation as mothers. We know we have failed. Guilt takes over.

Now I've finally accepted that Hannah was sexually abused, and I'm learning to live with it. I can think of myself in a role other than the mother of a molested child. I can introduce myself without feeling the urge to say, hi, my name is Patricia Crowley, I'm thirty-seven, and my daughter was sexually abused at her day-care center.

And still I berate myself for not knowing my daughter as well as I thought I did. Sometimes I think back to the self-portrait she drew at school in April 1985, just before Kelly Michaels left Wee Care. All the children in Hannah's class sat in front of a mirror one day and made pictures of themselves with colorful markers. The teacher wrote their names on them and hung them on the wall.

I remember standing in front of the display at school, comparing Hannah's drawing with the others. Some of the youngsters had drawn stick figures with just one or two colors. But Hannah had obviously spent a lot of time and effort on her picture: a smiling blond girl in a pink dress with a purple daisy in the center, standing in a field of green grass, with puffy blue clouds floating in the sky.

I was so proud of that portrait. I took it to work and hung it over my desk. Whenever I looked at it, I would think to myself that only a happy, well-adjusted child could draw such a bright, cheerful picture.

Two years later, in 1987, I showed the drawing to Sara McArdle, who pointed out something I hadn't noticed before: the little girl in the picture had no arms. Sara said this indicated that Hannah had felt powerless, not in control. I was skeptical at first. Perhaps four-and-a-half-year-olds just don't draw hands in their artwork, I reasoned. So I asked Ellen, who was the same age then as Hannah had been when she did her self-portrait, to draw a picture of herself. The little girl in Ellen's drawing not only had hands but also fingers.

Things aren't always what they seem with children because they don't necessarily tell us outright what's happening to them. We have to probe a little, be watchful, ask questions to find out what's beneath the surface.

The Wee Care experience taught me many lessons, most of them painful. Never again will I depend on someone else to teach my children about their bodies, their sexuality. Though I've known it all along, I recognize as if for the first time that as their mother, I am responsible not just for being my children's primary caretaker, but their first and most influential teacher.

And one of the things that I have tried to teach them, ingrain in them even, is that they can question grown-ups, that adults are not infallible. I want them to grow up to respect authority, and yet to know when to disregard it. I want them to trust, and yet not be naïve. I want them to have a strong sense of who they are, and to be comfortable but not preoccupied with their bodies.

I don't advise my sisters and other mothers I know not to put their children in day-care centers. In the majority of families I know, both parents have to work in order to make ends meet, and day care is a necessity. But when I'm asked, I do strongly urge parents to be active in their children's schools, to look for cooperative programs if possible, where parents take turns working one day or several hours each month.

Above all, I've learned to be a better listener, to hear what my children are telling me even when they don't say it out loud. Wee Care brought home to me how short and precious their childhood is. I love my children more than anything in the world, and the time for letting them know this is now.

"THE WORLD NEEDS MORE LIKE TOREY HAYDEN"

Boston Globe

JUST ANOTHER KID　　　　　　**70564-8/$4.95 US/$5.95 Can**
More than a moving story of one woman's personal battle, this is a loving tribute to all Hayden's "special" children and their remarkable strength of spirit.

MURPHY'S BOY　　　　　　**65227-7/$4.95 US/$5.95 Can**
Education Psychologist and bestselling author Torey L. Hayden tells the dramatic and moving true story of her confrontation with a fifteen-year-old boy who refused to speak—until the miracle of love penetrated the terrible silence.

SOMEBODY ELSE'S KIDS　　　　　　**59949-X/$4.95 US/$5.95 Can**
This is the true story of Torey Hayden's experience teaching four disturbed children who were put in her class because no one else knew what to do with them.

ONE CHILD　　　　　　**54262-5/$4.95 US/$5.95 Can**
Six-year-old Sheila never spoke, never cried, and her eyes were filled with hate. Abandoned by her mother, abused by her alcoholic father, Sheila was placed in a class for the hopelessly retarded and disturbed. Everyone said Sheila was lost forever...everyone except teacher Torey Hayden, whose perseverence finally revealed Sheila to be a child with a genius I.Q.—and a great capacity for love.
